Free Agency and Competitive
Balance in Baseball

Free Agency and Competitive Balance in Baseball

Ronald W. Cox
with Daniel Skidmore-Hess

McFarland & Company, Inc., Publishers
Jefferson, North Carolina, and London

Photographs provided by the National Baseball Hall of Fame Library.

Library of Congress Cataloguing-in-Publication Data

Cox, Ronald W., 1962–
    Free agency and competitive balance in baseball / Ronald W. Cox with Daniel Skidmore-Hess.
    p.   cm.
    Includes bibliographical references and index.

    ISBN 0-7864-2220-3 (softcover : 50# alkaline paper)

    1. Baseball — Economic aspects — United States.   2. Baseball players — Salaries, etc. — United States.   3. Free agents (Sports) — United States.   I. Skidmore-Hess, Daniel, 1964–   II. Title.
GV880.C69   2006
331.2'817963570973 — dc22   2005029545

British Library cataloguing data are available

©2006 Ronald W. Cox and Daniel Skidmore-Hess. All rights reserved

No part of this book may be reproduced or transmitted in any form or by any means, electronic or mechanical, including photocopying or recording, or by any information storage and retrieval system, without permission in writing from the publisher.

On the cover: Comerica Park, home of the Detroit Tigers

Manufactured in the United States of America

McFarland & Company, Inc., Publishers
   Box 611, Jefferson, North Carolina 28640
      www.mcfarlandpub.com

To my mom, who gave me the love of baseball, and
my dad, who made it possible for me to create
a wiffle ball field in our backyard. — RC

To Cathy. — DSH

Contents

List of Tables viii

Introduction 1

ONE / Money and Myth in Major League Baseball   7

TWO / Team Competitiveness in Major League Baseball   47

THREE / Stadium Revenues and Competitiveness   79

FOUR / The Globalization of Baseball: Cost Cutting and Outsourcing   120

FIVE / The Politics and Economics of Expansion   148

Notes 191

Bibliography 195

Index 197

List of Tables

1 — Success Ratios for ML Franchises, 1946–1976 17
2 — Success Ratios for ML Franchises, 1977–1999 18
3 — Major League Metropolises, United States 39
4 — Major League Metropolises, Canada 39
5 — Success Ratios for ML Franchises, 1995–2001 49
6 — Revenue Trends, 1982–1993 55
7 — Summary of MLB Financial Data 56
8 — Payrolls and Profits, 2001 60
9 — Low Payroll Franchises and Owners 61
10 — NL Team Payrolls, 1997 176
11 — Beinfest's Trades 182
12 — Beinfest's Pitcher Trades 183
13 — Distributional Effects of Revenue Sharing System 186
14 — Market Size and Revenue Sharing 187

Introduction

As early as the late 19th century, the owners of major league baseball and the leading sportswriters covering the game were decrying the greediness of players as the foremost threat to the national pastime.[1] Columnists for *The Sporting News* continued in this tradition through the formation of the Major League Baseball Players Association in 1966, attacking the audacity of the players for threatening the competitive balance of the sport. The issue of competitive balance became a public rallying cry for the owners in their efforts to forestall free agency. When the Players Association succeeded in tearing down the permanent reserve clause with the assistance of an arbitration ruling in 1976, the owners kept insisting that the fundamental integrity of the game — competitive balance — would be undermined and that the players had become their own worst enemy. This rhetoric continued through the 1980s and 1990s, at the very same time that the sport was enjoying the most competitive balance in its history.

In this book, we label the period from 1981 to 1993 the golden age of competitive balance, when all twelve National League teams and eleven American League teams finished first at least once. At the same time, the number of teams repeating as champions declined precipitously from previous eras, which were much less competitive. From 1901 to 1968, about one of every three races was won by the defending champion (about a 36 percent repeat rate); from 1969 to 1980 it was 36 percent once again, but from 1981 to 1993 the rate had dropped to about 17 percent.[2]

Still, the owners chose to ignore these numbers in pursuit of their claim that free agency was destroying the game. This book examines the issues behind the owners' claims and locates the battles between owners and players in a larger set of revenue distribution issues that includes national and local television money, stadium income, recruitment of foreign athletes, and the politics behind the addition of four major league expansion franchises during the 1990s. Through all of these issues, what becomes clear is how the battle waged by the owners in the court of public opinion has been designed to maximize the owners' share of revenue. The public statements from the commissioner's office about the poor financial health of the sport contrast markedly with a relatively robust period of competitive balance, especially during the period 1981–1993. However, we do document a decline in competitive balance indicators from 1994 through 2001, which coincides with rising inequality between the very top big league spenders, the New York Yankees, and bottom feeders such as the Tampa Bay Devil Rays or the Montreal Expos — the latter of whom the owners have helped run into the ground by an unprecedented three years in which the team was jointly owned by all of the other MLB franchises.

In this book, we expand on various explanations for the golden age of competitiveness, as well as explanations for why the sport moved into a competitive decline from 1994 to 2001. We also analyze why the current economic circumstances favor a repeat of the golden age of competitiveness. The central thread of our argument is that periods of competitive equality tend to be caused by a sharp rise in national television revenue, which is shared among all the major league clubs. During the 1980s, as we show in chapter one, the sport enjoyed its biggest leap in the growth of such revenue, which meant that for the first time, if only for a brief period, national television money became more important as a source of revenue for most clubs than local revenue. That situation led to an unprecedented period of competitive balance, as very little local revenue is shared, although that has changed somewhat with the adoption of the latest collective bargaining agreement. The period 1994 through 2001 saw the national television revenue drop compared with local revenue, as some teams built new stadiums and others were able to secure lucrative local television contracts with the establishment of networks that paid for exclusive coverage of games. (Most notable among these was the YES network established by the Yankees,' which further reinforced the Yankees position as the most extreme example of competitive imbalance that the sport has ever seen.) The signing of new national television contracts in 2000 and 2001 with ESPN and Fox heralded the potential for a renewed era of competitive balance, as the amount of money from the new contracts increased the revenues available for distribution to all major league teams by about 50 percent over the previous national television contracts.

The upshot is that revenue distribution does matter, although the issue is much more complex than the owners acknowledge in their public war with the Players Association. At one level, it's only natural that there should be some correlation between winning percentage and team payroll, since good teams typically are rewarded with more revenues at the gate and in advertising and merchandising opportunities. On the other hand, some large-market franchises, such as the Yankees and Red Sox, have a built-in market advantage. Compensation for this advantage should come from league efforts to distribute revenues in a way that recognizes this disparity. Our analysis of the current revenue-sharing plan negotiated by the owners and players in the latest collective bargaining agreement identifies serious flaws that may well undermine its long-term effectiveness, although over the short term it is likely to contribute in a modest way to greater competitive balance. Rather than attempt to identify markets that have a built-in revenue advantage due to their geographic location, the current revenue distribution scheme simply penalizes teams whose revenues result from their winning traditions, and then gives revenues to teams such as the Philadelphia Phillies (prior to their move into Citizens Bank ballpark) who by any objective measurement are a large-market franchise. Still, even a flawed revenue-sharing scheme may well be better than nothing, and it is likely that at least some of the newly distributed revenues played a role in making the 2003 and 2004 seasons among the most competitive and interesting in recent memory. Much more important, however, has been the surge in national television revenues, which had undergone a dramatic decline in the mid to late 1990s before recovering in 2000-2001.

We also examine noneconomic factors that contribute to competitive imbalance, including the quality of a baseball organization in evaluating talent and how such talent evaluation can catapult a small-revenue club from the basement to a division title: witness the repeated success of the Minnesota Twins and Oakland Athletics. In chapter two, we spend considerable space exploring the extent to which organizational cohesion, sophistication and skill can make a difference in franchise success.

With this in mind, we argue that the amateur draft established in 1965 has allowed smart franchises to showcase their skills on an even playing field with other clubs, at least until the explosion of bonus money in 1991 began to make the player draft less of a leveling tool and more a part of the rising competitive problems faced by the sport in the mid-1990s. Still, organizations that are willing to take an unconventional approach emphasizing Sabermetrics, such as the Oakland A's, can be successful despite these rising costs. Other organizations, such as the Minnesota Twins, have been successful by relying heavily on the traditional tools of scouting and player development to supply them with an enviable collection of young talent capable of displacing expensive free agents. At the same time, organizations such as the Arizona Diamondbacks borrowed heavily to sign free agents, counting on getting their money back through the success that follows a championship run, which the D-Backs enjoyed in 2001. In contrast, Florida Marlins owner Wayne Huizenga treated his 1997 championship club like cheap champagne, dispensing all ingredients in an unprecedented fire sale that put the future owners of the club in an extremely difficult situation. The turnaround for this franchise came during the current ownership by Jeffrey Loria, who invested enough in the team to capture a second World Series title for the franchise despite having the worst stadium lease in baseball.

As all these examples illustrate, major league baseball teams have followed divergent paths to success and failure, with market size and revenue streams accounting only partially for the outcome. As we document in our chapter on the economics of stadium financing, publicly funded stadiums often do not deliver a winning product to the localities, counties and states that help finance such projects. The honeymoon effect associated with rising attendance at a new ballpark appears to be increasingly brief and can evaporate after the first season if a team performs poorly in its new facility. Clubs in smaller markets are more dependent on stadium revenues than their large market counterparts and have much less revenue from local television and radio contracts. These teams can remain trapped in a vicious cycle of losing if the organizational dynamics are not in place to help guide a franchise turnaround. We analyze these organizational dynamics in chapter three in the context of clubs that were able to maximize their utilization of stadium revenues to help build a winning tradition, such as the Cleveland Indians; clubs that achieved mixed results, such as the Baltimore Orioles; and clubs that have continued losing even after moving into their new facility, such as the Pittsburgh Pirates, Milwaukee Brewers, and Detroit Tigers.

Chapter four continues the discussion of team strategies to minimize their costs and maximize their revenues by examining the globalization of the sport, with a focus on the competitive process of player recruitment in the Dominican Republic and Venezuela from the 1980s to the present. Faced with spiraling bonus payments in the early 1990s and rising player salaries on the free agent market through the 1980s and 1990s, all teams have established academies in the Dominican Republic, and most teams have training facilities in Venezuela, in an effort to recruit low-cost Latin athletes to fill slots on minor league rosters. This process is extremely unregulated and involves a fair number of under-the-table agreements with Latin scouts in an effort to keep prized players out of the reach of competitors. Extensive studies of player recruitment indicate that teams often have not provided Latin players with full disclosure of the terms of their initial contracts, often providing English-only versions of contracts. Although that practice has changed and evolved as Major League Baseball now requires and circulates Spanish-language contracts, Latin players still find themselves without any protection when it comes to the negotiation of bonus clauses, injury risks, unsafe training facilities, and local talent scouts, or *buscones*, who often try to pocket a share of an athlete's bonus money as "compensation" for providing assistance and training prior to signing by a major league club. The Wild West atmosphere of player recruitment in Latin America is part of Major League Baseball's efforts to expand the reach of the sport for both commercialization and cost-cutting purposes. The concept of a worldwide draft, proposed by the commissioner's office and included in the last collective bargaining agreement, promised to promote a greater regulation of the process of player selection in Latin America. Although it appears that a worldwide draft may not materialize any time soon, due in part to disagreement over the scope, logistics and necessity of the draft among big-league clubs and the Players Association, we examine the implications of a hypothetical draft for big-league owners and Latin players. Then we explore the possibilities of greater regulation of the process of recruitment in Latin America with the goal of establishing greater rights for Latin players and greater responsibilities for major league teams.

The final chapter explores the politics and economics of expansion teams. Major League Baseball has long sought gradual limits on expansion to provide the league with greater leverage in pressuring cities, counties and states to finance new ballparks. By not allowing expansion clubs in certain prime markets, Major League Baseball can use the threat of relocation to those markets when authorities balk at public financing of a new stadium for an existing franchise. However, the politics of expansion often become intermingled with the politics of Washington, D.C., and congressmen and senators threaten to eliminate baseball's prized antitrust exemption unless the league adds an expansion club to a particular district favored by a powerful political figure. This political pressure, combined with Major League Baseball's desire to generate short-term revenue for the league as national television money declined during the early 1990s, contributed to the decision to award new franchises to Miami and Denver. Losing cities, including Phoenix and Tampa Bay, then kept the political heat turned up in demanding franchises for themselves at a latter date. The process, then, has ultimately been driven less by the best interests of the sport and more by short-term considerations of political influence and revenue generation.

The central focus of all these chapters is the factors that contribute to a competitive league alongside the economic and organizational factors that help us understand why some teams are successful and others are not. We argue that league-wide decisions regarding allocation of revenue are important, as are league decisions that help to maximize the potential revenue available for distribution, in determining how competitive and successful the league will be. At the same time, individual teams can help themselves by practicing sound organizational decision making that maximizes their revenues and allows them to buy more talent at less cost than their opponents. As a cursory examination of baseball from the 1980s to the present suggests, we have been living in an unusually competitive period when the sport has seen more teams compete successfully than ever before in its history. We use this book to document this trend and to identify the various reasons for the recent golden age of competitiveness. We also discuss how such a golden age might be replicated for future generations of fans.

ONE

Money and Myth in Major League Baseball

The history of owner-player conflict is littered with owner claims that the elimination of the "cradle-to-grave" reserve clause would destroy baseball, that free agency would lead to bankruptcy for franchises and that a competitive imbalance caused by escalating player salaries would drive fans away from the game. In the free agency era, the owners have tried to use the end of each collective bargaining agreement to extract concessions from players ranging from the attempted imposition of a salary cap to taxes on high-payroll teams in an effort to slow the spiraling rise of player salaries. In recent years, owners have asserted that more than half of all the major league clubs have no chance to reach the postseason due solely to payroll considerations. Owner claims of financial crisis were elevated to astounding heights when commissioner Bud Selig stated after the end of the 2001 season that 25 of the 30 major league clubs had lost money during the 2001 campaign, with this contention providing the backdrop for the failed plan to eliminate two franchises, which would have been an unprecedented move in modern sports history and was most likely an ownership bargaining chip in a desperate attempt to win concessions from the players' union in the last collective bargaining agreement.

The owners' declarations of financial crisis rise with renewed urgency every time a new collective bargaining agreement is being negotiated. In fact, if the ownership's rhetoric of financial loss was matched by events, there would certainly have been numerous franchise bankruptcies by now. Instead, all reports by independent sources at a safe distance from the commissioner's office have concluded that Major League Baseball franchises have steadily escalated in value. Owners' claims of losses do not square with their ability to profit from the sale of their franchises to bidders who are willing to pay ever higher prices to own a piece of this industry, including a record-setting $720 million purchase price for the Boston Red Sox in 2001, a franchise which sold for $17 million in 1978, or the $350 million price for the Los Angeles Dodgers in 1997. Baltimore, which sold for $13 million in 1979, was bought for $173 million in 1993. But even the small-market franchises have seen their assets soar in value, including the Pittsburgh Pirates, sold for $22 million in 1985 compared to $85 million in 1995, hardly an increase that can be accounted for by inflation.[1]

Then why the owners' claims of losses? The answer has more to do with the battle over who gets the bulk of the revenues generated by the sport-owners or players — with actual losses by franchises. In the days of the reserve clause, owners pocketed over 80 percent of all revenues pouring into major league baseball. Since free agency began, the owners have seen a larger share of their profit margin slip to the players' pockets, with the players now receiving about 55 percent of all the revenues generated by the sport. The escalation of salaries over the past decade has been more dramatic than at any time during the history of the game, and the salary scale is increasingly established by those franchises that have the highest revenue streams and can set the bar for the cost of top-line free agents. Corporate conglomerates that purchase franchises in large markets with ample television and local media revenue are able to use their ownership of major league teams to enhance the profitability of their other assets, whether it be media, real estate, or merchandising. Increasingly, the battle between the owners and players is also a battle between groups of owners who are playing under different financial capabilities. The cries of financial crisis are partly posturing by the owners, part of every negotiation with the players association, and partly reflect the growth of revenue inequalities that have increasingly divided the large-revenue teams from their smaller-revenue competitors.

As if to unwittingly reinforce the owners' claims of financial crisis, some of the best historians and sportswriters invoke memories of baseball from their childhood during the 1940s and 1950s with the appellation of "golden age." Yet while this golden age is to be heralded for bringing us cherished memories of some of the greatest ballplayers who have ever lived, the free agency era has provided better competitive balance than the period before free agency. Since free agency, a wider range of major league clubs have gone to the postseason than during the so-called golden age of the 1950s, when two teams dominated their sport to the detriment of fan interest and attendance, as baseball experienced spiraling declines in gate receipts that helped lead to the last extended period of franchise relocation in the sport's history. Despite the owners' claims, the ability of players to offer their services to the highest bidder has coincided with greater competitive balance during the free agency period than during the decades of the 1950s through 1960s. At the same time, owners have fought rearguard actions during the free agent era to reign in their cost margins by attempting to limit player salaries through collusion, lockouts, and the brief but failed attempt to field replacement players during the longest stoppage of play in major league history, in 1994-1995.

This last go-round, the owners utilized a new strategy in an attempt to gain bargaining leverage with the Players Association: the public attempt to eliminate two major league franchises, and thereby 50 major league jobs, for the stated purpose of helping to ease the financial crisis faced by the sport. The owners argued that they could undertake this step unilaterally, while the Players Association pointed to contractual stipulations that require the owners to bargain with the union over the conditions, extent, and terms of eliminating franchises, including the manner in which the eliminated teams disperse their players to other major league clubs. Ultimately, the owners cashed in their contraction chips, bargaining away their self-proclaimed right to eliminate franchises as part of the new four-year collective bargaining agreement with the Players Association (although reserving the right to contract in 2007). In return, the owners were able to talk the Players Association into extending the luxury tax for the duration of the agreement and to establish a date at which the four-year agreement would end at a point more favorable to ownership: December 19, prior to when new contracts have to be tendered.

What is striking about the owner's negotiating ploy to contract teams is how such a posture contradicted the recommendations from the owners' own Blue Ribbon Commission Report, in which a panel of experts were authorized by the commissioners office to produce a study of the game's financial health and issue recommendations designed to address the current financial problems faced by the sport.² Interestingly, the commission's report limited its focus to the years following the last strike and lockout that canceled the last two months of the 1994 season, including the elimination of the World Series and the delay of the 1995 season. Clearly an owners' document, absent any representation from the Players Association on the Blue Ribbon Panel, the commission's report did not recommend contraction or a salary cap as answers for the current "financial crisis." Instead, the commission appears to have recognized that the emergence of serious revenue inequities among franchises escalated dramatically during the mid– to late 1990s, long after free agency had been established, and coincided with the gap between large- and small-revenue franchises around the spiraling differential in local television and radio revenue during the 1990s, with the effects most apparent between 1994 and 2000. The commission concluded that any effort to address the growing gap between the top and bottom payroll teams has to include a willingness on the part of the owners to share 50 percent of their local net revenues with the rest of Major League Baseball. However, this recommendation rests alongside other measures suggested by the Blue Ribbon panel that were opposed even more forcefully by the Players Association, including a dramatic escalation of the luxury tax on team payrolls that would place a 50 percent levy on all MLB payrolls above a designated payroll threshold. Ultimately, compromises were reached on both revenue sharing and the luxury tax, with revenue sharing set at 34 percent of net local revenues, a figure comfortably between the owners' original 50 percent proposal and the Players Association 22 percent figure, while the luxury tax was well below the 50 percent figure desired by the owners. The players bargained for no more than a 17.5 percent luxury tax in 2003 for payrolls over $117 million, which would only marginally escalate over the lifetime of the agreement.³

Prior to the negotiated agreement following the last work stoppage in 1994, the owners shared less than 20 percent of gate receipts, a small fraction of pay television money (cable and superstation) and nothing of local television and radio money. Starting in 1995, owners were required to share only 20 percent of net local revenues with the rest of the league. Unlike other sports, which have mostly increased the revenue distribution derived from gate receipts, Major League Baseball had minimized revenue distribution by allowing all teams to pocket 80 percent of home gate receipts and other local revenue. More importantly, MLB relies more heavily on local media revenue as a significant source of income for individual franchises than do other sports, and local radio and TV money has risen steadily as a percentage of overall team revenues, especially during the 1990s. The lack of any greater redistribution of this media money has coincided with a weakening of the improved competitive balance that accompanied the period of free agency from the late 1970s to the early 1990s. From 1994 to 2000, the growing inequality among franchise payrolls was due in part to skyrocketing disparities in local media money that have allowed the New York Yankees, Boston Red Sox, Baltimore Orioles and other northeastern franchise giants to earn more from this source of revenue than the bottom franchises pay in team salary. Although, as we will document in this book, the recent period from 2001 to 2004 has seen a return to greater competitive balance once again, due mainly to the infusion of more money being distributed to all major league teams as a result of the 2001–2006 television contracts with ESPN and Fox, which collectively increased television revenue by about 50 percent over the previous television contract.[4] Still, there remains a tension between small-revenue and large-revenue franchises to this day.

The owners of mid-revenue franchises, with less access to local media revenue, have argued that they can compete only by securing increasingly lucrative taxpayer subsidies for new state-of-the-art ballparks, equipped with ample luxury boxes and a potpourri of amusement park themes, concession facilities, and parking facilities that ensure a wealth of revenue to narrow the gap with their upper-tier, media-rich cousins, at least for a time. As for franchises that simply draw well, such as the St. Louis Cardinals' perennial attendance mark of three million-plus that announces the city as a great baseball town, the ownership has successfully pushed the city of St. Louis, the county and the state for the construction of a new ballpark, with a combination of private and public financing, to open in 2006, all in the name of increasing team payroll to ensure a healthy and competitive franchise for the future. It seems that the current plan, orchestrated and approved at the highest levels of Major League Baseball, is to continue to insist that cities up the ante with the most modern facilities possible, thereby helping to increase revenue streams and leveling the playing field between the media-rich and the stadium-poor clubs through taxpayer subsidies toward new stadiums and all their revenue-enhancing possibilities, despite the fact that new stadium construction has often coincided with *reduced* spending on player payroll and non-competitiveness (see the recent histories of Milwaukee, Pittsburgh and Detroit as exhibits A, B, and C). Still, never allowing reality to stand in their way, the owners' push for the contraction of franchises was intended as yet another threat to cities, counties and states of the possible consequences of failing to approve publicly financed stadiums. The owners view the public financing of state-of-the-art modern facilities as short-term solutions to the severe revenue imbalances between the top- and bottom-payroll clubs, though little evidence for this position exists outside of the early examples of Cleveland and, to a lesser extent, Baltimore.

While the last seven years have seen an escalation in disparity between the high- and low-revenue clubs, the reasons have more to do with the escalating importance of local media revenue as a percentage of team income, and as we will show in our final chapter, these income disparities appear to have become much less significant in the last three seasons than they may have been for the period from 1994 to 2000. During the 1970s, 1980s and early 1990s, revenues were more evenly divided among baseball clubs than they have been since the mid–1990s. The reasons have to do with the escalation of national media revenue as a percentage of team revenue during the period of the late 1970s through the early 1990s, as national media contracts are evenly divided among all major league clubs and thereby lessen revenue inequalities. During the 1994 strike and subsequent lockout, the owners saw their national television money decline, well short of the value of the lucrative 1984 television deal with CBS that coincided with the lowest disparity of revenue among franchises in the history of the sport.[5] However, despite growing revenue imbalances between 1994–2000, there appears to be little evidence of a singular long-term correlation between team revenue, payroll and winning percentage. For example, the early effects of free agency have not resulted in any consistent correlation between money spent on free agents and high team winning percentages. As Andrew Zimbalist has argued "Team owners since 1976 have done a singularly unimpressive job of signing top-performing free agents or of paying a player according to his output. Consequently, average team salary has been related only tenuously to team performance: from 1984 to 1989, average team salary explained less than 10 percent of the variance in team win percentage and less than 12 percent of the variance in team standing."[6] Instead, a combination of factors seem to have been more essential to team success: a productive player development strategy through the minor league system, strategic signings of free agents to complement an existing base of talent, and the ability to evaluate the worth of players in trade negotiations. These factors, during the bulk of the free agency period, have been more important than money in predicting success, although a more equitable distribution of revenue also contributes to competitive balance.

Measuring Competitiveness: A Statistical Method

In order to demonstrate that the free agency era has been more competitive than the pre–free-agency era, we have developed a statistical model of competitiveness that broadly compares the two periods. Our competitiveness index is based on an examination of whether or not there has been an increased variation of different teams succeeding in making it to the postseason during different years and eras. In other words, there is no variation if the same teams make the postseason each year, indicating a noncompetitive environment. By contrast, if every team in the league reaches the postseason over a limited span of years, that would be defined as a highly competitive environment. Just such a highly competitive pattern emerged in the National League in the 1980s, when each of the existing twelve teams won a division title (even the Expos, in strike-shortened 1981).

Arguably, success in reaching the postseason is not the only measure of competitiveness. However, as a savvy baseball friend of ours, Carlos Barrera, recently commented to us, good organizations don't compete; they either win or they rebuild. As any longtime fan knows, when a member of management says something along the lines of "I think we'll be competitive this year," your team is not headed to the playoffs. More to the point, when a supposedly "competitive" club fails to reach the postseason over a stretch of several seasons, then we must either blame it on bad luck, the likelihood that the franchise is poorly managed, or some flaw in the competitive environment, creating systemic inequities between franchises' abilities to succeed.

Over time, luck will even out. Therefore, looking over longer ranges of years is a better way to look at baseball's competitive environment, because the "bad luck" factors, such as injuries to key players, will even out between clubs over time. Even the likelihood of franchises being poorly managed will even out over eras as teams are bought and sold and management teams turn over. The point here is that over many years of major league baseball history, there should be increasing variety in the specific teams that succeed in making it to the postseason. Every dynasty should eventually collapse and, as the saying goes, every dog (or Cub, as the case may be) should have his day.

If, over longer stretches of many seasons, variation among successful teams does not occur, then we should consider perhaps that flaws in the structural environment are the cause of a lack of competitiveness. But is this the case? And how does the presence of free agency correlate to the competitiveness of major league baseball?

To measure the correlation between the presence of free agency and the competitive environment, we compare the free agency era (1977–present) to the era immediately preceding free agency (1946–1976). We don't go back any further on the assumption that World War II created an alteration in the competitive environment when many top players were in the service. Further, for purposes of statistical analysis, we want to keep the two eras comparable in time spans. However, in so far as the pre–free-agency era studied here is seven seasons longer (due to the absence of a postseason in 1994), it should, all other things being equal, be an era of greater variation in franchises achieving success in reaching the postseason. It is not.

Baseball fans will immediately recognize that the New York Yankees dominated much of the earlier era in the American League at least up until their shocking, sudden collapse in 1965. Over in the NL, the Dodgers were disproportionately successful during the pre–free-agency era. While much of the relevant financial information is unavailable for major league baseball franchises prior to recent decades, what we do know suggests that the Yankees and likely the Dodgers as well had even greater economic advantages in the pre–free-agency era than they do now.

In order to compare the different eras, we have devised an index of competitiveness. Our index would provide a perfect score of 100 to any era in which teams would reach the postseason an equal number of times, and a score of zero would be given to any purely monopolistic era in which one team wins all of the time. To the extent that there is variance from a long-run egalitarian outcome, the era's score falls. According to our index the free agency era has close to a passing grade (59), while the pre–free-agency era of 1946–1976 scores much lower (20).

What we can see from these tables is that there has been a clumping of teams toward the expected average rates of success in reaching the postseason. For the pre–free-agency era, the complete lack of success among the expansion teams (and the Cubs) pushes the mean ratio below one, while the success ratio of the pre–free-agency Yankees (and to a lesser extent, the Dodgers) creates a higher degree of variances in rates of success in the pre–free-agency era, as indicated by the standard deviations. Calculating variance filters out, to some extent, the fact that there are more opportunities to go to the playoffs in the current era. This is because standard deviation is derived from a calculation of variance within the data set. In any period, regardless of the number of teams that get to go to the postseason, the variance would approach zero under conditions of pure competition/equality of outcomes.

The competitiveness index may be a more convenient shorthand comparison. It is calculated by subtracting the variance from one and then multiplying by one hundred. Under conditions of pure competition, in which success rates converged toward equality over time, the competitive index would approach 100. Conversely, if it falls to zero or enters negative territory, we have calculations that the federal courts would likely regard as prima facie evidence of monopolistic practices. For the earlier era, the index would have been zero if the Yankees had maintained their success after 1964, or if the Dodgers' rate of success had approximated that of the Yankees.

Expansion and the addition of extra rounds of playoffs also contribute to increased variation of the number of teams that succeed. Very likely, if there had been divisional playoffs in the 1950s, the Yankees would not have won the World Series or even the pennant as often as they did. Our measure of competitiveness controls for these changes. For each franchise, we have developed a composite average of what the frequency of success for that team should be if the environment were one of pure competition and luck was not a factor. For example, prior to 1961, there were only eight teams and one postseason spot in each league. Hence, for those teams during that era, each should get to the post season $1/8$th (12.5 percent) of the time. After the two additional teams were added to each league in 1961-62, then each existing franchise should succeed $1/10$th (10 percent) of the time. Similarly, beginning with the introduction of divisional play and the LCS in 1969, the ratio of expected success rises to $1/6$th and so on. At the present time, the ratio of expected success for NL teams is 1/4, 2/7 for AL teams. (The wild card format obviates the need to break this down by division.) For each franchise within each era, we calculated a composite ratio of expected success to account for changes in the number of teams and playoff spots available to each franchise over the course of its particular franchise history. For example, the Seattle Pilots/Milwaukee Brewers had a 1/6 opportunity (over time, opportunity should equal expected success) to make the postseason from 1969 to 1976. From 1977 to 1993 they had a 1/7 opportunity. For 1995–1997, the Brewers were in a league where 4/14 teams went to the post season (or 2/7), and after realignment they entered a 4/16 or 1/4 opportunity framework. That complicated franchise's history works out to a composite figure of 17.6 percent as the expected frequency at which the Brewers should have reached the postseason during the free-agency era. In fact, they actually got to the postseason 8.7 percent of the time (twice in 23 seasons).

Franchise Success Ratios

By comparing franchises' actual success in each era to their expected rate of success, we can derive a success indicator for each team. If we divide actual success (A) by expected success (E) then A/E equals the success ratio (SR). The score of one indicates a team whose actual success is equal to the expected. Any score below one indicates a franchise that succeeded less often than it should have, and a score above one indicates a better-than-expected rate of success. If a franchise scores a two, then it succeeds twice as often as expected and so on. The tables on the following two pages show the success ratios for each franchise in each era.

It should be noted that these indices do not prove or disprove anything about the impact of free agency on competitiveness. They do, at best, emphasize the reality that the free agency era has been more competitive but they do not (and cannot) tell us why. We argue in this book that the most consistent predictor of competitiveness, is the leveling factor associated with dramatic increases in national television money. During the 1980s, a decade that saw the strongest growth in competitiveness, there was a corresponding surge in national television money as a result of new contracts signed by Major League Baseball with major networks. From 1982 through 1984, national television revenues more than tripled

Table 1
Success Ratios for ML Franchises, 1946–1976

Franchise	Actual Success % (A)	Expected Success % (E)	Success Ratio (A/E)
Yankees	51.6	12.9	4.00
Dodgers	35.5	12.9	2.75
Browns/Orioles	19.4	12.9	1.50
Pirates	19.4	12.9	1.50
Reds	19.4	12.9	1.50
Athletics	16.1	12.9	1.25
Braves	12.9	12.9	1.00
Cardinals	12.9	12.9	1.00
Giants	12.9	12.9	1.00
Mets	13.3	13.6	1.00
Senators/Twins	9.7	12.9	0.75
Royals	12.5	16.7	0.75
Red Sox	9.7	12.9	0.75
Indians	6.5	12.9	0.50
Tigers	6.5	12.9	0.50
Phillies	6.5	12.9	0.50
White Sox	3.2	12.9	0.25
Cubs	0		0.00
Colt .45s/Astros	0		0.00
Angels	0		0.00
Senators/Rangers	0		0.00
Pilots/Brewers	0		0.00
Padres	0		0.00
Expos	0		0.00

Variance = .80
Competitiveness Index (maximum score = 100): 20

in value, from $53.4 million to $163 million, the biggest increase in the history of the sport. This money was evenly distributed to all major league clubs, and as such contributed strongly to greater competitive balance. Conversely, when national television money declined sharply from 1994 through 2000, there was a corresponding decline in competitiveness, as indicated by the fall of the competitiveness index during the period from 1995 to 2001 (documented more extensively in chapter two). Due to a poorly conceived contract with NBC and ABC and less up-front money from ESPN, as well as the effects of the strike and lockout of 1994-1995, the league received less national television revenue per year from 1994 to 2000 than in 1992 and 1993. That resulted in less money to distribute to

Table 2
Success Ratios for ML Franchises, 1977–1999

Franchise	Actual Success % (A)	Expected Success % (E)	Success Ratio (A/E)
Yankees	43.5	18.0	2.42
Braves	43.5	19.2	2.27
Dodgers	34.8	19.2	1.92
Red Sox	26.1	18.0	1.45
Royals	26.1	18.0	1.45
Athletics	26.1	18.0	1.45
Phillies	26.1	19.2	1.36
Astros	26.1	19.2	1.36
Diamondbacks	33.3	25.0	1.33
Indians	21.7	18.0	1.21
Blue Jays	21.7	18.0	1.21
Cardinals	21.7	19.2	1.13
Orioles	17.4	18.0	0.97
Giants	17.4	19.2	0.91
Pirates	17.4	19.2	0.91
Mets	17.4	19.2	0.91
Angels	13.0	18.0	0.72
Rangers	13.0	18.0	0.72
Mariners	13.0	18.0	0.72
White Sox	13.0	18.0	0.72
Padres	13.0	19.2	0.68
Reds	13.0	19.2	0.68
Cubs	13.0	19.2	0.68
Marlins	14.3	25.0	0.57
Rockies	14.3	25.0	0.57
Brewers	8.7	17.6	0.50
Tigers	8.7	18.0	0.48
Twins	8.7	18.0	0.48
Expos	4.3	19.2	0.22
Devil Rays	0		0.00

Variance = 41 percent
Competitiveness Index (maximum score = 100): 59

teams and more revenue inequality, which resulted in a move away from the competitiveness trends of 1981–1993. However, with the more recent signing of a lucrative national television deal with Fox and ESPN covering the period from 2000 to 2006 (ESPN) and 2001 to 2006 (FOX), there has been a significant jump in national television money in recent years. The Fox deal by itself increased revenues by 45 percent over the previous package by raising the payout to Major League Baseball from an average of $290 million per year to $417 million per year. This is likely to have contributed to a return to greater competitive equality during the past three seasons, 2002–2004.

The golden age of competitiveness occurred between 1981 and 1993, when every National League team made the playoffs and only two American League clubs failed to advance to the postseason. Despite ownership cries that the end of the reserve clause would doom the sport, just the opposite has occurred: the game has never been healthier than immediately after the beginning of free agency, when more teams competed for championships than during any other comparable period of baseball history, and when more teams won championships than in any other period. During this free agent era, Major League Baseball overcame the serious competitive imbalances that plagued its misnamed "golden age" of the 1940s and 1950s, when the unrivaled dominance of just a few well-endowed franchises confused their continuity and glory with the health of the sport. Ordinary fans weren't confused by the economics of the so-called golden age, as evidenced by progressively lower attendance during the 1950s, a financial reality that helped lead the sport to the relocation of franchises.[7] At that time, the owners, under considerable challenge to their cherished antitrust exemption, moved franchises to high-growth regions in an effort to combat declining attendance in the northeast and midwest. The strategy proved to rebound in baseball's favor, as many of the new markets prospered initially, although the shifting of franchises could not ultimately conceal the weaknesses of a system that held players in perpetual bondage. Teams that were able to purchase players held the edge over their second-division counterparts, relying on a market position of wealth and privilege to allow them more room for error in their evaluation of talent.

Teams that were not so well endowed, however, could and did rise to the top if they were willing and able to take advantage of the ability of franchises to develop talent through a low-cost minor league system, tied through antitrust exemption to the control of Major League Baseball teams and maximized to full advantage by clubs that learned to rely on a talent strategy that eschewed paying large salaries to veteran big-leaguers in favor of recruiting an abundance of low-paid minor league talent, paying them while they came cheap and trading them away after they had outlived their usefulness. This, otherwise known as the Cardinals model, when combined with a willingness to embrace the sport's belated allowance of racial integration, helped propel certain franchises past others. In other words, money has never been enough by itself, but talent evaluation and willingness to take risks and adjust to new market circumstances have been very important ingredients for success. The owners used the reserve system to their full advantage, holding down player salaries well below inflation, so that player salaries during the cradle-to-grave reserve system stagnated in real terms during the so-called golden age of the 1950s, when a significant number of baseball players still had to supplement their baseball income with off-season jobs in order to provide for their families. This system ensured that owners would pocket the vast majority of revenues generated by the sport, which at the time were highly concentrated around gate receipts, with concessions and media money playing a secondary role. In the entertainment age of the 1990s to the present, the ticket price is only about 50 percent of the cost of attending a major league game, as teams depend much more on concessions revenue, parking, and the sale of luxury suites for overall revenue, as well as the value of a club's local radio and TV contract.

As the subject of our book involves an analysis of the financial health and competitive structure of the sport, we need to locate the emergence of the free agency era in the context of the pre–free-agency period. In comparing and contrasting the two periods of baseball history, we will focus our analysis on the post–World War II trajectory of the sport by first delineating the major institutional features of baseball during the pre–free-agency periods, including the changes and continuities surrounding the transition from one period to the next. With that in mind, no analysis of the revenue dynamics of the modern game would be complete without an understanding of the importance of the baseball's cartel structure.

Baseball as a Cartel

Throughout its history, Major League Baseball has operated as a cartel that gives the league monopoly power in the distribution of revenues generated by the sport, the location of franchises, the movement of players, the creation of new franchises, and the player development system that allows major league teams to own rights to players through minor league affiliates. During the period immediately after World War II, Major League Baseball had already institutionalized the key features of this cartel, aided by an exemption from U.S. antitrust law upheld by the Supreme Court decision of 1922. Prior to free agency, the owners exercised almost total control over the various aspects of the cartel, buttressed by a reserve clause that had defined the relationship between the players and the owners for close to a century. The reserve clause allowed Major League Baseball teams to own a player from cradle to grave at the moment the player was signed to a big-league contract. This clause coincided with a reserve system that allowed major league clubs to maintain ownership of an extensive farm system of young talent whose promotion to the big leagues were left to the discretion of team owners. The fact that baseball teams concentrated their farm systems in the Deep South was no accident of geography, as the reserve system was dependent on a low-cost minor league structure that operated best in an environment devoid of unions and collective bargaining agreements.[8]

Whatever else has changed about the relationship between Major League Baseball teams and players, the central features of the reserve system, especially its minor league structure, have remained in place to this day. The abolition of the cradle-to-grave reserve clause, made possible by an arbitrator's ruling in 1976, did not eliminate the tight major league control over the minor league system, nor did it necessarily free players to become free agents after their contracts expired. Instead, the reserve system has been retained, but modified, allowing for free agency only after a six-year period of service time in Major League Baseball, with the requisite service time negotiated between Major League Baseball and the newly powerful Players Association under the leadership of Marvin Miller. The Players Association recognized that complete free agency would work against player salaries by allowing too many free agents to flood the market, thereby driving down the players' bargaining position and allowing the owners to maintain lower salaries for top-flight players. Charles Finley, alone among Major League owners, urged his brethren to push for complete free agency for all players whose contracts had ended, regardless of service time, a proposal rejected by both the owners and eschewed by Marvin Miller in negotiating a partial reserve clause in the collective bargaining agreement finalized after the 1976 season.[9]

In exchange for paying minor league salaries and bonuses that allow minor league franchises to fill their rosters, Major League Baseball gets virtually unlimited rights regarding the utilization of minor league talent. Alongside this arrangement, minor league teams are expected to finance the costs of their facility and operations expenses, which these days usually involve considerable public subsidies to cover the costs of playing equipment, infrastructure and officiating necessary to league competition. The relationship between the major league clubs and their minor league subsidiaries is central to understanding the ongoing reserve system in Major League Baseball. First, Major League Baseball created their own minor league affiliations in response to competitive threats from other professional baseball leagues, and to secure talent more cheaply than if teams continued to purchase talent from independently owned minor league franchises. As early as 1916 and well before Branch Rickey firmly institutionalized the large-scale minor league system that would replenish the St. Louis Cardinals with young, inexpensive talent year after year, Cleveland's owner Charles Somers had secured minor league franchises in Eastern League Waterbury, Southern League New Orleans, and AA Toledo in an effort to counteract salary escalation driven by competition from the rival Federal League. The subsequent development of the minor league system by Branch Rickey was utilized to control a low-paying reserve system of labor that allowed Rickey, and soon all other baseball owners and general managers, the institutional advantages of being a "supplier, rather than a buyer," of playing labor. In Rickey's own words, his system was based on a parent organization signing a player at a "production expense" that was lower than the subsequent "market value" for that player.[10]

The ability of Major League Baseball to control its minor league subsidiaries has been a central feature of baseball's antitrust exemption, which would be periodically challenged whenever the league decided to move franchises from one market to another, a process that would be accom-

Opposite: The legendary Branch Rickey, who managed the St. Louis Browns, St. Louis Cardinals, Brooklyn Dodgers, and Pittsburgh Pirates. Rickey pioneered the development of a farm system that revolutionized the sport; under his watch, the Cardinals won five pennants in nine years, due in large part to Rickey's keen eye for developing and trading players. With the Dodgers, Rickey kept ahead of the competition by signing Jackie Robinson, giving Brooklyn an advantage over clubs who were slower to integrate. Rickey challenged Major League Baseball's monopoly in 1960 by helping to establish the short-lived Continental Baseball League, a move that spurred Major League Baseball to add expansion franchises in 1961.

panied by congressional inquiries into the antitrust exemption enjoyed by the sport. A congressional hearing in 1953 examined the relationship between Major League Baseball and its minor league affiliates by noting that Major League Baseball had profited from control over minor league affiliates during the 1930s and 1940s, with parent organizations receiving more from their minor league subsidiaries than they paid in expenses to those clubs.

> Until 1950, the net cost to the major leagues of owning minor league subsidiaries never exceeded $400,000; 1933 and 1943 appear to have been the costliest years. In normal times, however, the major leagues have operated their minor league subsidiaries at a profit; from 1939–1942, 1944–1947, and 1949, the net flow of funds was not from parent club to subsidiary, but from minor league affiliations to the majors.[11]

This report contradicted claims by Branch Rickey that major league control of minor league subsidiaries saved the minor leagues from bankruptcy. In fact, the economic vitality of the minor leagues reached its ascendancy during the 1940s, when the minors could be divided into three categories: those teams that were controlled outright as subsidiaries of major league clubs, those teams that had working agreements with major league clubs that involved limited major league rights to players under terms negotiated by the major league and minor league franchise, and those teams that operated independently of Major League Baseball. The antitrust exemption granted to Major League Baseball by the Supreme Court in 1922 allowed the league to exercise considerable control over both its operating structure and the supply network of players that were developed in minor league organizations linked to major league teams. The tensions between commissioner Kenesaw Mountain Landis and Branch Rickey over the development of this minor league system, with Landis opposed to its extension and Rickey taking liberties to pioneer an extensive system of minor league subsidiaries, could not deter the adoption of a minor league network that was firmly integrated into Major League Baseball. By 1951, MLB teams owned 207 minor league clubs and controlled some 9,000 minor leaguers, while the average pay at the top classification level was almost 25 percent of the major league average.[12]

Major league clubs looked to reduce the expenses of player development during the 1950s as the costs of the farm systems had skyrocketed in the context of a revenue crisis that was the product of several factors. First, competition among big-league clubs for expensive amateur signings intensified after World War II, as total bonus payments came to $4.5 million in 1951 alone, a figure equivalent to 14 percent of combined MLB revenues. Second, the demographics of major league franchises remained concentrated around the old urban population centers of the northeast, with St. Louis the westernmost franchise despite the considerable population growth of Midwestern and Western cities without teams, including Los Angeles and San Francisco, the third- and ninth-ranking cities in total population by the late 1940s.[13] Without a franchise relocation since 1903, MLB remained locked out of emerging cities with growing populations and potential revenues that could have provided a net gain to what had become a stagnant and declining revenue base. Robert Burk summarizes the financial problems faced by the sport during the 1950s:

> ...major league turnout slipped to 14.4 million by 1953 and did not reach 20 million again until 1960. The American League felt the crisis the worst; given the Yankees' dominance and the circuit's laggardness in signing African-American talent, AL attendance dropped from 9.1 million in 1950 to 7.3 million by 1958. In 1950, big-league profit margins suddenly slumped 7.5 percent to only 2 percent on net revenue of $65 million. By 1956, revenue had shrunk $5 million more, and the average club profit stood at but $30,000. Reflecting baseball's decline relative to other forms of recreation, the industry's share of the U.S. entertainment dollar, 68 cents in 1948, slipped to 49 cents as early as 1950 and kept falling.[14]

These financial problems coincided with, and were likely exacerbated by, a marked disparity among revenues generated by franchises, reflected in significant disparities between the top- and bottom-payroll clubs. During the 1950s, the Yankees outspent the bottom quintile of Major League Baseball franchises by a margin close to 5–1, coinciding with a period of franchise domination that virtually ensured that the poorest teams would be feeding grounds for the Yankee acquisition of talent. As Donald Dewey and Nicholas Acocella explained in their seminal history of major league organizations:

> When new pitchers were needed, as they were in 1954, the organization dipped into the farm system for Rookie of the Year Bob Grim

(20–6) and pulled off an eighteen-player trade (the largest in history) with Baltimore that brought to New York right-handers Bob Turley, the 1958 Cy Young Award winner, and Don Larsen, best remembered for his perfect game against the Dodgers in the fifth game of the 1956 World Series. After 1955, when the Philadelphia Athletics moved to Kansas City, Weiss used the new franchise as a Yankee farm club, reaching out to make seventeen separate deals between April 1955 and May 1960 that netted New York frontline pitchers Art Ditmar, Bobby Shantz, Ralph Terry, and reliever Ryne Duren; third baseman Clete Boyer; and outfielders Roger Maris, Enos Slaughter, Hector Lopez and Bob Cerv. The Kansas City connection centered around Arnold Johnson, who had owned Yankee Stadium before taking over the Athletics, and Kansas City GM Parke Carroll, who had worked for Weiss in the Yankee front office.[15]

Thus the clubs that generated the most revenues, usually located in the largest markets with the largest fan base and buttressed by ownership groups with the deepest pockets, could acquire players by purchasing them from cash-strapped franchises, in addition to committing considerable money toward player development. The system worked well for large-market giants such as the New York Yankees and Brooklyn Dodgers, whose payroll advantages over the rest of the league allowed them to consistently appear at the top of the standings in their respective leagues.

The Yankees and Dodgers benefited from their privileged market position, allowing these teams to exceed other major league clubs in operating revenue, and in team payrolls, by a substantial margin. Over the course of the post–World War II period, Major League Baseball clubs have relied on three main sources of revenue: gate and stadium revenues, broadcasting revenues, and licensing revenues. Prior to 1945, almost all of a baseball team's revenue came from ticket and concession sales, while over time radio and television broadcast revenues have grown substantially, from "3 percent in 1946, 10 percent in 1950, 17 percent in 1956, 28 percent in 1970, 38 percent in 1985, 42 percent in 1988 and 50 percent in 1990."[16] In terms of aggregate revenues, baseball has never been healthier than it is now, but showdowns over the distribution of that revenue, between teams and between players and owners, continue to cast a depressing shadow over the sport.

Anxiety in a Booming World Market

As a business, baseball's prospects were never so bright in the past as they are now. Revenue and attendance are at all-time-highs, while the industry's potential market in this age of globalization is virtually unlimited. The fans, as Bill James points out, attend baseball games with greater frequency than ever.[17] Cable television and other media revenues have grown in comparison to gate receipts as sources of cash flow for MLB franchises. Merchandising provides a further source of income and, as the industry's fan base extends into emerging international markets, even more money.

In 2001 Ichiro Suzuki capped off a successful North American debut by winning the American League Rookie of the Year and Most Valuable Player awards. With the world's second largest consumer market now tuned in, savvy entrepreneurs will not miss the multimedia and merchandising opportunities presented by the cross-cultural appeal of Suzuki and other star players from Japan now to be seen in major league venues. Unlike its U.S.–centric commercial rival, American football, baseball draws player talent from throughout the Americas, East Asia, and Australia. Through the appeal of its international cast, Major League Baseball has the realistic potential to rival soccer as the world's biggest and most profitable professional game.

In the age of the dot-com boom, baseball remains a reliable brick-and-mortar venture with dependable revenue streams and loyal customers. This is a product so popular that even when the main event is cancelled, i.e., the World Series, as a consequence of the strike of 1994, there is only a very short-term pause in the ever-upward growth of revenue and fan attendance at games (a trend which certainly took a backslide in 2002, undoubtedly affected by the ongoing threat of a work stoppage). Product identification with major league baseball is so strong that even the game's worst scandal, the "Black Sox" of 1919, is the stuff of highly marketable folk legend. Nor is nostalgia the limit of the game's appeal. As Tygiel points out, the virtual world of rotisserie and fantasy baseball, well adapted to the computer, has emerged as the cutting-edge marketing device.[18] The game is marketable across a wide spectrum of popular taste, from old-fashioned nostalgia in movies and books to the technically sophisticated simulations.

Global investors are well aware of baseball's value. The Los Angeles

Dodgers were until very recently part of the Murdoch empire, while the Atlanta Braves provide programming for the Turner/AOL/Time Warner communications network. Donald Watkins, an Alabama-based investor, recently declared two of the sport's "small-market" franchises (Tampa Bay and Minnesota) to be "undervalued" assets that he seemed eager to buy. A capital idea, since there is no living financier who has ever lost money in the buying and selling of Major League Baseball franchises.

Despite the global boom times, the commissioner of Major League Baseball claimed before a congressional committee in late 2001 that 25 of 30 franchises were currently operating at a loss due to ever-higher labor costs. A claim of this kind can hardly be taken seriously in light of revenue growth and the fact that player salaries are actually not rising as a percentage of overall revenue. By the commissioner's own numbers, the industry's revenues rose by 156 percent from 1995 to 2001, while player salaries increased by 113 percent for the same period.[19] Since many Major League Baseball franchises are subsidiary to larger multimedia and even multinational enterprises, it is difficult to abstract the profits and losses of the baseball teams from their roles within these larger conglomerates. In the cases of four franchises such as the Chicago Cubs (owned by the Tribune Company, which also owns the WGN superstation), the baseball team is owned by a larger media concern and so probably is best regarded as a programming cost. In other cases, such as the Philadelphia Phillies, the franchise is part owner of its own cable network and therefore the cash value placed on its television contract ought not be taken too seriously as an indicator of a team's market value. Claiming a "loss" in such contexts is akin to McDonald's claiming that it is losing money in hamburgers due to the high cost of beef, but arriving at that conclusion by failing to calculate the full measure of revenues generated by the Big Mac.

Current IRS rules permit MLB League franchise purchasers to depreciate the present value of player contracts over the first five years of ownership. As such, any team that has changed hands within the past five years will be claiming such "costs" and resultant book losses. All practical experience indicates that such "losses" can be recouped with ease by any investor who wants to sell the franchise. As Commissioner Selig tells Congress his industry is losing money, he is making a perverse claim that is a function of the favorable tax laws that Congress itself has proved to the industry. Given all the accounting shenanigans that are afoot, it makes far more sense to pay attention to the value of franchises rather than to statements about yearly profit and loss.

Beyond the tax laws, public policy is favorable to Major League Baseball in a number of other crucial ways. More often than not, state and local governments will provide public subsidies to build stadiums and have done so with increasing frequency in recent years. Additionally, the federal courts have upheld an antitrust exemption for Major League Baseball that provides a firewall against a range of potential litigation (an advantage that Microsoft would surely love to have).

As we have described, MLB is a cartel. The industry's franchise owners control access to the market and limit it stringently. Despite the owners' posture of being in favor of eliminating two, and perhaps four, clubs from existence, the collective bargaining agreement that expired in 2001 actually foresaw expansion to 32 teams. MLB franchising represents the creation of artificial scarcity of an enormously popular product, a reality that has prompted *Forbes* to suggest that if market forces dictated supply, the number of major leagues and teams would proliferate radically. Some fear that expansion of the number of franchises dilutes the quality of play, and there is a kernel of truth to this concern. If investors were freer to enter the major leagues of baseball and expand the number of teams at a rate faster than the growth of the player talent pool then there would logically follow a dilution of the overall quality of play and the caliber of the average player's skill levels. The fact of the matter, however, is that any such fear is misplaced insofar as the growth of MLB teams from 16 (in 1960) to 30 (by 2000) does not outstrip the growth and globalization of the available talent pool nor of the fan base.

Another way in which the talent pool could be degraded would be to compensate the players below their fair market values. Yet this does still occur. Under the current labor market structure as negotiated by the owners' cartel and the players' union, players, unlike workers in any other capitalist industry, may not work for whatever firm they choose until such time as they complete six years of service time at the major league level. Six years is longer than the average player's major league career, which averages between three and four years, so only a minority of players ever have the opportunity to sell their labor power to the highest bidder. Most are under the restrictions of a reserve clause that few acknowledge is still very much in effect.

If MLB is to continue to thrive as a global entertainment enterprise, it needs to excite and entice the consumer with a high-quality product. To do so, MLB must recruit a cadre of the world's best athletes, people whose reflexes and other relevant physical and mental attributes allow them to perform to a world-class standard. If MLB fails to offer world-class compensation to these rare talents, then future generations of young athletes will find their dreams and fortunes on other fields or courts of play. A key fault line of the ongoing battle between owners and players, and for that matter owners versus owners, is the extent to which the current revenue sharing and luxury tax policies are seen by the conflicting parties as a genuine aid to competitive balance or as a soft salary cap that does little to enhance competitive balance. To be sure, both parties will be monitoring the progress of the current agreement with a discerning eye toward its effects. When the agreement expires in 2006, complete with a set of rollover terms for 2007, again a precedent-setting move, the small-revenue owners may be hungry for a greater redistribution. At the same time the Players Association may have decided that they gave up too much, once again locking arms with the large-revenue owners in an attempt to either preserve the status quo or win an agreement more to their liking. How the conflicting sides deal with these distributional issues, and how they maneuver to expand overall revenues to the game, will ultimately chart the economic future of major league baseball, where money and power will continue to rest uneasily with on-field performances, even the record-shattering variety. Whether or not the commissioner's office can actually bring itself to celebrate the on-field success of low-revenue franchises like the Minnesota Twins and Oakland A's, rather than bemoan their small-market status, will have more to do with the tug-of-war over the distribution of revenues across the game, rather than any sustained trends in actual competitive balance.

Competitiveness and Payrolls

During the free-agency era, the game has seen increased competitiveness. No franchise during the 1980s and early to mid–1990s, not even the superbly well financed New York Yankees, have been able to dominate MLB like the Yankees of the "golden era." As defined by turnover in the teams winning championships, pennants, and other postseason berths, MLB has never been more competitive than in the last two decades of the twentieth century.[20] Perhaps as a further indication of competitive balance, during the 2000 and 2001 seasons, no team in the National League finished the season above .600 or below .400 in win-loss percentage. With the addition of "wild card" playoff slots in the late 1990s, this has meant that an increasing number of teams have remained in contention late into the season.

At the advent of the free-agency era, Tom Seaver made the claim to Roger Angell that players who are more free to move on to a better deal or preferred alternative playing situation would take the opportunity to move from situations where their playing time was limited by the presence of established players to venues where they could have increased opportunities. Said Seaver, "Free agency is going to help the game by cutting loose the good players that some clubs have kept sitting on the bench."[21] In practice, free agency appears to work the other way around. Under the current system, six-year veterans move to greener pastures, thereby creating openings for rising talent in their old organizations. The upshot is that with free agency limited by the six-year rule and transfer of draft picks in the compensation for loss of players to free agency, teams with lower payroll capacities can, and often do, remain competitive by emphasizing minor league player development. Further, as veterans' salaries have become more function of supply and demand, but younger players remain restricted by the cartel, the financial incentive has increased for clubs to move talented younger players into major league roles sooner rather than later with the effect that mediocre veteran players often get caught in the squeeze between very high-priced stars and comparatively very low-paid "up-and-comers." These are stressful working conditions for the experienced but marginal, yet nonetheless an incentive structure that may well, on balance, enhance both competitiveness and increased emphasis on talent development.

Some complain that player movement from team to team associated with free agency is bad for the game because it breaks up teams and leaves lower-payroll teams bereft of their top talent from one season to the next. As Bob Costas puts it, "No player of consistent All-Star quality is going to remain in Minnesota [or another "small market"] throughout his career."[22] Yet common perception to the contrary, the fact of the matter is that player movement has not increased during most of the free-agency era. "From 1961, the beginning of expansion, to 1993, the movement of players from one major league team to another was exactly the same, a range of four to six per year. Nor was it a matter of second-line players moving and stars staying put. A check of all the Hall of Famers who played before 1960 would show that more than a third of them had been traded during career peaks in the 'old days.'"[23]

Why the perception otherwise? Both the commissioner's office and the memorabilia industry have a strong role in perpetuating the myth that free agency has had a negative impact on the game. The owners, ever eager to win back some of the gains secured by the players with the elimination of the reserve clause and the advent of three-year arbitration, have repeatedly claimed that free agency has made it impossible to keep teams together, as "greedy" players perpetually flock to greener pastures and thereby help to destroy continuity and tradition, undermining competitiveness and weakening the game. This rhetoric, used by owners in their war with players throughout the 1980s and 1990s, contrasts with the facts: competitive balance was greater than ever during the period between 1981 and 1993; player movement remained constant before and after free agency; and the industry was bringing in more revenue than ever before. But such rhetoric appealed to the commercialized autograph and memento collecting industry, who had a vested interest in creating profitable nostalgia. The middle-aged, and relatively wealthy, older fan base of major league baseball tapped into the nostalgia craze, eager to agree that baseball would never be the same as it was during the "golden age" of their youth. Both seller and customer depended on an environment that romanticized the past and encouraged the buying of older collectibles that were somehow infused with the "purity" lacking in the modern incarnation of the sport. The ideology of lack of competitive balance was thus fueled by the political and economic factors surrounding the sport during the 1980s and 1990s and too often reinforced by reminiscing from hosts and fans on sports talk radio, which habitually extolled the virtues of the mythical good old days when a kid could follow his team with the assurance that players would be there from year to year. In reality, the good old days only meant continuity in team rosters for the habitually dominant franchises, especially the New York Yankees and Brooklyn Dodgers, with the Yankees treating other major league organizations as extensions of their minor league system.

Although Major League Baseball's competitive environment has been keen for the past three decades, there are signs, albeit of limited duration, of a re-emergence of competitive imbalance, especially for the period from

1994 to 2000. Since the resumption of play after the 1994 work stoppage a noticeable trend has arisen in which the same teams seem to succeed year in and year out: Yankees, Braves, Indians, Astros, Mariners, while "small-market" teams such as the Minnesota Twins, who were very successful in the early 1990s, and the Montreal Expos, who appeared on the verge of success when the strike was called, were for a short time on the commissioner's contraction list and have steadily lost ground in revenues and payroll compared to the top and middle-tier clubs. This growing imbalance may be superficially reinforced by the apparent inability of several of the top teams of the post–1994 era to win in the postseason (Braves, Indians, Mariners, Astros) in contrast to the mighty Bronx Bombers. Serious students of the game of baseball will recognize that the postseason does not actually tell us which team is best with anything like the statistical validity of the long 162-game season. Yet even when we bracket out the misleading small sample sizes of postseason success and failure, the fact remains that competitiveness declined from the mid–1990s to the present.

As competitiveness declined after 1994, the disparities between team payrolls increased. In 1994 the ratio of the highest team payroll to the lowest was 3.3 to one (Yankees' $45 million to Padres' $13.5 million). By 1999, the discrepancy had risen to better than a six-to-one gap from the Yankees to the Expos. For the period from 1994 to 2000, it did often seem that come Opening Day, many of the lower-payroll teams were already out of contention in a way similar to the lowly Kansas City Athletics in the 1950s (although not true in 2002 for the Minnesota Twins and Oakland A's, as well as the moderately priced World Series competitors Anaheim and San Francisco). The current payroll discrepancies in MLB are rooted in radical and increasing discrepancies between franchises in local media revenues. These locally generated revenues have escalated to the point where the minimal sharing of 20 percent of local revenue has not been able to check the disparity in payrolls between the top and bottom clubs. The latest move toward distribution of a higher percentage of local net revenues may help alleviate some of the extreme growth in payroll disparity, although how much remains to be seen. Most economists suggest that the recently negotiated enhanced revenue sharing will transfer only a modest amount from rich teams to poor teams, in fact just a small fraction on top of what poor teams were already receiving in revenue sharing. This will not make up the gap in spending between top clubs like the Yankees and everyone else, but it may allow small-revenue franchises to sign a player or two that they otherwise could not afford. It is highly doubtful that the small luxury tax will prevent the top-revenue teams from spending above the designated thresholds. A more important ingredient for a return to competitiveness in recent years, 2001–2004, appears to have been the substantial rise in national television revenue that was the product of a newly negotiated contract with Fox (2001–2006) and ESPN (2000–2005).

Some argue that revenue sharing needs to be coupled with a salary cap for the players, as is done in pro football and basketball.[24] Advocates of radical reform should be cautious, however, and consider the possible unintended anticompetitive consequences that could result from a league structure that virtually guarantees profitability for every franchise, as is arguably the case in the NFL. So long as MLB is fundamentally designed as a capitalist enterprise it probably makes sense that profits should be associated, though not necessarily strictly correlated, with on-field success. The combination of a salary cap with revenue sharing could have the perverse effect of encouraging some franchises to combine shared revenues with restricted payrolls to profit in a short-run manner that diminishes long-term capacity to develop talent and/or broaden its market appeal to the fans. Indeed, some argue that the current revenue-sharing plan negotiated in the latest collective bargaining agreement actually encourages small-revenue teams to spend less, as they become perpetually dependent on handouts from Major League Baseball to supplement for declines at the gate that their penurious policies contribute to. Advocates of the salary cap acknowledge that a salary floor is also necessary to prevent penurious, profit-taking owners from undercutting the industry as a whole. We argue that MLB probably needs greater revenue-sharing than attained in this last collective bargaining agreement, but also a revenue sharing plan more attuned to the differences in market size, where more money goes from franchises in the large markets to those truly small-market franchises that are disadvantaged by their local TV/radio contracts and their smaller fan base/population. The current revenue-sharing plan devotes most of the money to a straight pool arrangement where the funds are redistributed equally to all 30 teams. We would advocate a greater emphasis on a split pool arrangement, where money from a central fund is delivered from large-market to small-market teams in larger increments, with those franchises at the bottom receiving most of the contributions. This latter component is part of the current revenue-sharing deal, but limited to a $72.2 million base figure, which is distributed unevenly to clubs based on their distance from the average local revenues in the game. Teams that are farthest below average local revenues get more money than teams just below the bar, while teams above the average revenue are net contributors to the fund. Still, the $72.2 million is a small amount, and the emphasis of the current agreement is on the distribution of revenue equally among clubs, which will likely help the mid-market clubs more than the small-market or small-revenue organizations.

The players' union, the Major League Baseball Players Association (MLBPA), bargained hard to limit the percentage of locally generated revenues distributed among clubs to a percentage that is significantly lower than the owner's 50 percent. The players' union originally favored a split pool concept, which would distribute the largest share of the money from large-revenue to small-revenue franchises. The owners' plan, ultimately framing the final agreement, sought to distribute revenue equally across teams, a so-called straight pool plan, and to pocket $80 million of the fund inside the commissioner's office to be used at the "discretion of MLB!" The players succeeded in lowering the discretionary money available to the commissioner's office from $80 million to $10 million. The players saw the owners' original revenue-sharing proposal as less about improving competitive balance for small-market franchises and more as a way to limit spending on player salaries. The final revenue-sharing formula represented a compromise in this area, with the 34 percent figure coinciding with both a straight-pool plan favored by the owners alongside a central fund component distributed according to distance from average revenue. The players' union, while willing to move on the revenue sharing issue, had been more reluctant to accept the owners' other major agenda item: a luxury tax that would, under the owners' original plan, have affected as many as seven MLB franchises, who would have been asked to pay 50 cents for every dollar spent over a $102 million payroll, which the owners were sticking to until the final two days of negotiation. The players' union argued, with a great deal of justification, that such an extensive luxury tax would have been equivalent to a salary cap in disguise, and that the primary effect would not be to improve competitive balance but to depress salaries. The critics of the Players Association's opposition to the luxury tax seemed to be suggesting that the owners needed to be saved from themselves and their own lack of prudent judgment in the marketplace. If such is the case, such a profitable industry as MLB would do well to find more competent investors or alternative management structure that would better encourage responsible fiduciary behavior. Ultimately, however, there was even compromise on this issue, despite strong opposition from the bureaucracy of the Players Association, who reportedly were willing to consider the luxury tax proposal as a deal-breaker, only to be encouraged to bargain by the voices of players themselves, according to Jayson Stark in an ESPN website report of August 15, 2002. The extent to which the powerful union bureaucracy actually listens to its membership is an ongoing testament to the democratic culture instilled by Marvin Miller, the founder of the modern union.

In addition to agreeing to a compromise on the luxury tax issue, players have also been willing to give ground from time to time to aid their franchises in circumstances outside the bargaining table. Recently, some MLB franchises have asked players to defer their receipt of salary payments in order to help a few teams manage cash flow. The Arizona Diamondbacks, for example, spent only about $40 million in cash payroll expenses during their 2001 championship winning season. Yet during this same season, Arizona management incurred liabilities for deferred salary equal to or greater than cash payroll expenses. Further indicating the possibility of fiscal irresponsibility, managing general partner Jerry Colangelo made cash calls to his fellow owners and also needed to draw credit lines from banks and even the league itself in order to meet operating costs. The Diamondbacks, in other words, are deeply leveraged, and by one estimate they join eight other franchises: Boston, Detroit, Florida, Milwaukee, Montreal, Minnesota, Philadelphia and Tampa Bay with a debt/value ratio above 50 percent. The average baseball team has $109 million in debt and is worth $286 million, a debt/value ratio of 38 percent. By contrast, the ratios for the NFL and the NBA are 25 percent and 34 percent, respectively. Even so, it is a truism that it takes money to make money.[25] MLB marketing experience shows that a team's revenues typically rise most rapidly not during a winning season but afterwards, in the happy afterglow of success. Chances are that Colangelo et al. will turn out to be successful risk takers whose entrepreneurial efforts will be rewarded with increased ticket sales and merchandising, not to mention likely improvement in their market value on cable television (although as of this writing the Diamondbacks were facing the inevitable task of rebuilding an aging and costly franchise, but nonetheless had a set of World Series rings for their efforts — no small achievement).

Even if a club experiences declining fortunes to the point of monetary losses that cannot be sustained by the incumbent owner, as long as the baseball industry itself has broad appeal and revenue-generating popularity, it is assured that there will be investors available to purchase any franchise. Probably the only thing that could do the industry serious harm would be to do something that would so offend the fan base that revenues would be significantly affected. Had there been another major work stoppage, severe contraction in the number of teams, or a plethora of payroll-slashing "fire sales" of the kind undertaken by former Florida Marlins owner Wayne Huizenga, the game itself would surely have succeeded in killing many of its most profitable revenue sources, whether nationally or in the markets most immediately affected by the decisions. The most competitiveness-enhancing decision that MLB's owners could make would be to avoid making such choices in the future, and the completion of the latest collective bargaining agreement without a lockout or a strike at least shows some recognition of this economic environment, in which MLB has more sports competition than it has had in the entirety of its existence.

Myths and Market Realities

The sports media commonly use terms such as "small market" and "large market" to distinguish between MLB's rich and successful (N.Y. Yankees, L.A. Dodgers, etc.) and its revenue-challenged franchises (Milwaukee, Kansas City, Montreal, etc.). Yet the conventional "big versus small" dichotomy of major league baseball markets is actually based on a significant degree of myth and misconception. As a matter of fact, many of the supposed "big market," high-payroll clubs have markets no larger than those of low-payroll teams. Also, cable and merchandising revenues do not correlate neatly with market size. Markets in any business are made, not found, and the revenue base for a high-payroll professional baseball team is a matter of investment and development, or, within the risk-avoiding structure of a cartel, a problem of market decline through mismanagement and neglect of the consumers' wants.

There was a time in the not-too-distant 1980s when the Montreal

Expos enjoyed one of the largest home market television contracts of all the MLB franchises that then existed. Montreal since dropped to the lowest-payroll and least valued franchise in MLB and was relocated to Washington, D.C. This decline in Montreal's economic status came only after two decades in which the Expos fans watched a profitable and competitive franchise decline into a kind of glorified Triple-A squad, unwilling or unable to afford contracts that could retain the many star-quality talents who were developed in Montreal's once-premier farm system. Adding insult to injury, the Expos never had a chance to enjoy the fruits of their successes. The team's two most successful seasons on the field were 1981 and 1994, strike years in which the disruption of the season undercut the Expos' potential. Thus they could not cash in on their success via the typical revenue spike that comes after a successful season. MLB appears to have squandered the Montreal sports market, which is not a "small" market (second largest in Canada and 15th in the U.S. and Canada combined). Investors who in Washington, D.C., have succeeded in purchasing the team, and with it went MLB's stake in that 15th largest market.

As Table 3 illustrates, 24 of the 27 most populous metropolitan regions within the United States host one or more MLB teams as of the 2002 season. Additionally, Canada's largest city has a single team as well (see Table 4). Of other Canadian urban centers only Vancouver (2000 population: 2,048,800) would appear to be large enough to sustain an MLB franchise, although its proximity to Seattle makes it difficult to imagine the cartel permitting the placing of a big-league team on Canada's west coast. The three largest U.S. cities that lack a major league club are San Juan, Portland, and Sacramento. Of the three, Portland is probably most viable as a future MLB location as San Juan residents' per capita income is only half that of the U.S. median while Sacramento is proximate to San Francisco–Oakland, the smallest metropolitan area to host two teams. A Portland team would clearly be "small market," however, ranking ahead of only Kansas City and Milwaukee. The next largest U.S./Canada metro area after Milwaukee is Orlando, which is close to the already relatively small market of the Tampa Bay Devil Rays and so not a viable new market either (although Orlando has been mentioned as a possible relocation site for a post-contraction single MLB team to remain in Florida). At the top end of the population spectrum, the U.S.'s five largest metropolitan centers host two MLB franchises. The latest top-

Table 3
Major League Metropolises, United States

Metropolitan Area / # of MLB franchises	Population, 2000
New York / 2	21,199,865
Los Angeles / 2	16,373,645
Chicago / 2	9,157,540
Washington-Baltimore / 2	7,608,070
San Francisco-Oakland / 2	7,039,362
Philadelphia / 1	6,188,463
Boston / 1	5,819,100
Detroit / 1	5,456,428
Dallas-Fort Worth / 1	5,221,801
Houston / 1	4,669,571
Atlanta / 1	4,112,198
Miami-Fort Lauderdale / 1	3,876,380
Seattle / 1	3,554,760
Phoenix / 1	3,251,876
Minneapolis-St. Paul / 1	2,968,806
Cleveland / 1	2,945,831
San Diego / 1	2,813,833
St. Louis / 1	2,603,607
Denver-Boulder / 1	2,581,506
San Juan (Puerto Rico) / 0	2,450,292
Tampa-St. Petersburg / 1	2,395,997
Pittsburgh / 1	2,358,695
Portland-Salem / 0	2,265,223
Cincinnati / 1	1,979,202
Sacramento / 0	1,796,857
Kansas City / 1	1,776,062
Milwaukee / 1	1,689,572

Source: U.S. Census Bureau

Table 4
Major League Metropolises, Canada

Metropolitan Area / # of MLB franchises	Population, 2000
Toronto / 1	4,751,400

Source: Statistics Canada

five metro area adding a second team is Washington-Baltimore, a growth region that is almost 10 percent larger and growing faster than the San Francisco Bay area. The move of the Montreal Expos to Washington was viable from a population base standpoint, and strategic marketing and/or sitting of the team in Virginia could also draw on the better than two and a half million residents of the markets of Norfolk and Richmond, numbers 31 and 51 respectively in the U.S. (this approach would also lessen the obvious conflict of interest with the ownership of the Baltimore Orioles, who were privileged by their sole occupancy of this large market).

Looking at the base population figures we can note that a number of relatively "small market" franchises actually operate as big spenders with high payroll and high attendance and revenue. These include St. Louis and Denver (18th and 19th largest markets, respectively), two urban centers that are smaller than Minneapolis/St. Paul (15th), a market designated as unviable according to the MLB commissioner's office previous plan to "contract" the Minnesota Twins out of existence through a profitable buyout for franchise owner Carl Pohlad, who also happens, in apparent unconcern for propriety, to be a competitor for the upper Midwest regional market with the Selig family's interest in the Milwaukee Brewers, as well as a past provider of low interest loans to Commissioner Selig. After an initial period of resistance, the state and local government in Minnesota are now expressing a willingness to subsidize a new stadium for the Twins, which was true even as the threat of franchise elimination hung over the Twin Cities' baseball fans.

Based on experience in other cities, new stadiums have yet to be shown to be even a short-term means of successfully building consumer enthusiasm in local baseball markets, as teams have an increasingly short one to two-year stadium honeymoon period, after which the maintenance of sellout crowds are mostly dependent on a team's winning percentage. For the first couple of years, new facilities provide teams a comfortable public subsidy that can temporarily disguise mediocrity. And as the example of the St. Louis Cardinals indicates, a new stadium is not necessary to small-market success. Also, as recent trends associated with the newest stadiums indicate, if teams lose, fans won't come, or won't keep coming. Building and maintaining a solid baseball tradition, including a good relationship with the loyal fans, is far more important, as is providing the fans with a winning and competent product year in, year out. New stadiums in Detroit and Pittsburgh have already worn out their capacity to fill seats by themselves, shortly after the first year of being built, as those franchises have continued to flounder in the standings, although that fact finally prompted the Detroit owner to increase payroll in the 2004 season and thereby reverse the slide in attendance. In addition, we can also observe that poor marketing and lousy community relations destroyed the Major League Baseball franchise in Montreal and created tremendous obstacles for resuscitating the market for baseball in South Florida, even after new ownership spent enough money to win a second World Series title.

Bill James describes the current political and economic tensions in baseball as the latest in a series of historical "wars" between MLB's various conflicting interests. This latest "war," according to James, is said to pit large urban areas against small ones, as big-market teams outspend their less endowed rivals and monopolize top talent and championships.[26] While there is a degree of truth to this description of MLB's current situation, it is based on the fuzzy distinction between big and small markets, and even more problematically, it obscures the conflict between ownership groups of "small market" franchises and the public interests of those small urban areas. MLB's recent contraction threats and plans, for example, were, at least in part, directed at local governments in order to apply pressure on those governments to subsidize new facilities in Minnesota, South Florida, and Oakland. In these cases, as might be expected, the local owners want and have lobbied for public support for their proposed new parks, albeit unsuccessfully up to this point. If there is a large vs. small market conflict, it is one of ownership in general against the public sectors of small markets, especially in those cases where local politicians, fans, and other stakeholders are confronted with what appears to some as nothing more than the blackmail ploy of threatened franchise loss if local and state government refuse to join the trend toward public subsidization of the baseball business. Of course, the large-revenue teams do resent having to share their local TV and radio revenues, but the only loudmouth among rich franchises in the latest collective bargaining deal has been the Yankees and Steinbrenner has recently been outnumbered and outmaneuvered by his fellow owners.

In order to protect state and local public interests, we propose that Major League Baseball be required to provide state and local authorities with an equity stake in any franchise that is the beneficiary of the public's capital support, commensurate with the public's investment in the facilities used by the franchise. This is no more than basic fairness and serves to protect the public's stake in baseball and provide something in return for the risk that the public is being asked to share with baseball's owners. Our idea of shared public-private ownership is already in use in baseball's minor leagues and so hardly represents a radical proposal from the viewpoint of regional planning and development policy, where a body of experience and research is already available to assist state and local governments that might choose to support MLB as a matter of reasoned public policy rather than under duress.

Bill James suggests as a solution to the problems confronting small-market teams that they ought simply to refuse to play in markets where they do not receive a greater share of net local revenues. This is a plausible suggestion that is not nearly so radical as it may seem and could lead to the sort of revenue sharing that many think is necessary. After all, the sharing of gate receipts with visiting teams has been the normal practice throughout the history of professional baseball and remains the prevailing pattern in the present day. However, for this Jamesian suggestion to work, "small-market" team owners would have to make common cause with fans and local interests against the power and interests of

Right: Shipbuilding magnate George Steinbrenner assembled an ownership group that purchased the New York Yankees in 1973. Though suspended from baseball from 1974 to 1976 because of a conviction for illegal presidential campaign contributions, it was he nevertheless who approved the signing of free agent pitcher Catfish Hunter in 1975. Hunter's signing marked the start of the Yankees' dominance of the early free agent market, as Steinbrenner preferred costly veteran talent at the expense of player development. This approach initially looked promising but quickly fizzled. The latest Yankee dynasty has proved more durable, supported by the greatest revenue advantage in baseball history along with a smart front office that has acquired more autonomy from Steinbrenner.

larger-market owners. This has not happened, and so long as MLB functions as a cartel it seems less than likely to occur. The current posture of MLB owners indicates an internal unity against all other interests headed up by a commissioner whose family has owned the franchise in MLB's smallest market and publicly advocates contraction, an aggressive stratagem that would seem to be aimed directly at the heart of small-market fans and taxpayers' interests and is likely aimed at the players' union as well.

The Players' Union

The Major League Baseball Players Association (MLBPA) has to date triumphed in every major conflict with management over the past three decades, although the union did make some concessions in the latest collective bargaining agreement of 2002. The MLBPA remains opposed to salary cap schemes whereby total player salaries would be limited to a specific share of total industry revenues as is done in other pro sports. As discussed earlier, such a cap potentially encourages non-entrepreneurial profit taking combined with team mediocrity, as arguably occurs in the NFL, rather than competitiveness unless the cap is combined with a payroll floor. Such a floor in turn would also almost surely require some form of revenue sharing. Given these considerations, the players' union is probably correct to insist that a salary cap remain off the bargaining agenda until the owners agree amongst themselves on a revenue-sharing plan.

However, the players' union has taken an almost theological position against both significantly greater revenue sharing and a salary floor, which can only be explained by their calculation that, past a certain threshold, revenue-sharing plans act as such a significant drag on large-market expenditures that teams will lower their spending on high-priced free agents, thereby lowering player salaries across the board. This notion is akin to supply-side economics, which argues that any form of revenue distribution from top to bottom depresses investment and therefore discourages the growth of revenue. However, it is very hard to imagine that the owners' original plan to increase shared revenue from 20 to 50 percent would have discouraged revenue growth among top clubs, where local media and TV contracts are increasing by a sixfold rate over the past decade. Such a distribution, if structured properly, would provide more revenues for a wider range of franchises, increasing the ability of lower-revenue clubs to spend money on a wider range of players. Too often, the players' union has focused their attention almost exclusively on ensuring high contracts for superstar free agents, while not addressing the interests of a majority of players who fail to even qualify for free agency. Spreading the distribution of revenues could allow for more clubs to compete and to sign players to higher-salaried contracts than would be the case if revenues continue to be concentrated among seven or eight large market franchises. Ultimately, the players' association agreed that some compromise on the revenue-sharing issue was desirable, but now the only question is how both the owners and players will evaluate the effects of the current plan by the time it ends in 2006 and whether either side will declare further war on the other.

The players' union did help matters by insisting on a more progressive revenue distribution scheme, which ultimately helped result in a central fund component, discussed earlier, that distributed a greater fraction of money from rich to poor teams. Yet the players' union once again was trapped by supply-side economics in opposing any minimum payroll, and the owners' paltry $40 million payroll across entire 40-man rosters seemed far too little anyway. Ultimately, no minimum payroll was included in this final deal, which has many analysts suggesting that the small-revenue owners may simply pocket the extra change from revenue sharing and the luxury tax, blocking the goal of competitive balance and exacerbating long-term tensions among franchises and between the commissioner's office and the players.

The only public statements against the minimum payroll coming from the players' association was that it violated the free market ethos that the players have rested their economic case on. Yet there is little question that a higher minimum payroll could offer significant benefits to the average major league player who will not acquire enough service time to qualify for free agency. If a lower-payroll club that relies on its farm system to compete is able to meet the minimum payroll, it may well have to raise the salaries of those pre-arbitration players who are now completely at the mercy of their clubs. The current agreement relies on internal peer pressure and fan pressure to encourage owners to spend the redistributed money on player salaries or player development, and how effective has this ever been in encouraging spendthrifts to unload their money on improving the product on the field?

All this being said, the players' union is rightly critical of the owners' luxury tax proposal, which would target a range of teams in a manner that would almost certainly depress spending on player salaries and act as a salary cap. The difference between a revenue-sharing plan and a luxury tax is significant. While a distribution of revenues would still keep money in the pot to be potentially spent on player salaries, bonuses, etc., a luxury tax would simply discourage a range of MLB teams from increasing spending at all, thereby transferring money from players to owners. To agree to such a plan would likely lead to the loss of the union's effectiveness as a collective bargaining agency, which would in turn lead to probable rollbacks in the limited form of free agency and salary arbitration rights that the players have gained.

The union is often criticized for its recalcitrance on the salary cap issue and its apparent refusal to take seriously the problems of "small market" franchises. There is some validity to these criticisms insofar as the union represents the elite of baseball's workforce by excluding minor league players, and thus the union is not focused on equity issues. Yet it is difficult to see how the MLBPA can be expected to be more "responsible" until such time as its position and the gains made by the players under its leadership are accepted by ownership as permanent features of the industry by an ongoing willingness of the commissioner's office to include the union in its institutional decision-making structures and to provide the union with an open and accountable ability to check and verify the owners' claims of monetary losses. Our suggestion would be that baseball's governing body or office (i.e., the role currently played by the commissioner) be changed to one that incorporates the players' voice in its selection. The current commissioner is not merely a creature of the owners but has for much of his tenure been an owner himself. All pretense of the commissioner's independence was lost when the owners replaced former commissioner Vincent with Selig. Until such time as MLB creates something like a autonomous leadership structure, the union must be expected by any reasonable observer to maintain a strong defensive posture over its membership's interests.

We think it best not to make detailed proposals for reform of the baseball industry, for the detail work must be the work of the collective bargaining and policy-making processes. What we do argue here, however, is that Major League Baseball needs fundamental structural change to protect all of the game's stakeholders from the concentration of power and its abuse. The remaining chapters explore the ways in which the economics of baseball are producing new trends in all areas of the sport, including an analysis of why the sport moved from the golden age of competitiveness between 1981–1993 to the increased competitive imbalance of the late to mid–1990s; the importance of stadium politics in shaping competitiveness; the monetary factors leading to the globalization of player recruitment; and the way that the politics of expansion have shaped the sport over the past decade.

Above all, our conclusions reinforce the complexity of the revenue imbalance and competitiveness issues. As the recent history of this sport has demonstrated, team competitiveness most often depends on smart business decisions, wise investments, an effective utilization of player development strategy, free agent signings, and trades to produce winning baseball. While revenue streams play a role, by itself money is less important than many think, an observation which became steadily reinforced in recent years (2002–2004), as baseball seems to have returned to the strong competitive balance of the 1980s and early 1990s, a subject that will frame the arguments of this book by examining the question of when, if ever, revenue disparity becomes a serious issue for Major League Baseball, and how such trends as new stadiums, globalization, and expansion are affecting the competitiveness of the sport.

TWO

Team Competitiveness in Major League Baseball

The nostalgia industry, along with the commissioner's office, has perpetuated the myth that spiraling player salaries in the free agency era have widened the gulf between haves and have-nots, with only a few teams able to compete for playoff spots and a world championship. This myth runs completely against the realities of the 1980s and early 1990s, when baseball competitiveness reached an all-time high. Whether measured by the gap in winning percentage between the top and bottom teams or by the number of teams reaching the postseason or winning championships, the period of 1981–1993 was the true golden age of competitiveness. This runs counter to much pontificating about the sorry state of baseball economics during this time. The question becomes: How did baseball competitiveness improve during this timeframe? And why did the competitiveness of the sport decline from 1995 to 2001, only to rebound rather aggressively the past three years? Fortunately, we have a sizeable body of research to draw on, combined with our own competitiveness index that measures the history of competitiveness across much of the post–WWII period. This research advances several plausible reasons for improved competitiveness during the 1980s and the early 1990s, as well as the most recent period of rising competitive imbalance from 1995 to 2001.

From 1995 to 2001, the level of competitiveness in Major League Baseball fell precipitously. A point had been reached where baseball's competitive environment may have accurately been labeled one of "negative competition." In other words, MLB became during these years more like a monopolistic enterprise in which outcomes are determined by status privileges, rather than an open market in which each participant has a reasonable chance of achieving success. This degradation of the competitive environment cannot blame player free agency; otherwise the 1981–1993 period could not have been the greatly competitive period that it was. The current decline of competitiveness is much more clearly explicable, at least partly, as a result of increasing revenue disparities, which are reflected in payroll disparities as well. In other words, during the 1981–1993 period most franchises had the revenue capacity to compete even as payrolls rose due to free agency and salary arbitration for many players. From 1995 to 2001, on the other hand, fewer franchises had the fiscal capacity to bid for the services of the highest-priced players. However, as we elaborate in this chapter, there is likely no single causal factor that explains the period from 1995 to 2001. High revenues do not in any simple way equal high payrolls and success. Most of the time, revenues are simply one factor in the equation of competitive balance, and during the period of the golden age of competitiveness, revenues often did not predict success. How those revenues are deployed are typically more important. However, it is clear from the data that high revenues were more statistically significant in predicting the teams that would qualify for postseason play from 1995 to 2001, making this period more similar to the 1950s than were the 1980s and early 1990s.

To support this assertion, we provide data in Table 5 that illustrates success ratios for MLB franchises from 1995 through 2001. These ratios of success indicate the proximity of each franchise's success to the median ratio (1.00), where success is defined as making postseason appearances. In an environment of perfect competition, we can postulate that over time these success ratios would converge toward the median point as the on-field fortunes of various teams went through cycles of rise and fall. Of course, luck and other qualitative factors such as the contributions of the general manager, talent scouts, and the player development programs would prevent perfect balance from ever being achieved, but over time our competitiveness index should rise rather than decline.

Our competitiveness index indicates the level of competitiveness in MLB, in any given time period, relative to perfect competition (+100) or perfect monopoly (-100). For the contemporary era, the index is in negative territory, largely due to two efficient factors. On the one hand, in each league, a single franchise has monopolized a playoff slot through-

Table 5
Success Ratios for ML Franchises, 1995–2001

Franchise	# of playoff appearances	Actual Success rate % (A)	Expected Success rate % (E)	Success Ratio (A/E)
Atlanta	7	100%	26.5%	3.77
New York-AL	7	100%	28.6%	3.50
Cleveland	6	85.7%	28.6%	3.00
Houston	4	57.1%	26.5%	2.15
Seattle	4	57.1%	28.6%	2.00
Arizona	2	50%	25%	2.00
St. Louis	3	42.9%	26.5%	1.62
Texas	3	42.9%	28.6%	1.50
Boston	3	42.9%	28.6%	1.50
New York-NL	2	28.6%	26.5%	1.08
Los Angeles	2	28.6%	26.5%	1.08
San Diego	2	28.6%	26.5%	1.08
San Francisco	2	28.6%	26.5%	1.08
Baltimore	2	28.6%	28.6%	1.00
Oakland	2	28.6%	28.6%	1.00
Cincinnati	1	14.3%	26.5%	0.54
Chicago-NL	1	14.3%	26.5%	0.54
Florida	1	14.3%	26.5%	0.54
Colorado	1	14.3%	26.5%	0.54
Chicago-AL	1	14.3%	28.6%	0.50
10 others	0	0%	26.5–28.6%	0

Competitiveness Index = -5

out the period. In the American League, the Yankees, and in the National, the Braves, have each made the playoffs every year without fail, and the remaining teams at the top of our success ratio index have been, like the Yankees and Braves, overwhelmingly dominated by top-spending teams. For fans of these two teams during this time span, the regular season appeared to be no more than a prelude to the real test of the postseason. The second factor contributing to the negative measure of competitiveness is the large number of teams, 30 percent of the total, that did not reach the playoffs at all during this time period, which generally, though not exclusively, included teams whose revenues were low compared to the top-tier teams.

If it is in fact the case that MLB is a noncompetitive sport over this most recent period, as our index strongly suggests, then it is of significant interest to those concerned with the overall state of the game to understand the reasons for the lack of competitiveness during this time period. The first thing to understand is that it does not have to be this way, which is illustrated by the simple fact that it was not always this way. Indeed, the index shows that the most competitive era in MLB's history immediately precedes the present one.[1] For the years 1977 through 1993 the competitiveness index is a positive 56, which is a stark difference from the -5 score that the 1995-2001 period has generated. For the first sixteen years after its implementation, free agency contributed to rising player salaries in an environment that became more and more, not less, competitive. Our analysis in this chapter seeks to identify the sources of both the rising competitiveness from 1981-1993 and of the decline in competitiveness from 1995 to 2001, which in our view is related to financial imbalances, although not in a simple manner easily reducible to clichés about greedy players, an arrogant union leadership, or the need to return to some utopian golden age when MLB was a game rather than a business. In fact, there may be reasons to conclude that the period from 1995 to 2001 was merely an aberration, a bump in the road on the way to baseball having returned to greater competitiveness between 2002 and 2004. In fact, the early indications are that baseball has, in the past three seasons, returned to the golden age of competitiveness of the period from 1981 to 1993. Still, we will focus our attention now on how to think about competitiveness in Major League Baseball, whether it be the period of rising competitive equality, 1981-1993, or the more recent period of a growth in competitive inequality, 1995-2001, with the goal of thinking about competitive balance in a more complex and multifaceted fashion.

In any attempt to analyze competitiveness in baseball or other sports, there are several factors to consider, and they extend well beyond the distribution of revenues and the size of team payrolls, although these certainly must be considered. The first is the source of revenue for each team in the league, including the distribution of the local and national sources of revenue throughout the league and the changes in such distribution over time. A closely related factor is league management, or in this case how Major League Baseball determines, governs and maximizes the overall pool of revenue that can be distributed to all teams in the league The third factor is the quality of organizational and player development, which includes how teams maximize their revenues by spending their money wisely and judiciously or wasting it foolishly and inappropriately. For the sake of analysis, we can divide the third factor into two component parts that are essential for an analysis of competitiveness in baseball: management of player development, including a deep and productive farm system, and management skills in the front office that enable clubs to identify trade opportunities that can help a team compete. Due to the fact that all three variables play a role in competitiveness, any assessment of the causes of league competitiveness should be sensitive to the complexities of the issue. As we will argue, just because free agency preceded the advent of the most competitive period in baseball history does not mean that free agency was the cause of such competitiveness. Correlation does not equal causation. A careful analysis of competitiveness needs to examine the issue in historical context, to draw out the interplay among these diverse factors that affect the rise of competitive balance and imbalance across different periods. Statistical methods, which we also employ, are useful in demonstrating the plausibility of theories, but they cannot explain why one era has been more competitive than another. For that we need a discussion of history so that we can better understand the present-day context and get beyond the bluster of the owners' arguments that equates their own desire for a greater share of overall revenues with the competitive health of the game.

Revenues and Competitiveness

In the 1950s, which is often discussed as the "golden age" of baseball history, the sport experienced its most severe gap between the revenue of the richest teams and the poorest teams compared to any subsequent decade. As economist Rodney Fort has demonstrated using a gini coefficient to measure revenue disparity by year and decade, the disparity between top and bottom clubs was .202 during the decade of the 1950s and .184 during the 1980s with a larger coefficient representing greater disparity among team revenues.[2] The disparity of team revenues was much greater in the American League, given the overwhelming market position of the New York Yankees, which, according to data obtained from congressional hearings of the early 1950s, were generating revenues four times higher than the revenues of the bottom AL teams during this period. The Yankees drew on their enormous population and market size advantage to eclipse the revenue of other teams in the areas of gate revenues, which were the primary source of team revenues during the 1950s.

The dominance of the Yankees rested on their ability to draw greater local revenues than their opponents, and the gap between their revenues and other clubs widened during the 1950s, reflected in their overwhelming dominance in the World Series — a reflection, of course, of both revenues and the ability to utilize those revenues effectively. The perennial challenge from either the NL's Brooklyn Dodgers or New York Giants, whose revenues eclipsed their lowest National League counterparts by a 3–1 margin, provided a staid predictability to the pennant races of the decade. Between 1947 and 1957 a New York team appeared in every World Series but one. This lack of competitiveness coincided with a dramatic decline in attendance throughout Major League Baseball, including in New York, where the revenue advantages of the metropolis could not conceal the steady drop in attendance compared to the immediate aftermath of World War II. While 5.6 million attended Yankees, Dodgers and Giants games in 1947, that figure declined to 4.3 million in 1951, reflecting a broader trend.[3] From 1947 to 1949, the major leagues drew approximately 20 million fans a season.[4] In 1951, the clubs barely passed the 16 million mark and would only draw a collective 14.3 million in 1953.

Despite the overall decline in attendance, the top clubs maintained a revenue advantage, in part because they compensated for a decline in gate receipts by acquiring the most lucrative local media contracts available. By the mid–1950s the Dodgers earned more than $750,000 for television and radio rights, which exceeded their player payroll by $250,000.[5] Still, the media contracts during the 1950s remained less important overall than gate revenues, so that long-term declines in attendance remained a serious concern for franchises. This was especially true during a decade of population shifts that led fans away from the metropolitan areas that housed baseball clubs. Historians have argued that suburbanization and a geographic migration from the Northeast to the West contributed to a decline in baseball's attendance figures. The suburban culture and the advent of television coincided to provide fans with opportunities to watch games in the comfort of their homes, without having to take the time and the trouble to venture back to the cities that they had recently left behind.

At the same time, the geographic map of major league baseball was increasingly out of sync with the population shifts in the U.S. census.

Los Angeles and San Francisco, the third- and ninth-ranking cities, had no teams until 1958, when the Brooklyn Dodgers and the New York Giants moved to these respective destinations. Meanwhile, Montreal, Baltimore, Toronto, Buffalo, Havana and Milwaukee all had larger populations than Cincinnati, but no representation in the ranks of major league baseball clubs. At the same time, four cities had two teams entering the decade of the 1950s: Boston, Chicago, Philadelphia and St. Louis, while New York had three. St. Louis represented the farthest western and southern outpost, long after the population trends suggested that more potential fans had gathered along the West Coast in California.

The cartel structure of baseball meant that owners have been reluctant to change patterns of behavior and to relocate teams unless prodded by serious financial and political circumstances. Congressional investigators began a detailed investigation of baseball's antitrust exemption in the early 1950s, in the midst of political complaints that the sport had dragged its feet in refusing to make franchises available to cities in the Midwest and Western U.S., a fact which did not go unnoticed or uncriticized by influential congressional representatives during the decade of the 1950s. This political investigation, together with the financial crises confronting a number of franchises, led to the largest pattern of franchise shifts ever seen in any decade of the sport's history. On balance, the shifts were good for the sport, as they injected new fans into the sagging attendance base at a time when baseball was experiencing severe revenue decline. This was true in every case where baseball shifted a franchise, whether it was the move of the Boston Braves to Milwaukee in 1953, the St. Louis Browns to Baltimore in 1954, the Philadelphia Athletics to Kansas City in 1955 and the dual move of the Giants and Dodgers to San Francisco and Los Angeles, respectively, in 1958. In each case, the franchise shifts resulted in a wave of new fan interest and excitement and a reversal, at least for a time, in the dismal attendance figures that had dogged the previous franchises. For example, the Milwaukee Braves drew the highest attendance in National League history in their debut season of 1953 and won two pennants and a World Series over the next five years while selling 10 million tickets.[6]

At the same time, the commissioner's office did little to improve the distribution of national sources of revenue among teams until the mid–1960s. The most significant failure was the fact that national television money was not evenly distributed to all major league clubs until 1965, when the first shared national network TV contract was signed with ABC-TV at the urging of Tigers owner John Fetzer. Fetzer had made his fortune in TV and radio stations and understood the power and utility of the new medium much better than the other owners. This sharing of national television revenue lagged well behind professional football, which had already begun to take advantage of the equalizing effects of an evenly distributed national television contract, eclipsing professional baseball in timing, scale and scope. However, by 1965 major league baseball had secured a $5.7 million contract that grew to $11.8 million in 1968, $49.5 million from 1969 to 1971, $72 million from 1972 to 1974 and by 1980, for the first time, "network revenue exceeded local TV rights."[7] The share of national television revenues over time have become much more important as a percentage of all media revenues, as the value of national contracts rose from 25 percent in 1960 to 30 percent in 1971 to 44 percent in 1979 to 40 percent in 1990.[8]

This growth in the importance of national broadcast revenue relative to local broadcast revenue is central to our analysis of greater competitive balance between 1981–1993. The fact that national broadcast revenues are evenly distributed, combined with their increasing importance as a percentage of overall team revenues, helps explain why revenue imbalances had improved in the decades after the 1950s — when teams were overwhelmingly dependent on local gate receipts and concessions for the bulk of their revenues. As media contracts have increased to almost 50 percent of team revenues, and as the percentage of national media revenue has grown over time, the revenue and payroll disparities among clubs began to taper off, especially during the decade of the 1980s and early 1990s, which, using Rodney Fort's data, coincides with the lowest recorded revenue disparities among major league clubs. The biggest single jump in national television revenue, from $53.4 million to $163 million, occurred between 1982 and 1984, helping to usher in the conditions that would contribute to the greatest revenue balance that the sport had ever seen (1984, according to Fort's estimates, when the gini index was at a (then) all-time low of .149). As Table 6 demonstrates, the favorable trends continued through the early 1990s, as national TV money escalated from $163 million in 1984 to $181 million in 1986, $197 million in 1988, and $365 million in 1990.

However, by the early 1990s, two trends were starting to occur that tilted the balance toward greater revenue disparity. First, as indicated in

Table 6
Revenue Trends, 1982–1993 (figures in millions)

Year	Attendance	National TV	Gross Revenue	Player Costs
1982	44.6	$53.4	$422	$185
1984	44.7	$163	$600	NA
1986	47.5	$181	$746	$317
1988	53.0	$197	$958	$335
1990	54.8	$365	$1,336	$494
1991	56.8	$351	$1,537	$695
1992	55.9	$377	$1,668	$950
1993*	70.3	$377	$1,880	$1052

*28 teams instead of 26
Source: Leonard Koppett, *Concise History of Major League Baseball*, 399.

Table 6, the national television income had tapered off, rising to only $377 million in 1993; thus the geometric growth in television revenue was no longer occurring. The revenue declines were attributable to two factors. The first was an ill-advised agreement with ABC and NBC that based revenues on advertising sales. The second factor was the effect of the 1994 work stoppage, which contributed to a temporary stagnation in national television revenue that contrasted with the dramatic escalation of such revenue during the 1980s. From 1994 to 2000, the national television contracts averaged $365 million per year, lower than the figures reported from 1993. The fact that the 1994 work stoppage lowered the ESPN deal from $100 million in 1993 to $42.5 million in 1994 helped depress the most important source of distributed revenues for the league.[9] The correlation with Fort's data on revenue imbalance is clear: there was a dramatic jump in the gini index for major league baseball team revenues from .140 in 1993 (the lowest gini index ever on record, indicating that the sport had reached an all-time high point of revenue equality) to .201 (a gini index that indicates considerably higher levels of revenue inequality, surpassed only by the decade of the 1950s and one year, 1980, in recent decades).[10]

As a further contribution to greater revenue imbalances, there was a dramatic escalation in local revenues for franchises able to secure new stadiums and new local media contracts, whose value escalated dramatically in large and medium-sized markets during the 1990s, while stagnating in the smaller markets. The new stadium revenue was especially important for the 11 clubs able to get new facilities since 1989, as the gate receipts for teams in the upper third of gate revenues increased from an average of $39.1 million per team in 1990 to an average of $60.5 million per team in 1999.[11] The costly effects of the 1994 work stoppage, which drained immediate income from franchises that were extremely vulnerable to losing local revenues, also contributed to alarming new disparities between the top and bottom clubs. The clubs that did the worst across the board during the 1990s were those low-revenue franchises that did not acquire new stadiums. The lowest-revenue club, the Montreal Expos, saw their gate revenues drop from $9.9 million to $9.1 million. Also for Montreal, local media revenues stagnated during the 1990s, rising only from an already low $2.9 million in 1990 to $4.1 million in 1999, falling farther behind the top-tier clubs (see Table 7). For the first time ever recorded, the top team was spending almost six times more on their payroll than the bottom team, slightly eclipsing the payroll disparity of the 1950s, when competitive balance was also very low.

By 1999, the New York Yankees were pulling in revenues of about $170 million, a figure that was over $121 million larger than Montreal's league low. The local media money represented about one-third of this revenue, and by 2001 the Yankees were pulling in $56,750,000 in local media money, way ahead of the Montreal Expos' paltry $536,000 and far beyond the $5 million to $7 million brought in by the next four lowest clubs: Milwaukee ($5,918,000), Kansas City ($6,505,000), Minnesota (7,273,000) and Cincinnati (7,861,000).[12] This gap in aggregate local rev-

Table 7
Summary of MLB Financial Data ($ million)

1990	Gate Revenues	Local Media Revenues	Total Revenues	Payroll
High	39.1	55.3	98.0	23.6
Mean	17.4	12.1	52.0	17.4
Low	9.9	2.9	34.0	8.1
1999	Gate Revenues	Local Media Revenues	Total Revenues	Payroll
High	60.5	57.2	169.5	85.0
Mean	33.5	17.2	90.4	47.4
Low	9.1	4.1	48.7	16.2

Source: Paul Kagan Associates, *The Business of Baseball*, 1999.

enues and local media revenues, combined with the tapering off of national television revenues, correlates very well with the increased disparity in the sport between 1994 and 2001. However, it's important to note that the latest television deal with Fox (2001–2006) and ESPN (2000–2005) promises a much more lucrative bounty to divide among teams. As of 2001, these collective contracts were worth about $559 million per year, a substantial escalation over the television deals of the previous decade. This combined with the latest collective bargaining agreement, which promises modest revenue sharing and an even more modest luxury tax, should contribute to a lessening of the revenue disparities that developed during the mid- to late 1990s, although as we have argued the current revenue-sharing plan will hardly be sufficient to address the problems. However, if our thesis is correct, then the increased national television revenues, divided equally among major league teams, may well help explain the return to greater competitive balance during the period of 2002–2004, which we will explore in our final chapter.

Of course, the players accurately pointed out that there was more than enough income generated by the sport to pay the costs of player salaries, even during the revenue imbalances of the 1994–2001 period. And this certainly was true. Overall revenues generated by the sport rose by more than $1 billion from 1996 to 1999, while player salaries rose by about $550 million over this same period.[13] Yet Commissioner Bud Selig nonetheless testified to Congress in 2001 that the sport had lost $519 million in 2001 alone! The bookkeeping tricks utilized by Selig and MLB to reach this loss figure included understating the local value of superstation contracts and erroneously including bigger salaries for executives and staff, tens of millions of dollars spent on the new MLB website, and money stashed to fund operating expenses away in the event of a work stoppage. In addition, MLB arrived at the $519 million loss figure by taking advantage of accounting gimmickry to include amortization, depreciation and interest expenses as "losses" even though they do not represent operating expenses to run a business. In the case of amortization, MLB has taken advantage of precedents established in tax law that allow baseball franchises to "attribute 50 percent of the price they pay for a franchise to the value of player contracts and then amortize that value over five or fewer years."[14] If a team is purchased for $300 million, then $150 million of the purchase price can be amortized at $30 million over five years. This wrinkle in federal tax law then allows a team with operating profits of $20 million to show a loss of $10 million. The deduction is also illogical in that it allows a team to depreciate player salaries over the course of the first five years of ownership, despite that fact that major league players on average do not depreciate in value, in contrast to buildings and machinery.

MLB also counts interest expense as "losses." Owners who borrow money to purchase a franchise can deduct the interest incurred on that loan as an expense. In addition, general partners of an ownership team can lend the partnership "$100 million at 10 percent in order to raise sufficient capital for the purchase."[15] Because it is a loan instead of equity capital, the team may then deduct the 10 percent interest payments toward servicing the loan as an expense. According to Andrew Zimbalist, Jr., "If we make the same adjustment to Selig's $510 million book loss in 2001 by deducting depreciation, amortization, and interest charges, the result is an operating loss of $232 million — less than half of the book loss."[16]

Another inflation of loss estimates is derived from the systematic undervaluation of superstation contracts. The fact that several major league teams own superstations, including the Chicago Cubs' ownership of WGN, allows them to lower the value of their baseball TV deals by shifting money from one pocket (the Cubs) to another (WGN). According to Andrew Zimbalist, Jr., if the Cubs' local broadcasting earnings reflected the real value of the contract, "their reported $1.8 million loss would become a $33.6 million profit in 2001."[17] At the same time, if baseball properly counted the revenues to its central office from national TV, radio, the Internet and property, without deducting as operating expenses the salaries of execs or the MLB website and money stashed away in a central fund, then the league's "losses" would automatically be reduced by another $144 million, falling to $88 million in losses, in contrast to Selig's $519 million figure.[18]

A more accurate portrayal of MLB's financial situation may be found in a source that describes itself as a "capitalist tool" and well-known information source for investors. *Forbes* magazine's 2002 report on profits, losses, and franchise values in MLB provided Commissioner Selig with a serious case of heartburn, as it gave the lie to his claims that the industry had suffered an aggregate loss of $232 million that year. Table 8 (pg. 60) parallels team payrolls for the 2001 season with the *Forbes* tabulations of profit or loss. By their reckoning, MLB's collective profit was $76.7 million for the year, making Major League Baseball a good enough investment that the market value of franchises rose by about 10 percent over the previous year. Scrutinizing the discrepancy, Doug Pappas notes that for "most clubs, the biggest difference comes from *Forbes*'s refusal to accept teams' reported expenses at face value. These adjustments, which presumably reflect non-baseball costs, related party transactions, or money taken out of the team by its owner as salary or bonus, come to almost $20 million for the Mets and Blue Jays, and $25 million for the Diamondbacks. *Forbes* also imputes considerable additional revenue to the superstation teams: $23.8 million for the Braves, $7.2 million for the Cubs."[19]

An interesting aspect of the data in Table 8 (pg. 60) is that it suggests that unless your MLB franchise is located in New York or Montreal, low payrolls correlate with profitability and high payrolls correspond with losses. Apparently, trying to keep up with Big Apple baseball is more than most markets other than Atlanta can bear. A "profit squeeze" appears to set in for most franchises as payroll increases, perhaps indicating a kernel of realism within the obfuscating husk of the commissioner's disinformation campaign. MLB owners are, as should be expected, following divergent business strategies. Some act as "profit takers" who turn profits by keeping costs down (cellar dweller Milwaukee, for instance). Others play the game as entrepreneurial risk takers, spending much more on player salaries, presumably in hopes of transmitting on-field success into building the value of the franchise (2001 world champ Arizona exemplifies this approach).

Table 9 (pg. 61) indicates who are the owners of the low-payroll franchises. Notably, there is only one corporate conglomerate in the bottom half of the payroll standings for 2001. That anomaly franchise is Anaheim, owned by the Walt Disney Corporation, which in 2001 decided to sell its Major League Baseball franchise. Nonetheless, in a nice example of the organizational skill factors discussed in the next section of this chapter, the team triumphed on the field in 2002. In the top half of the payroll standings, there are four conglomerates: Toronto, Atlanta, Chicago-NL, and Los Angeles. In general, it seems reasonable to generalize that in MLB, the higher-payroll teams are conglomerates or well capitalized partnerships that are better able to "ride it out" and absorb losses in expectation of future gains than are the more risk-averse low-payroll teams.

The owners of MLB want us to believe that the sport is in such a

Table 8
Payrolls and Profits, 2001

Team	Payroll $	Profit or (Loss) $
*New York Yankees	109,791,833	18,700,000
Boston Red Sox	109,558,908	(11,400,000)
Los Angeles Dodgers	108,980,952	(29,600,000)
New York Mets	93,174,428	14,300,000
*Cleveland Indians	91,974,979	(3,600,000)
*Atlanta Braves	91,851,587	9,500,000
Texas Rangers	88,504,421	(6,500,000)
*Arizona Diamondbacks	81,206,513	(3,900,000)
*Saint Louis Cardinals	77,270,855	(5,100,000)
Toronto Blue Jays	75,798,500	(20,600,000)
*Seattle Mariners	75,652,500	14,100,000
Baltimore Orioles	72,426,328	3,200,000
Colorado Rockies	71,068,000	6,700,000
Chicago Cubs	64,015,833	7,900,000
San Francisco Giants	63,332,667	16,800,000
Chicago White Sox	62,363,000	(3,800,000)
*Houston Astros	60,382,667	4,100,000
Tampa Bay Devil Rays	54,951,602	(6,100,000)
Pittsburgh Pirates	52,698,333	9,500,000
Detroit Tigers	49,831,167	12,300,000
Anaheim Angels	46,568,180	5,700,000
Cincinnati Reds	45,227,882	4,300,000
Milwaukee Brewers	43,089,333	18,800,000
Philadelphia Phillies	41,664,167	2,600,000
San Diego Padres	38,333,117	5,700,000
Kansas City Royals	35,643,000	2,200,000
Florida Marlins	35,504,167	1,400,000
Montreal Expos	34,774,500	(3,400,000)
*Oakland Athletics	33,810,750	6,800,000
Minnesota Twins	24,350,000	3,600,000

Sources: ESPN.com & *Forbes*

dire financial crisis that lower player salaries and more public subsidies are crucial for its survival. But it's clear that the revenue imbalances among teams have not prevented the sport from dramatically increasing overall revenues for the game, which have accrued at a phenomenal and unprecedented pace over the past decade. Furthermore, the separation between high-revenue and low-revenue clubs is not solely reducible to factors such as market size and population base, although those elements

Table 9
Low Payroll Franchises and Owners

Chicago White Sox	Jerry Reinsdorf, ltd. partners
*Houston Astros	Drayton McLane, Jr.
Tampa Bay Devil Rays	Vincent Naimoli group
Pittsburgh Pirates	Kevin McClatchy group
Detroit Tigers	Michael Ilitch, principal
Anaheim Angels	Walt Disney Co.
Cincinnati Reds	Carl Linder, principal
Milwaukee Brewers	Selig-Prieb, principal
Philadelphia Phillies	Giles, Montgomery & 3 others
San Diego Padres	John Moores group
Kansas City Royals	David Glass
Florida Marlins	Jeffrey Loria
Montreal Expos	MLB
*Oakland Athletics	Ken Hoffman & Steve Schott
Minnesota Twins	Carl Pohlad

Source: *USA Today*

are clearly important. Well managed franchises can often increase their revenues over time in a manner that elevates them from a "have-not" to a "have." Franchises that excel in player development can compete quite effectively, challenging for championship titles more than franchises that have lots of local revenues but lack skill, acumen and sophistication in the player development and acquisition business. It is this next component of competitiveness that we turn our attention to in the following section.

Organizational Skill and Player Development

Our analysis has shown that revenue imbalances do have an impact on league competitiveness over various historical time periods. Clubs with a relatively large supply of local revenues have a greater ability to acquire better and higher-priced players than their low-revenue brethren. The structure of major league baseball, though, makes it highly unlikely that a team can be successful for an extended period of time simply by buying talent. Typically, a winning franchise has to have at least two of the following elements to be successful over the long haul: a high revenue base; a quality player development system; and a front office capable of making sound decisions regarding player retention and trades. The operating rules of the league affect which of these three factors become more important over time. If a league has no regulations that allow low-revenue teams to acquire young talent inexpensively, then the odds of that franchise ever being able to consistently compete with the high-revenue clubs are greatly diminished. Indeed, it is a catch-22 in that good franchises are rewarded with higher attendance and a higher revenue base, but to get there requires the ability to acquire talent inexpensively when a club is still stuck in a low-revenue environment. The fact that baseball's losers cannot fix themselves by simply purchasing a few high-priced stars is evident, look at the range of clubs that have attempted to use the free agency system to buy a winner, without having laid the foundation for this process through the stockpiling of young prospects.

Prior to the introduction of the 1965 amateur player draft, major league clubs with high revenues were able to use their revenue advantages to pay the spiraling costs of bonuses to attract and sign amateur talent, in addition to keeping their veteran superstar players under contract for the duration of their careers. The use of bonus money to buy young talent coexisted with a reserve system that encouraged large-revenue clubs to purchase talent from small-revenue clubs, thereby monopolizing the distribution of talent of both superstar and young players — who, under the reserve system, could be kept on major league rosters indefinitely, particularly if a team could afford to pay for the costs of retention and a farm system that became increasingly expensive by the 1950s. Under the reserve system, the poor teams often functioned as a kind of cheap labor market for the rich teams, whose purchase of players from their small-market competitors helped subsidize small-revenue owners while players' salaries were kept low. The reason that both large-revenue and small-revenue owners liked the reserve clause had nothing to do with its role in keeping baseball competitive. Owners treasured the system because it allowed for a much greater distribution of revenue to the owners and much less to the players, who during the decade of the 1950s received no more than 15 percent of the overall revenue of the sport, only to see that figure increase to 28.2 percent by 1978 (two years after free agency) to 42.8 percent in 1984 and to 55 percent by the early 1990s.[20]

The impact of free agency was not decreased competitiveness, as the owners predicted, but quite the opposite, as free agency coincided with the greatest period of competitive balance that the sport had ever seen. Free agency did not cause greater competitive balance. Its main effect was simply to shift the distribution of revenues from owners to players. A greater amount of shared national media revenue, combined with earlier changes in the sport that helped equalize and standardize access to young talent through such innovations as the amateur player draft of 1965, contributed to greater competitive balance. The introduction of the draft helped to stop revenue-rich teams from acquiring young talent strictly by paying higher bonuses than their competitors. It regularized the process by which talent was acquired and gave poor-performing clubs, often with a low-revenue base, a better chance to stockpile talent than they had when forced to compete in an unrestricted high-bonus environment. At the same time, the advent of a National Scouting Bureau, utilized to varying degrees by all major league clubs, helped to standardize a scouting process that was previously subject to much more rigorous competition among scouting organizations whose ability to get to a prospect with the right offer and the right incentives was previously the key in getting a player signed.

That being said, the league's decision to implement an amateur player draft in 1965 did not guarantee that there would be greater competitive balance, as the baseball draft is so far from being an exact science as to preclude such a connection. But it did allow low-revenue clubs to increase the sheer numbers of quality prospects in their system at a much lower price than existed in the previous period of escalating bonus payments. Still, organizations would only succeed under the new system if they were skilled and lucky enough to take advantage of the years in which they landed the highest draft picks in round after round. In many ways, the player development draft saved organizations from themselves, as the Milwaukee Braves' general manager John McHale acknowledged after witnessing six teams shelling out the largest bonuses in club history in 1961.[21] From 1958 to 1963, "an estimated $45 million was spent on bonuses and first-year player salaries. In 1964 bonus payments continued to go through the roof ... a record $7 million-plus was paid out that year to amateur players, more than was spent on major league salaries. Teams such as the Yankees and Los Angeles Dodgers were buying up much of the talent in sight, and were prospering."[22]

The introduction of the draft brought baseball into line with other sports that had used such a system to distribute amateur talent, with football leading the way in 1936, followed by basketball in 1947 and hockey in 1963. Of course, baseball was not in the same league as the other sports in terms of the talent evaluation process, with a much higher failure rate dotting the landscape of baseball draft picks over the first three decades of the process. Only two of every three first-round picks reached the big leagues, compared to a near 100 percent success rate for first-round picks in football and basketball. At the same time, only 18 players went directly to the major leagues in the draft's first 32 years, while 14 of those had to be returned to the minors for additional seasoning.[23] Still, successful low-revenue franchises used the draft to turn their clubs around, producing mini-dynasties for the Oakland A's between 1972 to 1974 with the selection of Rick Monday, Sal Bando, Gene Tenace and Reggie Jackson in 1965–1966, the first two years of the draft. The Los Angeles Dodgers produced a contending team throughout the 1970s in part because of a bonanza of picks in the 1968 draft, which produced 15 big-leaguers, including Bill Buckner, Ron Cey, Steve Garvey and Dave Lopes. The Chicago White Sox made astute selections from 1987 to 1990, building the foundation for later success by acquiring pitcher Jack McDowell, third baseman Robin Ventura, first baseman Frank Thomas and pitcher Alex Fernandez with first-round picks. The Atlanta Braves lifted their organization from one of the worst low-performing, low-revenue franchises in the sport by judicious drafting and superb player development, including superstar Chipper Jones, their first-round pick in 1990, and the nucleus of the team's superb pitching staff.

    The amateur draft held down the costs of prospects through the first 25 years of its existence, allowing the stockpiling of talent across the landscape of baseball's high- and low-revenue clubs, as long as clubs were astute (and lucky) in their player development policies and were not overly stingy in their allocation of money to this process. Few realize that the Seattle Mariners paid Ken Griffey, Jr., just $160,000 to sign, less money than the $205,000 bonus given by the Los Angeles Angels to outfielder Rick Reichardt in 1964! The fact that it took 23 years before players topped the $200,000 bonus that Reichardt had received indicated the extent to which the amateur drafting process had held costs down. This, together with the escalation of national media revenue in the 1980s, contributed to the golden age of competitiveness, whereas the explosion of bonus payments from 1993 to the present has coincided with the greater competitive imbalance of the 1994–present period.

The introduction of the amateur player draft in 1965 represented a response to both the escalating bonus payments of the 1950s and early 1960s and the revenue disparities between the top and bottom major league clubs. During the 1930s and 1940s, major league teams with relatively lower revenues could compensate by creating minor league affiliates, helping to guarantee a cheap infusion of talent when it became necessary to sell their major league veterans for cash. The Branch Rickey/St. Louis Cardinals model of purchasing minor league teams to provide a cheap infusion of young major league talent was increasingly a precondition for success in the 1930s and 1940s. Teams that were slow to develop a farm system in the 1930s were invariably the teams that were the least successful in the 1940s. The Phillies, Athletics, White Sox, Senators, Cubs, Giants, Braves and Pirates had the thinnest farm systems during the 1930s, and these clubs were the least successful teams of the 1940s, alongside the St. Louis Browns. But despite the poor overall showing of the Browns during the 1940s, both the Browns and the Cincinnati Reds had established extensive farm systems in the 1930s, helping them become the most improved teams of the 1940s.

By the 1950s, major league teams had cut back dramatically on their minor league affiliates, part of a general crisis of minor league baseball that saw plummeting attendance for both affiliated and independent clubs. In 1946, "the portion of minor league teams affiliated with major league teams dropped from 62 percent in 1946 to 47 percent in 1951 as major league farm systems collectively dropped from 280 to 175 clubs and outright major league ownership of minor league clubs dropped from 125 to 75."[24] Baseball historians have argued that a number of factors contributed to a crisis in minor league baseball during the 1950s, when there was a dramatic reduction of minor league affiliates and the eventual collapse of the independent minor leagues. These include the impact of television and the movement of major league clubs to minor league markets. The explosion of bonus payments was a third factor that contributed to the crisis, as major league teams could no longer afford to run a farm system that comprised 20 or more teams. The spiraling bonus payments, combined with the poor science of talent evaluation, led many clubs to take monetary risks with unproven talent in the environment of the 1950s and early 1960s. Bonus payments grew to the point where the big-market clubs had a distinctive and overwhelming advantage in acquiring young talent. The advent of the 1965 amateur player draft leveled off bonus payments over a long period of time, thereby helping to perpetuate a cycle of greater competitive balance that reached its apex in the 1980s and early 1990s.

However, by the late 1980s and early 1990s, the escalation of bonus payments had begun to alter the stakes of the amateur player draft. Flush with cash and basking in the financial well-being of the game, owners opened the purse strings to give unprecedented bonuses to early-round draft picks. After 1991, average bonus payments to first-round picks began to escalate dramatically, rising from $355,000 in 1991 to $482,000 in 1992, to $611,000 in 1993. These escalating payments were hardly a function solely of revenues, however, despite the fact that it was the Yankees who helped to open the floodgates by signing pitcher Brien Taylor to a record $1.55 million bonus in 1991, more than double the previous mark. Major league teams posted a dramatically differentiated record of using their picks wisely, and some clubs foolishly threw money at draft picks that they could ill afford. The difference was that the Yankees combined relatively sound judgment and a monetary ability to "eat their mistakes" that other clubs simply did not possess. Despite the revenue advantages possessed by the Yankees, it is very hard to sympathize with revenue-poor organizations that continued to lavish huge bonus payments on high school pitchers, especially when the history of the draft suggests that the overwhelming majority of those pitchers, even those taken in the highest rounds, never have a successful career in the big leagues. By 1997, faced with the fallout from a system that had seen an explosion in bonus payments, low-revenue clubs began to focus on signability in making their first-round selections, thereby contravening the purpose of the draft as a vehicle to help distribute talent to underperforming, low-revenue clubs. In recent years, the ability of a low-revenue team to differentiate themselves from other clubs often hinges on deviating from the norm in creative ways, including a willingness to spend money on long-term player development alongside a willingness to incorporate the insights of cutting-edge research and evaluation methods into the organization.

Just as Branch Rickey pioneered a minor league player development strategy well before other clubs saw the wisdom in this approach, GM Billy Beane of the Oakland A's, following in the footsteps of former GM and mentor Sandy Alderson, has been the first to incorporate the latest insights of a wave of baseball research known as sabermetrics into every facet of his organization, and as of this writing a number of major league clubs are emulating Beane's approach, including the Boston Red Sox and the Toronto Blue Jays. Every GM and organization is now aware of the sabermetric revolution, and many utilize its insights to some extent in player evaluation. However, Oakland was the first organization to utilize sabermetrics as a coherent strategy to link all aspects of its baseball operation. Sabermetrics was pioneered by such researchers as Pete Palmer, John Thorn and Bill James and recently popularized by well known columnists such as ESPN's Rob Neyer. But as writer Alan Schwarz has demonstrated in a recent book, it is hardly a novel approach. It was designed on a very simple premise: determine what facets of the game contribute to scoring runs and preventing runs from being scored. For sabermetricians, there is a consistent and compelling correlation between a high on-base percentage and runs scored, with on-base percentage being the single most important statistic measuring the offensive contribution of a player, while on-base plus slugging percentage gives an analyst a more complete profile of a player's overall offensive contribution. Sabermetricians value pitchers who have a relatively high

Billy Beane, the general manager of the Oakland Athletics from 1997 to the present, inherited the basics of sabermetrics from his predecessor, Sandy Alderson. Beane's introduction to sabermetrics changed the way he thought about the game and drove him to cut costs by targeting players with high on-base percentages who had been systematically undervalued in the baseball marketplace. Beane and his front office personnel, mainly college-educated statistical experts who measure performance in ways that go well beyond traditional scouting methods, show a preference for pitchers with college experience, eschewing what they feel are more risky and developmentally expensive high school selections.

strikeout-to-walk ratio and who give up few home runs. Unlike their tools-oriented counterparts in the scouting world, scouts for the Oakland A's value on-field performance in these categories as the most important gauge of future big-league success. Oakland's player development team also teaches players the importance of plate discipline from the earliest phases of the minor league system through their promotion to the majors and rewards hitters and pitchers who post favorable strikeout-to-walk ratios with quicker promotion up the rungs of the organizational ladder.

In the always unpredictable and baffling world of projecting young pitching talent, the Oakland A's have an approach that emphasizes drafting college athletes with a more extended track record on which to gauge major league performance, rather than high school pitchers whose record of success has lagged behind their more seasoned counterparts. Here, the A's have been both good and lucky in their talent evaluation strategy, as their track record for selecting quality college pitchers has arguably been the very cornerstone of their success thus far. The organization drafted their three star pitchers with sixth-round pick Tim Hudson from Auburn University in 1997, first-round pick Mark Mulder from Michigan State in 1998, and first-round pick Barry Zito from USC in 1999. With the drafting of these college pitchers, the Oakland A's achieved what no other major league club had achieved in the last 22 years of major league baseball: three star pitching performers who were drafted within three years of one another. This level of success is a combination of the skills of the A's player development team and organizational philosophy, as well as a good deal of luck. Most importantly for Oakland, this drafting

Left: Mark Mulder, whom Oakland selected with the second overall pick in the 1998 amateur draft. A top pitcher at Michigan State, Mulder fit the A's preference for college athletes. Much of the A's success can be traced to the consistent and dominating performances of their starting rotation, including Mulder, Tim Hudson, and Barry Zito, all college pitchers. Mulder posted seasons of 21, 19, 15 and 17 wins from 2001 though 2004. Together with Hudson and Zito, the trio combined to win 56 games in 2001 and 57 games in 2002. Nevertheless, as of this writing, the A's have traded both Mulder and Zito due to payroll constraints.

success has allowed the organization to acquire three pitchers who made a combined $1.97 million in 2002, freeing scarce revenues for other needs. That has gone a long way toward helping Oakland compete with the 28th-highest payroll in major league baseball at the start of the 2002 season.

The success of the A's organization reinforces the wisdom of such publications as *Baseball Prospectus*, which has long argued that careful attention to the right player performance numbers can allow a club to win with considerably less money than common wisdom would argue is necessary. The question, of course, is how long before other organizations adopt the Oakland A's philosophy? The widespread and more thoroughly institutionalized adoption of sabermetrics by a larger number of teams would be equivalent to the eventual rush to emulate Branch Rickey's innovative minor league developmental system of the 1920s and 1930s. When more teams jump on the bandwagon, the pioneers' competitive advantages are decreased, and creative GMs with less revenue than their counterparts have to find new ways to reinvent the wheel. Still, the A's represent a shot in the arm to a baseball scouting establishment that has been historically prone to ignore numbers in favor of tools, "character," and race in making judgments about who to sign, promote and reward with major league contracts. But as other organizations' success indicates, the A's approach to player development is not the only one that succeeds, as "tools" organizations such as the Atlanta Braves rely on their superior teaching techniques to get the most ability from their physically gifted athletes. The New York Yankees during most of the 1980s and early 1990s demonstrated that money was not enough to win, and the Los Angeles Dodgers and Baltimore Orioles demonstrated that rule repeatedly during the 1990s, by consistently overpaying mediocre veterans and being all too willing to sacrifice player development for quick fixes at the major league level. The astounding success of the Yankees was ultimately made possible only when the organization had a sound player development system in place that gave the club a pipeline of young stars to promote to the majors, complementing the revenue advantages that have allowed the club to add higher-priced players through trade to the mix. The Yankees not only spend well, but they have a superior player development strategy and are astute in evaluating trades, a troika that has made the club exceedingly difficult to dethrone during the late 1990s and across the turn of the century.

Ultimately, in baseball monetary disparities are not as important as in other sports, especially sports such as basketball where two great players can go a long way toward ensuring that your team competes effectively in the playoffs and possibly advances to the championship. In baseball, the unpredictability of pitching is often the great equalizer. Organizations can attempt to buy talent, but if that talent is not supported by a strong player development system and smart trades that lend depth to the club, then all the money that the club has to offer is not likely to ensure a winning team. The depth required in the pitching department to compete effectively over the course of an extremely lengthy season should not be underestimated, and such depth can rarely be "purchased" with any more certainty that it can be developed. That said, the richer teams do have a mistake-leeway that their less well capitalized brethren lack, and the kind of revenue disparity that emerged in the late 1990s was not particularly healthy for the sport. This is especially true when contrasted with the golden age of competitiveness of the 1980s and early 1990s, when a confluence of factors emerged to allow a wide range of clubs to compete for the title year after year.

The 2002 collective bargaining agreement between MLB and the MLBPA establishes a commissioner-administered payroll "tax" on high payroll franchises, which will be redistributed. The players' union had long resisted such a change, concerned that it will have the effect of curbing spending on free agent salaries. Initial indications from 2003 and 2004 are that the payroll tax may indeed be having such an effect on the free agent market as notably fewer long-term, high-profile signings have occurred. However, this apparent trend may also be attributed to generally sluggish economic conditions and/or owner concerns about decline in fan attendance and national television ratings during the 2002 season, played largely under the shadow of the threat of yet another work stoppage.

Other analysts have suggested that owners and GMs are simply getting wiser, refusing to relinquish the necessary payroll flexibility that is an important part of being able to retool and compete if high-priced players are underperforming. If high-priced players are signed to long-term contracts, teams are hamstrung in their ability to shift gears if those players fail to perform to the value of their contracts. The Florida Marlins, for example, were willing to orchestrate a complicated trade with the Colorado Rockies just to junk the expensive long-term salaries of Charles Johnson and Preston Wilson in favor of Juan Pierre, while the veteran Rockies pitcher Mike Hampton was acquired by the Marlins only to be shipped to the Braves for the inexpensive Tim Spooneybarger. During this transaction, the Marlins saved enough money to afford additions to their payroll, including veteran lefty starting pitcher Mark Redman and Ivan Rodriguez, who helped them make the playoffs and win the World Series. All this was achieved despite the Marlins having to pay the overwhelming majority of Mike Hampton's salary while he pitched for the Braves!

Just as the Marlins were able to succeed dramatically with a low payroll, Oakland has shown that smart investments in player development can do as much or more than large expenditures in the free agent market. In 2001, for example, the A's were 29th out of 30 in payroll expenditures, yet posted a .630 winning percentage and reached the playoffs as the American league's wild card team. Indeed from 1999 through 2002 the Oakland franchise has fielded a winning team without ever rising above 25th place in overall payroll.*

Oakland's success, while both impressive and providing a model that other low-revenue franchises ought to study closely, is an exception to the norm. Oakland's fellow cellar dwellers in the payroll standings, Milwaukee, Montreal, San Diego, Kansas City, have not been to the playoffs lately nor have they been fielding winning teams, although the Royals were improved in 2003 and the Brewers appeared to be better during the 2004 season. In 2002, when the well capitalized, Disney-owned Anaheim Angels won it all, there was a .444 statistical correlation between payroll and winning percentage at a .014 level of significance. In other words, it is almost a sure thing (98.6 percent likely) that payroll disparities indicate differences in on-field performance close to half the time (44.4 percent). Of course, there are other reasons that teams succeed and fail, not the least case certainly being baseball savvy management, as the Oakland A's so well illustrate.

High-revenue teams sometimes have foolish owners or mediocre managers who spend poorly, providing large long-term contracts to average players already past the peak of their abilities (the present day Baltimore Orioles and Texas Rangers come to mind here, as well as the New

---

*An earlier example of this kind of success is the Montreal Expos who remained competitive during the early 1990s with low payroll by maintaining a first-rate scouting department, especially active in the Dominican Republic, with emphasis on recruitment of "high ceiling" youthful talents who exhibited precocious athletic abilities.

York Yankees during the 1980s and early '90s). Yet of course, it is surely not the case that wealth correlates with bad business decisions. To the contrary, when intelligent baseball management is coupled with immense resources, a potent capacity to dominate emerges. The 1994–2001 period has witnessed such a development as the New York Yankees and, to a slightly lesser extent perhaps, the Atlanta Braves have combined these advantages. Each franchise has established and maintained a lock on a playoff spot throughout the era, and in fact it is this phenomenal performance of these two franchises that primarily explains the decline in the competitiveness index described earlier in this chapter.

We do not wish to disparage the achievements of the Braves and Yankees during recent years, when in point of fact, their achievements are often underappreciated due to the popular perception that they have bought their success. Our position is that baseball in both its whole and its parts is benefited as both business and as sport when there are highly competitive seasons with every team, in any given season, able to achieve postseason glory. In Atlanta a point of diminishing returns appears to have been reached, where attendance during the regular season and even the first round of the playoffs has fallen off. The fans, it would seem, now take success for granted. Even in New York, with its loyal fan base, the Yankees could probably increase their ratings on their own YES network if the quality of the opposition were stiffer and the outcome of the long season more in doubt. Of course, it almost goes without saying that occasional success for franchises that haven't been to the playoffs lately would improve the revenue flows for those franchises as well.

While we believe that a more level financial playing field is needed in baseball, we are leery of the impact of the payroll tax. The new payroll tax contributes directly to a sharp increase in marginal costs to high-payroll teams, thus presumably placing a drag on rising player salaries. These higher costs are then to be redistributed to lower-payroll teams, who presumably can use the additional resources to improve their competitive position. However, there do not appear to be adequate safeguards in the new arrangement to prevent low-revenue franchises from simply engaging in profit taking, rather than investing the redistributed monies in the franchise's payroll, farm system and/or scouting department. When one considers that present tax laws have the effect of encouraging owners to sell their franchises short, after the tax-sheltering effects of depreciation have been consumed, a picture emerges of an industry that could potentially be harmed, even disrupted by opportunistic owners who are in the business for short term write-offs and other quick benefits. The South Florida fiasco of the Huizenga ownership of the Marlins illustrates the damage that a rapacious, windfall-minded owner can do in what could very well have been one of baseball's great lost business opportunities, although the new ownership, rather surprisingly under Jeffrey Loria, has taken the team to the World Series for the second time in seven years, perhaps saving this franchise and revitalizing its fan base.

Revenue Distribution, Ownership and Organizational Strategies: Some Conclusions

We have argued that the heightened competitiveness of the 1977–1993 period was due to the escalation of shared national media revenue during the 1980s and early 1990s and the long-term effects of the amateur player draft of 1965. The decreased competitiveness of 1995–2001 was triggered by the dramatic increase in local sources of media revenue and a leveling off (for a time) of shared national media revenue; the construction of new publicly funded stadiums that provided some cities with a much greater infusion of local revenue; and the escalating bonus payments that diminished the equalizing effects of the amateur draft. The result has been a shift toward greater revenue imbalances that have impacted the competitiveness of the sport. Despite these developments, organizations could still compete if they followed a smart player development strategy coupled with sound business decisions regarding trades and long-term contracts. The early returns on the seasons following the last collective bargaining agreement of 2002 suggest that baseball is once again moving in a positive direction regarding competitive balance, as low-revenue teams have been able to retool and compete and as a wider range of teams have reached the All-Star break in 2004 with a chance to make the playoffs. This return to greater competitive equality is most likely fueled by the short-term effects of the revenue distribution scheme institutionalized by the latest collective bargaining agreement and, more importantly, by a substantial hike in national television revenue (evenly distributed to all teams) courtesy of new contracts with Fox (2001–2006) and ESPN (2000–2005). However, there is still little doubt that small-revenue franchises have much less leeway for mistakes, while the New

York Yankees are able to assemble a pitching staff that as of this writing includes eight starters, a luxury that would be economically prohibitive for the vast majority of franchises.

Despite the financial imbalances of recent years, there remain strong examples of divergent business strategies that suggest that ownership is not monolithic when it comes to navigating the new financial environment, especially when comparing the contrasting organizational strategies of two teams who claimed to be losing money after winning a World Series. The Arizona Diamondbacks and the Florida Marlins are recent expansion teams that won World Series in a record amount of time: the Marlins in five years and the Diamondbacks in four years. After each club won their respective titles, both claimed to be bleeding red ink due to free agent signings and long-term contracts that reportedly exceeded their capacity to generate revenue. However, the Diamondbacks' managing general partner, Jerry Colangelo, sought to meet the short-term financial challenges by convincing his group of co-investors to increase their monetary contributions to keep the world championship club intact, while Wayne Huizenga immediately ordered his general manager, Dave Dombrowski, to begin a fire sale that culminated in an unprecedented dismantling of a World Series–winning team.

The contrasting moves by Colangelo and Huizenga represented ownership choices more than economic imperatives. Colangelo made an assessment, based on overwhelming evidence in his favor, that the value of major league franchises increases over the lifetime of ownership and that local revenue streams increase dramatically the year after a World Series championship — due to increased attendance, greater merchandising sales, escalating media contracts, etc. Thus he successfully convinced co-investors to increase the short-term indebtedness of the franchise as a way to realize long-term investment gains. The choice by Colangelo and his co-investors can be defended as an economically rational one, given what we know about the escalating value of major league franchises. The Arizona managing general partner banked on a long-term strategy of increasing payroll and maintaining continuity and fan interest, over the short-term approach followed by Huizenga with the Florida Marlins.

Huizenga's decision to strip the Marlins of every recognizable player associated with the world championship club was indicative of his unwillingness to endure any short-term losses for the sake of potential long-term investment gains. Huizenga's strategy was to dramatically reduce the club's expenses in an effort to sell the club quickly and exit the business once and for all. The former Marlins owner claimed to have lost as much as $30 to $35 million in the World Series run of 1997, and he wanted to recoup his investments immediately to exit what he considered to be a flawed industry and an abysmal investment. Economist Andrew Zimbalist, Jr., examined the Marlins' bookkeeping at Pro Player Stadium, where the team shared a playing facility with the Miami Dolphins, and concluded that the Marlins' owner was perpetuating a "fish story" of significant proportions. Zimbalist pointed out that Huizenga had performed what many owners in all businesses have a habit of doing when it rebounds to their benefit: accounting tricks that allow them to claim losses by separating revenue streams into separate business accounts. Huizenga's "losses" were based on separating parking and concessions revenue between the Florida Marlins, Inc., and Pro Player Stadium, which Huizenga also owned. Both the parking and concessions revenues earned at Marlins games in 1997 were attributed to the stadium company, not to the Marlins. In addition, Huizenga diverted revenues from luxury boxes and club seats from the Marlins to Pro Player, thereby removing $16.5 million of revenue from the Marlins' books for the 1997 season. For Huizenga, the elevated losses claimed as owner of the Florida Marlins allowed him to reduce his tax expenses in a manner that would have been impossible had he included the full range of revenue streams in the profit margin.

Even if we accept both Huizenga's claims of monetary losses and the D'Backs' claims, that does not account for the divergent strategies pursued by each owner in the aftermath of World Series glory. Interestingly, Huizenga and Colangelo both were reporting losses in the neighborhood of $35 million, yet Colangelo viewed the losses differently from Huizenga. Colangelo made a business decision based on a long-term calculation that the Arizona franchise would appreciate steadily, especially on the heels of a championship. Huizenga had already decided to leave the business, as early as prior to the start of the 1997 season, well before the Marlins won the World Series, based on two factors: his displeasure with the Florida state legislature, which refused to give Huizenga a second public subsidy on Pro Player Stadium prior to the 1997 season, and his long-term anger at the players' union for blocking efforts by hardline owners, a group that included Huizenga, to force a renegotiation of the terms of the collective bargaining agreement in a manner that favored the owners. Huizenga was convinced that the players' union was getting far too much of the overall revenue generated by the sport and that the long-term financial health of the sport was problematic under the current economic environment. He was also convinced that, given his recent legislative defeat, he could not get a new publicly financed stadium in South Florida. So Huizenga bailed, while Colangelo stuck around.

Business decisions are affected by a diverse range of factors, often having little to do with the quality of a particular team and more to do with the business strategy of a team owner. That strategy is influenced by such factors as whether or not an owner has a stake in a cable outlet that broadcasts the team's games; whether or not the baseball team is viewed as a side-item tax shelter, a profit-making venture or a long-term investment; whether or not the club plays in a large media market; and whether or not the club has access to revenues generated by a new stadium. Ironically, it was Huizenga, not Colangelo, who had the cross-ownership advantages of a cable media outlet, as Huizenga owned Sports Channel, which continues to televise the vast majority of Florida Marlins games. Huizenga, however, always viewed the Marlins as a business that would only be worthwhile if it generated a consistent profit. He calculated that the likely long-term appreciation of the value of a world championship team did not outweigh the costs of maintaining the salaries of the players at the Pro Player stadium venue, which he owned but claimed that South Florida banks continued to receive significant revenue streams, namely from seat licenses. Furthermore, Huizenga felt that ownership of both the Marlins and Sports Channel had become a financial burden in terms of time and commitment that was detracting from his primary business ventures. Instead of continuing ownership, he sought to sell both as quickly and as profitably as possible in the short term. For him, this meant stripping the Marlins' payroll to make the club more immediately affordable to a future investor or group of investors. At the same time, Huizenga insisted that any future owner of the Marlins agree to a 10-year commitment to Sports Channel, a provision that has locked the Marlins into a long-term deal with the cable giant, which served to inflate the worth of Sports Channel while diminishing the opportunities for future Marlins owners to increase the value of this contract.

The value of the Marlins as a tax depreciation vehicle was also slipping away, as federal tax law allows major league baseball clubs to claim a certain percentage of player salaries as "depreciation losses" for only the first five years of franchise ownership. It is no coincidence that Huizenga looked to dramatically increase spending for player salaries during the fifth year of the organization, then to slash his payroll during year six, when the player depreciation period had been exhausted. The maneuvers by Huizenga have put future Marlins owners in a very difficult position, as Huizenga also negotiated for himself a share of parking (over 60 percent) and concessions revenue (over 30 percent) in the sale of the team to John Henry, alongside the stipulation that Henry honor a ten-year commitment to Sports Channel as a condition of the sale. Thus Henry, who ultimately would sell the team after three years just before becoming managing general partner of the Boston Red Sox, had limited flexibility in generating revenue at Pro Player stadium, while at the same time having failed politically to secure public financing for a new ballpark. Henry also was getting increasingly nervous about the five-year period of ownership, the end of which would have eliminated his ability to depreciate player salaries from his tax obligations. His initial goal was to secure public financing of a new stadium inside the five-year window, but once that proved impossible, he worked with major league baseball in a game of unprecedented musical ownership chairs. Henry quickly sold the club to Jeffrey Loria, former owner of the Montreal Expos, who was allowed by the commissioner's office to purchase the club from Henry at the same time that the Expos were targeted for elimination by the league. Major League Baseball, after much wrangling with the Players' Association, abandoned contraction and took over ownership of the Expos, while Loria moved into South Florida in a new position with little to lose, as the new five-year ownership clock bought him considerable time in being able to depreciate the costs of player salaries from his taxation obligations. A short-term tax writeoff coupled with an eventual push for new stadium financing is the economic future of the Marlins.

The contrasting strategy of the Diamondbacks was made possible by the long-term commitment of Colangelo to the investment in Major League Baseball, coupled by the realization that the new stadium's revenue could be considerably enhanced by a baseball strategy that promised continuity of a World Series team, as opposed to the loss of merchandising dollars and fan support that would most assuredly have accompanied a Marlins-type dismantling. The steady appreciation of major league baseball franchises supports Colangelo's decision. Major league clubs have without exception increased in value from the point of purchase to the sale of those franchises. The fact that there has not been a single exception to this rule suggests that the sport is much more financially sound than the commissioner's office has or will acknowledge and that the problems faced by the sport have more to do with the particular market advantages of a few well placed franchises than with the ability to generate overall revenue. MLB's own figures show that total revenue has risen by 156 percent since 1995, the first year for which such figures are available, while player salaries have risen just 113 percent. Major league baseball claims losses from "other expenses," but a close look reveals that such losses are closely connected to accounting tricks that allow teams that own cable affiliates to undervalue their cable contracts. At the same time, the commissioner's office never bothers to include permissible tax writeoffs into its profit/loss calculations, thereby further overstating the problem.

However, even though the commissioner's office dramatically overstates the case, there has been a rising revenue imbalance in the sport, especially noteworthy from 1995 to 2001, and one that is related to the factors that we have discussed in this chapter, although there does appear to be a return to strong competitive equality from 2002 to 2004. The manner in which the Florida Marlins rebounded to a second world championship in 2003 within the constraints of arguably the worst stadium lease in baseball indicates the extent to which competitiveness is tied most closely to player development and personnel decisions even more strongly than the immediate financial position of a franchise. The final chapter examines the politics and economics surrounding the Marlins' ownership exchange from John Henry to Jeffrey Loria, and the subsequent front office moves engineered by general manager Larry Beinfest to catapult Florida to the 2003 World Series.

In the next chapter, we will explore the impact of publicly financed stadiums on team competitiveness. In chapter four, we will examine the globalization of baseball as a strategic response to the economic changes in the game during the 1980s and 1990s. Chapter five provides a detailed examination of the political economy of expansion, including a case study of the Florida Marlins as a way to reexamine the myths about team competitiveness at the turn of the millennium.

THREE

Stadium Revenues and Competitiveness

The previous chapters have compiled evidence to suggest that team competitiveness in Major League Baseball is closely linked to creative and successful player development strategies and revenue streams available to clubs, with both facets of competitiveness so interlinked that it is hard to analytically separate the two. Teams that have succeeded in acquiring talented players at relatively low costs have typically reaped the benefits in the form of increased attendance and increased revenues. At the same time, the league can enhance competitiveness by negotiating a larger revenue pie for distribution, such as national television revenue, which increased exponentially during the 1980s compared to levels attained during the previous two decades. Major League Baseball also experienced the positive long-term effects of the amateur draft during this time period, as the draft served to limit the costs of signing and developing amateur ballplayers, which proved an important avenue for small-revenue clubs lacking the resources of their large-revenue counterparts.

During the 1980s and early 1990s, a wider range of teams were able to compete than ever before in baseball history. Contrary to much pontificating about the sorry state of baseball economics, the game has recently enjoyed an unprecedented era of competitive balance, a kind of golden age of team competitiveness marked by the fact that the overwhelming majority of franchises advanced to the playoffs during this period. A major reason was the lucrative national television contracts of the 1980s, which took a quantum leap with the signing of the most lucrative television deal in major league history in 1984, as discussed at some length in chapter two. At the same time, teams with low revenues could still take advantage of the long-term effects of the amateur draft introduced in 1965, which depressed bonuses to drafted players through the early 1990s, until loopholes in the system were exploited and utilized to introduce a bidding war that dramatically increased the costs of signing an amateur player.

From 1995 to 2001, a combination of factors has contributed to increasing inequality among baseball franchises. These have included the growth of local media revenue relative to national media revenue, as Major League Baseball was not able to generate the exponential growth in national television contracts that it enjoyed during the 1980s, a point discussed at length in chapter two. The strike and lockout of 1994-1995 had a significant, depressing effect on the value of Major League Baseball's new national television contract, which fell by over 50 percent, undermining the ability of small-revenue teams to compete effectively.[1] At the same time, bonuses paid to amateur players have escalated exponentially, making it difficult for low-revenue teams to utilize their first-round draft picks on the best talent available. For financially challenged clubs, signability has long since become more important than talent in determining whom to select in the early rounds of the amateur draft. Finally, the explosion of new stadiums has provided some clubs with greater revenue streams, while teams stuck in older low-revenue facilities have not been able to keep pace. A study compiled by Keith Sherony, Michael Haupert and Glenn Knowles concluded that the discrepancy in gate revenues among major league clubs widened considerably during the 1990s, attributable for the most part to the fact that 11 new publicly financed stadiums opened during this time. Those teams on the cutting edge of the stadium construction boom, such as Baltimore in 1992 and Cleveland in 1994, experienced the greatest growth in gate revenues during this period, contributing to the widening inequality in revenues during the competitive decline of the mid- to late 1990s.

As the examples of Baltimore and Cleveland illustrate, the teams that have benefited the most from new stadium construction were those that were the pioneers of new baseball only facilities, retro parks whose uniqueness could be a selling point to attract new fans to the gate. As recent trends have indicated, however, utilizing a newly built facility to attract a large body of fans to the park will rarely work beyond the first year at the new facility if the team is not winning. Of all the new ballparks constructed between 1992 and 2003, only Safeco Park in Seattle and SBC Park in San Francisco are enjoying continued success at the box office, measured by daily sellouts at each facility. The turnstiles keep clicking in Seattle and San Francisco in lockstep with the winning fortunes of each franchise, although Seattle experienced a losing season in 2004 and is beginning to draw fewer fans. At the same time, those teams that have garnered publicly financed ballparks but have failed to win have been unable to sustain capacity crowds at their new facility, a list that includes 11 of the 13 teams that have secured ballparks over the past 13 years. Even Cleveland and Baltimore have seen their attendance drop over the past two seasons alongside the declining winning percentages and rebuilding efforts experienced by these franchises.

New ballparks in Detroit, Pittsburgh and Milwaukee, now in either their third or fourth seasons, have seen severe declines in attendance. When Miller Park in Milwaukee and PNC Park in Pittsburgh were opened in 2001, each team set attendance records, with the Brewers drawing 2.8 million fans and the Pirates drawing 2.4 million. But those clubs experienced significant attendance declines in 2002 and again in 2003, just as the Detroit Tigers have during their second and third seasons at Comerica. During the opening season for Comerica in 2000, the Tigers drew 2.5 million fans; the following season Detroit slipped to .9 million in attendance. Clearly, attendance patterns are increasingly tied to a winning product on the field, but has that always been the case? What are the various factors responsible for a team's attendance figures and how important are gate revenues for competitiveness?

Stadium Revenues

During the better part of the century, gate receipts composed the lion's share of revenues for major league baseball teams. In 1950, "76 percent of all team revenues came from ticket sales and an additional 14 percent came from concessions, stadium clubs, stadium advertising and parking."[2] But there has been a steady drop in the importance of gate receipts as a percentage of overall team revenue from the 1950s through the 1980s. In 1975 gate receipts accounted for 61.5 percent of all revenues; by 1988 gate receipts had fallen to 40.6 percent; and by 1990 gate receipts had dropped still further to 33 percent. At the same time that gate receipts were declining as a percentage of revenue, stadium-related income, including concessions, stadium clubs, advertising and parking, remained roughly the same over this period, representing 14 percent of overall revenue in 1950, 12.8 percent in 1975, 13 percent in 1988, and 12 percent in 1990. During the 1980s clubs began to depend more on media revenue, which represented about 50 percent of team revenues by 1990, with aggregate national television revenue slightly eclipsing local media revenue as early as 1984. The rise of national television revenue, as already argued, contributed to the period of greater competitive balance during the 1980s and early 1990s due to the fact that national media revenue is split evenly among all major league baseball teams.

By the mid- to late 1990s, however, stadium revenues took on increased importance for club profitability, with serious implications for revenue disparities among franchises. For example, during the 1990s, gate receipts have steadily increased as a percentage of team revenue, rising from 33 percent in 1990 to 39 percent in 2001. At the same time, stadium-related revenues have increased even more dramatically, from 12 percent in 1990 to 23 percent in 2001. A greater reliance on stadium revenues as a source of club profits, combined with a 60 percent reduction in national television money in 1994, contributed greatly to increasing payroll inequality during the mid- to late 1990s.

However, it would be incorrect to argue that all teams with new stadiums utilized their growing venue revenue to build winning teams. Cases in contrast are Baltimore and Cleveland, which opened new baseball-only facilities in 1992 and 1994, respectively. Both franchises received a tremendous financial windfall from their new parks that elevated each from the bottom half of baseball's payroll structure to the top tier. But there the similarity ends. The Indians spent their money prudently to build a club that won its division year after year, while the Orioles made serious financial mistakes that kept them toiling in mediocrity and inconsistency during most of the decade with the exception of three seasons. Still, both teams maintained high payrolls and high attendance figures in the 1990s after moving into their new facilities, which indicates that attendance at Oriole Park at Camden Yards (Baltimore) was driven, at least over the short term, by factors other than winning baseball games.

Katherine Willers has compiled a statistical analysis that examines the factors that correlate with increased attendance among major league baseball teams. In her analysis, she finds that only two factors have been statistically significant in correlating with increases in attendance during the 1990s: player payroll and postseason success, with the latter being far more important over the long run. Willers concluded that a team most likely needed at least one of these elements to boost attendance. Cleveland enjoyed both a high player payroll and consistent postseason success throughout much of the 1990s after the construction of their new stadium, thus embodying the two routes identified by Willers to generate consistently high attendance. Baltimore did not have anywhere near the degree of postseason success, but did consistently rank in the upper tier of all clubs in payroll. According to Willers's statistical findings, Baltimore kept attendance high due in large part to maintaining a relatively large player payroll, which helped to draw fans to the park to see top-name stars despite the disappointing showing of the Orioles in the standings. Willers argues that only a high player payroll and/or postseason success correlates consistently with increased attendance patterns over the course of the 1990s. She finds that after 1994, the construction of new stadiums has not correlated with increased attendance.[3] In addition, it seems apparent that a high player payroll as a route to increased attendance is a strategy destined to run out of steam, especially if a team lacks an ability to either evaluate high-priced talent or to develop a cast of supporting talent in its farm system. As we will see in our case study of the Orioles later in this chapter, Baltimore chose the expedient method of buying big-name stars, a strategy which kept both player payroll and attendance high for a time. But by consistently overpaying for those stars and sacrificing the player development system at the same time, the Orioles are now paying the price for short-term and short-range decision making.

However, it is undeniable that the Baltimore and Cleveland franchises benefited from pioneering the retro stadium boom of the 1990s in both increased revenues and increased attendance. The idea of designing new stadiums to mirror the quirks and character of old-time baseball facilities was first established with the construction of Oriole Park at Camden Yard in 1992, and then followed by Jacobs Stadium in 1994. These parks have been constructed with retro-style playing surfaces and facades, combined with a myriad of new entertainment and food options for families that have served to bring in added concessions revenues not available in the older facilities. They also have featured a wealth of luxury boxes and high-priced luxury suites that contributed to an infusion of gate revenues that eclipsed what was possible in the older facilities.

There likely was a short-term burst in attendance in Baltimore and Cleveland due to the unique nature of the experiment in retro stadium construction, which stood in contrast to the new stadiums prior to the 1990s. The earlier baseball stadiums featured the multipurpose sameness of the artificial turf stadiums created en masse during the 1960s and 1970s, where baseball teams either had to share revenue streams with the hometown professional football club and/or lacked the added revenues from luxury boxes and suites that multiplied during the construction boom of the 1990s. When other clubs have tried to mimic Baltimore and Cleveland with the construction of retro parks in the latter half of the 1990s, but lacked both a competitive team and a high payroll featuring star players, the attendance numbers have tended to plummet after the first year or two of operation. And now that both Cleveland and Baltimore have reduced payroll and are rebuilding through losing seasons, both teams have suffered at the gate, no longer drawing the consistent sellout crowds that were a hallmark of their new stadiums in the 1990s.

Oriole Park at Camden Yards

The politics behind the construction of Oriole Park in 1992 established a pattern that other municipalities, counties and state governments soon emulated to publicly finance stadiums throughout the 1990s and the turn of the millennium. Like other venues, the public footed the vast majority of the bill for construction of the facility, acquisition of land and payment of rent. This public subsidy left the Baltimore Orioles with a handsome profit that the club could spend at the discretion of the private ownership. The price tag for the building of Camden Yards was $210 million, with the state of Maryland financing the costs of construction through a publicly created entity, the Maryland Stadium Authority. The governor of Maryland, former Baltimore mayor William Donald Schaefer, took office in 1987 after having been elected in November of 1986. A proponent of a publicly financed baseball stadium ever since the Baltimore Colts bolted the city for Indianapolis on March 29, 1984, the governor was instrumental in the politics of securing a public source of funding for Oriole Park. While Schaefer was in office, the Maryland state legislature, with the full support of the governor, passed a bill establishing a new instant lottery whose proceeds would go to finance the construction of new sports stadium. The legislature created the Maryland Stadium Authority to arrange the financing of new stadiums. The Authority had the ability to issue bonds that were backed by revenues from the state lottery to finance new sports facilities. At the same time, the Maryland Senate approved the financing of Camden Yards facilities, one for baseball and another for football, that allowed the Authority to proceed quickly toward a financing scheme for Oriole Park at Camden Yards. The state successfully blocked a challenge from organized opposition to the stadium financing plan when a state appeals court ruled in favor of the state's position that stadium projects constituted "an appropriation for maintaining state government," and were therefore not subject to public vote.[4]

The Authority then issued bonds backed by lottery money to finance $99 million for the purchase and preparation of land for Oriole Park, $106.5 million for construction of the facility (with costs overruns pushing the price well beyond the initial $78.4 million estimate). The Orioles were given a below-market rent arrangement that amounted to paying the Maryland Stadium Authority 7 percent of admission revenue, 7.5 percent of concessions, 25 percent of ballpark advertising revenues, 50 percent of parking revenues and 10 percent of suite revenues. According to figures provided by economists Bruce Hamilton and Peter Kahn, and from *Financial World*'s yearly reports, the Orioles "realized a net absolute return of approximately $23 million" per year from 1992 through 1996 after the move to Camden Yards.[5] The yearly costs of operating the stadium have fallen heavily on the public, as the Maryland Stadium Authority has spent about $14 million per year in servicing the interest rate on borrowed public money, and $6 million per year for operating costs for a total of $20 million. The team, meanwhile, pays about $6 million in yearly rent, and about $5 million in admissions tax revenue, providing the Authority with approximately $11 million in revenues. When added up, the Maryland Stadium Authority had provided a $9 million per year subsidy to the Orioles through the first five years of Camden Yards existence. At the same time, "the federal treasury has incurred another $2 million in interest subsidy. The private economy bears another $8 million in forgone return to crowded out investment and $2 million in deadweight loss resulting from the incremental taxes. The authority's deficit of $9 million must be financed by taxes."[6]

The Orioles, courtesy of the state of Maryland, were able to generate revenues of about $23 million per year from their new ballpark, which the consecutive ownership groups of Eli Jacobs and Peter Angelos used to increase the Orioles' payroll. In fact, during the first year at Camden Yards, the Orioles' payroll rose by $22 million, approximately the same as the revenues generated by the new facility. By plowing money into the club, the team may well have extended the honeymoon effect of the new stadium. Typically, economists have suggested that a new stadium will see a honeymoon effect that boosts attendance for the first three years of the new facility over and above what the club could have drawn in their old ballpark. The Orioles' attendance boost clearly exceeded the three-year mark, perhaps due to the fact that superstar shortstop Cal Ripken, Jr., established an all-time record for games played in 1995 and that the club made the postseason in 1996. At the same time, the team's fans may have perceived that the ownership was trying to field a consistently winning club and responded with ongoing sellout attendance that averaged a consistent 45,000 through the first five years of the new facility. Much could also be made of the Orioles being the first club to design a new stadium with a nod to the architectural history of the game, and in a manner that broke the tradition of all-purpose baseball/football stadiums of the 1960s and 1970s and the downtown domes of the same period.

Through the move to Camden Yards, the Orioles increased their revenue 65 percent in 1992, moving overnight from a club that was consistently in the bottom tier in franchise payroll (dead last in 1990) to a club that was one of the top-spending teams in all of Major League Baseball. From 1992 to 1999, the Orioles' revenue was 41 percent above the MLB average. This did help in producing wins, although never at the rate suggested by the spending increase. During the first eight years at the new park, Baltimore finished no worse than three games under .500, and they made the playoffs in 1996 and 1997. This mediocrity contrasted favorably with the Orioles' last seasons at old Memorial Stadium, where the club finished 67–95 in 1991 and had 21 straight losses in 1988. The spate of .500 seasons did not offset the honeymoon effect of the new stadium, as the club was committed to spending money each year on expensive free agents who succeeded in wooing the faithful back to the stands in sellout numbers, even when the expensive veterans failed to deliver the implicit promise of owner Peter Angelos to be consistent playoff contenders.[7]

The public subsidy of Oriole Park did not come with any guaran-

THREE / Stadium Revenues and Competitiveness

tees that the profits flowing to the club would be used to improve the competitiveness of the team. In fact, the state ensured the team would be able to generate about $23 million in additional net revenues, beyond what was possible at Memorial Stadium, due to the terms of the public financing scheme. The Maryland Stadium Authority had full authority to issue bonds backed by an ongoing state lottery, whose proceeds have been diverted to finance the yearly costs of interest and operating expenses totaling about $20 million per year. The Orioles only had to commit to $6 million in rent and $5 million in admissions tax, leaving $11 million that was financed exclusively by public funds each year.

The diversion of money from the public to the team is also a transfer of money from the poor to the rich, as studies have shown that the proceeds of the lottery tend to come disproportionately from poor and working class residents of Maryland. The new venue also has priced out many working-class fans, as ticket prices have increased substantially with the proliferation of luxury suites and club seats, not to mention the escalation of food prices inside the new facility. While Memorial Stadium had no luxury suites, Oriole Park at Camden Yards featured 72 such suites, which rented between $55,000 and $95,000 a season, and 5,000 club seats that costs $40 per ticket by 2002. The hefty increases in ticket prices meant that working-class fans, whose lottery dollars helped finance the stadium, have been hard pressed to afford to take their families to games at Oriole Park. For modern-day Orioles fans, Camden Yards has institutionalized a greater division and separation between classes. The rich fans take advantage of the amenities offered by club seating and a wide array of food facilities, while the poor and working-class fans are relegated to the cheap seats in the upper deck, if not the least expensive option of catching the game on radio and/or television.

The politics of stadium financing are also a politics of exclusion, which often features deliberate efforts by stadium supporters to bypass the democratic process in an effort to secure public financing. Financing Camden Yards involved a strong leadership role by the state governor, who convinced the legislature to authorize and finance the Maryland Stadium Authority as a vehicle that would operate outside the normal public scrutiny in securing public money for sports stadiums. Governor Schaeffer, to reduce the likelihood of having to submit public financing schemes to popular referenda, utilized the creation of a state lottery whose funds would be exclusively earmarked for stadium construction. Instead of using existing general revenues, which would be highly politically contentious, the Governor's office, with the support of the state legislature, simply created a new bureaucratic entity and vested that entity with a new revenue base. The use of state bonds to back up the financing of Camden Yards was also designed to ensure that the public would not be able to vote on the financing plan, as state and local governments typically have wide discretion in the flotation of bonds to raise money for public projects. In addition, the federal government has encouraged the use of state, county and local bond money for stadium financing by passage of 1986 congressional legislation that allowed such bonds to be free of federal taxation requirements. That, coupled with the federal transportation monies diverted to Oriole Park, which have amounted to an additional $30 million in financing, meant that taxpayers other than those in Maryland were helping to finance a ballpark for the Orioles.

The Baltimore Orioles used the cartel privileges of major league baseball to exert maximum leverage on state, county and city officials prior to the decision of the Maryland governor and state legislature to facilitate the public financing of a baseball park. When owner Edward Bennett Williams purchased the club in 1979, he declared that he had no intention of moving the Orioles to another big-league city. However, such declarations were always half-hearted and not nearly as frequent as the proclamations that the Orioles could not generate enough revenue at Memorial Stadium to compete. Furthermore, Major League Baseball gave signals that it would have approved a move to another city without the promise of a new publicly financed stadium. The cartel privileges of MLB provide the owners with the ability to create an artificial scarcity of baseball teams, with the league being allowed to control the number of professional franchises and with cities competing for the rights to obtain those limited franchises. That invariably means a one-sided arrangement when it comes to publicly financed stadiums, as terms have been overwhelmingly skewed to the benefit team owners, with states, counties and municipalities footing substantial portions of the bill. The close ties of team owners to the political establishment have also given them a lobbying edge, as the case of Edward Bennett Williams illustrates. In making arguments before the state legislature for a publicly financed stadium, Williams "was greeted as an old friend. It was all these senators saying, 'Oh, you were my professor in law school and you were so wonderful.'"[8]

Several factors converged to explain the success of Williams and subsequent owner Eli Jacobs, who bought the club in 1988 following Williams's death. The first was the role of politicians in important leadership roles, especially the state governor, who was able to use tools at his disposal to forestall voter challenges to his stadium plan and to help Williams get a political platform in front of the state legislature. Secondly, the timing of the spring 1984 decision of the Baltimore Colts to leave town provided a base of political support at the city, county and state level to prevent an exit by the Orioles. The 1984 decision by a federal judge that ruled that the NFL did not have the power to prevent the Oakland Raiders from moving to Los Angeles expedited the Colts' exit from Baltimore. The loss of the Colts also occurred in a context of ongoing complaints by Williams and the previous ownership groups that the Orioles had long been in a low-revenue situation at Memorial Stadium. Interestingly, the club did just fine in the "low-revenue" confines of Memorial Stadium during the late 1960s and the 1970s, producing teams that were of championship and playoff caliber. But in the free agent environment of the 1980s, Orioles ownership were worried that they would not be able to spend enough money to compete with longtime division rivals New York and Boston, whose revenue streams were far greater than that enjoyed by the Orioles. However, Baltimore demonstrated through their previous title runs that a formula for winning involved a strong farm system and a steady commitment to player development. In that sense, the increase in revenues generated by Oriole Park represented a temptation for the club, especially under owner Peter Angelos, to emphasize free agent acquisitions and trades for relatively expensive veteran players. The influx of new revenues proved to be no guarantee of success. Although the club did better in the 1990s than it did during the down years of the 1980s, the Orioles were never able to translate their newfound revenues into a consistently winning product.

Still, Edward Bennett Williams insisted that a new revenue base was essential, given the limitations of Memorial Stadium. The criticisms included lack of easy entry and exit from the facility due to its location in a residential neighborhood of two-story rowhouses and its distance (about 20 blocks) from the nearest expressway. Baltimore's rail station was also approximately 20 blocks from the stadium, making the park difficult to access for fans traveling from well outside the Baltimore city limits. The parking accommodations did not allow for more than 30,000 fans, and there were no luxury suites or club boxes that the club could use to increase its ticket revenues. Of course, all of this meant that the facility was affordable to working-class fans in ways that new facilities rarely are.

The arguments used to support public financing of Oriole Park have included the additional revenues that accrue to the city of Baltimore, and thereby the state of Maryland, from having a publicly financed facility in a downtown area that generates jobs and additional spending. However, the economic activity tied to Camden Yards, like other sports facilities, represents a very small fraction of the gross domestic product for a metropolitan area, as stadiums typically account for well under one-half of one percent of a the gross domestic product of an average U.S. city. The types of jobs generated by stadiums are at opposite extremes of the economic spectrum, from high-salaried professional athletes, whose incomes do not typically stay in the cities where they play ball, to an array of minimum-wage jobs that workers use to supplement other low-paying jobs in urban areas. Ballplayers typically own homes and spend money in several cities, reducing the economic impact of their salaries for their home communities. The low-paying jobs to be had in modern-day stadiums are often well below what could be created if economic development money was explicitly targeted to public works type projects that involved building and improving infrastructure such as roads, buildings and communication networks.

Furthermore, the amount of money that is diverted to stadium construction often outpaces projected estimates, forcing states, counties and municipalities to dip further into public funds that could otherwise have been used elsewhere. In the case of Oriole Park at Camden Yards, the costs of financing the stadium from year to year utilized so much of the state lottery money that the Maryland Stadium Authority was perpetually in debt, having to rely on general fund revenue and the flotation of bonds to cover their costs of operation. This money could have been directly spent on education, job training, and tax incentives for businesses to relocate to poor neighborhoods in need of better-paying jobs. The money targeted to Oriole Park meant that the revenues previously generated by city-owned Memorial Stadium were nonexistent, essentially diverting funds from one set of neighborhoods to another in the guise of economic development. The residential neighborhoods adjacent to old Memorial Stadium, Waverly and Charles Village, were already starting to show signs of economic decline by the mid–1990s. Cagan and deMause described the extent of the decay: "FOR SALE signs sprout like dandelions along 33rd Street and the shopping drag on nearby Greenmount Avenue is littered with empty storefronts. The Stadium Lounge, on Greenmount and 34th, bears two large signs in its window: "The Stadium Lounge Welcomes the NFL Baltimore Ravens" and "Checks Cashed in a Flash."[9] The Orioles have claimed that some of the public costs of its new facility are offset by the influx of out of state fans who come to downtown Baltimore strictly for the purpose of attending games at Oriole Park. Team officials have given estimates that as many as one-third of Baltimore fans come from out-of-state, suggesting that these fans spend tourist dollars that help generate revenue for the local and state economy that would otherwise be lost. However, independent studies suggest that the figure is much less than one-third, including a study commissioned by Virginia group trying to buy a MLB team for Northern Virginia, which provided evidence that only 13 percent of Orioles fans come from the greater D.C. metropolitan area.[10] According to economist Andrew Zimbalist, "Unlike some other such analyses, this study provided details of its methodology, and its sampling technique appeared to be appropriately random."[11] An examination of Baltimore's hotel tax receipts shows little or no growth attributable to Camden Yards during much of the 1990s,[12] again puncturing the contention that the Orioles have attracted significant additional sources of non-state revenues for the city of Baltimore and the state of Maryland due to the construction of Oriole Park at Camden Yards.

The costs of Oriole Park were borne by the entire state, meaning that Maryland taxpayers have paid approximately $14 per year just for the ongoing costs to pay for the interest and yearly operations of the facility. This diversion of money for Oriole Park is thus felt statewide, as taxpayer expenditures on Oriole Park literally substitute for other potential uses for this money. This is especially costly if one takes into account the money that could be diverted from interest expenditures to other immediate uses. What is diverted to the city of Baltimore ultimately comes from other parts of the state of Maryland, and there remains no evidence that even a majority of Baltimore's citizens wanted public money to go for a baseball stadium. The one-sidedness of stadium politics, including a bypassing of the democratic process in favor of decisions made by political elites close to team owners, is made possible in part by the aspects of the law that allow states, counties and municipalities to pass on some of the costs of floating bonds to federal taxpayers, taking advantage of a federal tax exemption on bonds used to finance stadiums. At the same time, the politics of stadium financing is often moved by the local interests that stand to benefit most from stadium construction: banks that handle the financing or the issuing of bonds, construction companies that benefit from lucrative contracts and thus have incentives to hire high-powered lobbyists, and real estate interests that benefit from the sale of land necessary for stadium construction. In other words, the politics of stadium financing work to the benefit of those interests who are already well positioned to influence local and state governments, while appealing to the wealthy fan base that can fully enjoy the perks of a new venue, from its luxury boxes to its choice club seats.

As the case of Cleveland illustrates, many of the same forces were at work in the politics behind the public financing of Jacobs Field. The next section examines the public financing of that stadium and looks at the similarities and differences between Jacobs Field and Oriole Park in assessing the benefits and costs of public subsidies for baseball parks. The following sections then approach the issue from a different angle by asking the question of how the Indians and Orioles spent their public monies. While the Orioles relied heavily on veteran talent and allowed their farm system to be utilized as bait for short-term returns, the Indians had a long-term vision that involved locking up their most promising young stars, most of whom were acquired with the idea of building a long-term winner that would coincide with an infusion of public money from a new stadium. The different methods utilized by the Orioles and the Indians suggest that franchises are most successful if they develop their farm system in addition to spending their money on select free agents. Because they pursued the free agent route to the exclusion of the development of young talent, the Orioles struggled through most of the 1990s to field a club better than .500. The Indians, on the other hand, utilized their infusion of public money more effectively by sticking with a long-term development plan that gave the club more options for maintaining excellence over a longer period of time.

Jacobs Field

The public financing of Jacobs Field is often equated with the redevelopment and rebirth of downtown Cleveland. This perception is due to the public relations efforts of politicians and Indians team officials who lobbied for public money for the construction of two sports facilities, a baseball stadium and a basketball arena, along the southern boundary of downtown Cleveland. Mayor Michael White, shortly after his election in 1989, joined other politicians and Cleveland's team owners to lobby for the use of public funds for both the Cleveland Indians and the Cleveland Cavaliers as part of a so-called Central Market Gateway Project. Billed as an effort to spur downtown development via the creation of an entertainment complex that would attract paying customers year-round, the actual impetus for the projects were to save the Indians for Cleveland and to lure the Cavaliers from the suburbs to downtown Cleveland. The threats of Major League Baseball to relocate the Indians spurred the efforts of politicians, led by Mayor White, to add the construction of both a baseball stadium and a basketball arena to the Gateway Project. While the baseball stadium was always included in the Gateway Project, Mayor White added the construction of a basketball arena in order to promote the package as a year-round entertainment complex with sports facilities spurring the development of restaurants, clubs, redeveloped apartments and condominium complexes.

Still, the mayor was responding first and foremost to the public statements of Major League Baseball, most notably commissioner Fay Vincent, that the Cleveland Indians would be relocated if a new stadium was not forthcoming. In his testimony before the Cleveland City Council, Vincent noted that the Indians were losing money, had poor attendance, and needed a new stadium to ensure long-term viability of the franchise in Cleveland.[13] According to Vincent, without a new stadium, the Indians would qualify for immediate relocation to improve the financial status of the club. The politics of the situation, including the threatened relocation of the Indians and the rush to expand the Gateway Project as a downtown development vehicle before any of the fine details had been worked out, gave additional leverage to both the Indians and the Cavaliers, as neither team was obligated to accept the facilities being constructed for them until the construction terms were to their liking. County politicians orchestrated a public vote without having discussions with either team about the specifics of the final stadium/arena design. Cleveland politicians at both the city and county levels simply based cost estimates for each of the facilities on comparisons with stadiums constructed in other markets. As a result, the dollar estimates for both facilities fell well below the final price tag. While county officials pegged the Indians' new stadium at $128 million, the actual cost was about $180 million, especially after Indians officials insisted on luxurious food facilities, office space and expanded luxury seating capacity as a precondition for accepting the new facility. The cost overruns were ultimately paid for by a bond issue guaranteed by property taxes.

Cuyahoga County commissioners drafted the wording of the Gateway Project as it would appear on a May 8, 1990, referendum. The Project was referred to as a public/private partnership to provide financing for an economic development zone that included a new stadium and arena. The public's share of the estimated "$344 million development package" was to be $170 million in the form of an excise tax on the purchase of alcoholic beverages and cigarettes.[14] The commissioners indicated that $99 million of this package would be financed by the Indians and the Cavaliers or from the sale of luxury boxes or club seats. However, it become clear prior to the May 8 vote that the commissioners and the mayor of Cleveland, Michael White, had rushed the referendum to the voters prior to getting accurate information about the costs of the facilities and prior to signing a final agreement with the Indians and Cavaliers that specified their responsibility to contribute $99 million to the Gateway Project. As Mark Rosentraub would put it in his comprehensive analysis of the politics of the financing scheme: "It did not matter that no one knew what was to be built, how much it would cost, or what amount the teams would contribute. Vote yes or lose the Indians was the clear and distinct message."[15]

The message from Indians co-owner Richard Jacobs was clear prior to the public vote, when he echoed the comments of commissioner Fay Vincent that the club would be relocated if the voters did not pass the referendum. The vote tally was extremely revealing in terms of class politics, as the working class/poor residents of Cleveland voted against public financing by a 56–44 percent margin, while the relatively affluent suburban areas voted for the referendum by a 55–45 margin. Given that more suburban residents voted, the referendum passed by a slight 51.7 percent of the vote. Once the Indians and the Cavaliers had been guaranteed public money for the construction of sports facilities, they had the upper hand in ongoing negotiations with County officials over the amount that each would contribute to the financing of the stadiums. The county's estimate of $99 million from both teams implied that the Indians, whose stadium cost more than the Cavaliers arena, would pay anywhere from $55 to $60 million as part of their private contribution to this "private-public partnership," as labeled by the commissioners themselves prior to the vote. However, the Indians knew that they could now drive a hard bargain with county officials over the precise terms of their contribution, as the Gateway Project had been approved without an agreement having been signed to ensure that the Indians or the Cavaliers would have to occupy the sports facilities being constructed. Ultimately, the Indians paid only $20 million, taken from the sale of premium seats, for the development of their stadium, with an additional $2.9 million pledged to underwrite the debt service of the new facility. The Indians did agree to pay rent to Gateway, but only if more than 1.85 million tickets had been sold in a given season, in which case rent payments would be 75 cents per ticket. When season ticket sales exceeded 2.5 million tickets, then rent payments would rise to $1.25 per ticket.[16]

Estimates for the total costs of the Gateway Project range from $460 to $470 million, about 35 percent more than the figure that county commissioners gave to voters during the referendum vote of May, 1990. The cost overruns of the project were not included in the commissioners' estimates, as no study was undertaken to determine the real costs of the project. The county commissioners simply rushed the referendum to the voters on terms that were vague and highly beneficial to the sports teams, who had not signed any working agreement prior to the public vote. The referendum was sold as a private-public partnership that would also provide money for Cleveland's jobless, homeless, and schoolchildren. However, the costs overruns of the sports facilities and the limited contributions from the Indians and Cavaliers to the construction of the facilities have contributed to the Gateway Project having to draw additional bond money to service the ongoing debt, backed up by the property taxes of county residents. As Joanna Cagan and Neil deMause have written, the benefits of the Gateway Project did not trickle down to the working class and poor residents of Cleveland:

> In the midst of a decades-long drop in population, the percentage of Clevelanders living in poverty rose from 17 percent in 1970 to over 40 percent by the mid–1990s. The city school system, drained of property taxes, is in shambles — only 38 percent of its students graduate high school, with only seven percent testing at a 12th grade level — and was placed in receivership in 1995. In fact, the day before the deal for

a new football stadium in Cleveland was approved by the Cleveland city council, the Cleveland public school system announced it would cut $52 million over two years, laying off up to 160 teachers and eliminating inter-scholastic athletics from a program that the Cleveland School Superintendent Richard A. Boyd described as "in the worst shape of any school district in the country."[17]

The economic structure of the public financing package for Jacobs Field is very similar to the favorable terms that major league teams have been able to negotiate in other cities. While the Indians were responsible for maintenance and repairs of the facility, the club was allowed to retain all revenues from advertising and the sale of food and beverages. The Indians were also allowed to use Jacobs Field for nonbaseball events, including concerts and meetings, and to retain a substantial portion of the revenue for these events.[18] The team was given use of two private stadium suites and office complexes without being required to pay rent for the privilege. Thus the Gateway Corporation, which was ostensibly created to manage the affairs of the sports complexes that public tax dollars helped to build, gave almost exclusive control of Jacobs Field to the Indians, who were ostensibly the tenants of the stadium. The Indians collected the largest percentage of revenues from Jacobs Field with no significant lease or rental obligations. The club had also passed on to the county the cost overruns associated with the facility, whose costs escalated by 37 percent during the construction of the stadium, from the estimated $128 million to approximately $180 million.

Both Cleveland and Baltimore earned average annual revenues during the 1990s that were $30 to $40 million higher than other clubs that did not build new stadiums. According to a study conducted by the University of Texas–Arlington, teams that moved into a new park between 1990 and 2000 produced an annual average of $20.2 million more in gate receipts and $35.7 million in revenue than other teams during that period. For the Indians and the Orioles, the novelty of the new facilities combined with ownership that was willing to spend money to lock up marquee players led to a dramatic rise in attendance. In old Municipal Stadium, the Indians trailed all American League clubs in attendance in 1983, 1984, 1985, 1987, 1990, 1991 and 1992. Shortly after the team moved into Jacobs Field, the Indians established a major league baseball attendance record by playing before sold-out crowds for 454 consecutive games from June 12, 1995, through 2000. The club reached almost 2 million in attendance during the first year in the new ballpark, climbing to 2.8 million the second year, and over three million from 1996 through 2000, when it had established a new attendance record.

Cleveland's reversal of fortune was tied to a variety of factors, including the novelty of the new facility and its baseball-friendly character compared to the previous venue, Municipal Stadium, or the "mistake by the lake," as the stadium (and Cleveland itself) had been referred to since the late 1960s, when the Indians' ownership made ongoing noises about the need for a new facility. In short, Municipal Stadium had been one of the most difficult venues in which to stabilize attendance and earn revenues throughout the history of the club. When Municipal Stadium was first built in 1932, a $2.5 million bond issue was used to publicly finance construction of the largest stadium that a baseball team had ever called home. The cavernous dimensions and capacity of Municipal Stadium, combined with the multiplex uses of the facility — it was originally intended (unsuccessfully) to attract the Olympic Games to Cleveland in 1932 — made it an especially unattractive venue for hosting major league baseball games. In its first year of operation, the stadium's seating capacity was 71,189, making it the "largest seating capacity of any outdoor arena in the world"[19] The location next to Lake Eerie, with its cold winds, combined with the enormous distance of the seats from the playing field, contributed to the dissatisfaction of the fans and the Indians' management with the facility in the 1930s. The club actually moved back into old League Park, which Municipal Stadium was designed to replace, from 1934 to 1936, and then shared both facilities from 1937 to 1946, to avoid having to play every game under the cold, cavernous environment of the new facility.

The contrast of Municipal Stadium to Jacobs Field could not be more stark, highlighting the fact that Cleveland, along with Baltimore, had been pioneers of the retro park phase of stadium construction, whose more intimate confines and baseball-only environment were designed to make fans forget about the huge multiplex facilities that Municipal Stadium represented. The Indians benefited from being one of the first two teams to unleash the new dynamic of old-fashioned ballpark construction as a selling point for attracting a new base of fans. The Indians also had a successful organizational blueprint that combined astute player development with free agent signings to produce a consistently winning product. Cleveland made the playoffs five straight years from 1995 through 1999, including World Series loses in 1995 and 1997. The club used the revenue streams from a new stadium to plough money back into the franchise and to build a winning tradition that Cleveland not had for several decades, helping to ensure record-setting attendance figures for Jacobs Field.

The success of the Indians and the Orioles in attracting sellout crowds to their new facilities should not obscure the failure of other clubs to copy their results. Over the past five years, eight franchises have opened new parks with the promise of using the new revenue streams to build teams that were consistently competitive. In contrast to the top-tier payrolls maintained by the Indians and Orioles for years after their new ballparks opened, none of the eight teams that have opened new stadiums from 1998 to 2003 had a payroll in the top five in 2003. Only two of the teams, Seattle and San Francisco, had payrolls in the top ten in 2003. Two of the clubs, Detroit and Milwaukee, were in the bottom third. The average payroll of the eight teams was $64.8 million, less than baseball's median payroll of $69.4 million. Below is a capsule summary, from Barry Jackson of the *Miami Herald*, of each team that has had a new ballpark since 1998:

BANK ONE BALLPARK
Arizona Diamondbacks
City: Phoenix
Opened: 1998
Capacity: 49,033
Cost: $249 million
Team Contribution: $111 million
Playoff Appearances
Since Stadium Opened: Three
2003 Opening Day Payroll: $80 million
 (11th)

SAFECO FIELD
Seattle Mariners
City: Seattle
Opened: 1999
Capacity: 47,116
Cost: $517.6 million
Team Contribution: $75 million
Playoff Appearances: Two
2003 Opening Day Payroll: $87 million
 (7th)
2003 Record: 93–66

COMERICA PARK
Detroit Tigers
City: Detroit
Opened: 2000
Capacity: 40,120
Cost: $300 million
Team Contribution: $185 million
Playoff Appearances: None
2003 Opening Day Payroll: $49 million
 (25th)
2003 Record: 43–119

PACIFIC BELL PARK
San Francisco Giants
Opened: 2000
Capacity: 41,467
Cost: $255 million
Team Contribution: $245 million
Playoff Appearances: Three
2003 Opening Day Payroll: $82 million
 (9th)
2003 Record: 100–61

MINUTE MAID PARK
Houston Astros
City: Houston
Opened: 2000
Capacity: 40,950

Cost: $250 million
Team Contribution: $52 million
Playoff Appearances: One
2003 Opening Day Payroll: $70 million
 (14th)
2003 Record: 87–75

PNC PARK
Pittsburgh Pirates
City: Pittsburgh
Opened: 2001
Capacity: 38,365
Cost: $262 million
Team Contribution: $85 million
Playoff Appearances: None
2003 Opening Day Payroll: $54 million
 (19th)
2003 Record: 75–87

MILLER PARK
Milwaukee Brewers
City: Milwaukee
Opened: 2001
Capacity: 43,000
Cost: $400 million
Team Contribution: $90 million
Playoff Appearances: None
2003 Opening Day Payroll: $40 million
2003 Record: 68–94

GREAT AMERICAN BALLPARK
Cincinnati Reds
City: Cincinnati
Opened: 2003
Capacity: 42,036
Cost: $297 million
Team Contribution: $17 million
Playoff Appearances: None
2003 Opening Day Payroll: $57 million
 (17th)
2003 Record: 69–93

Teams that have sustained losing records after moving into their new ballparks have seen attendance plummet after the first year's novelty wears off. For Detroit, Pittsburgh, Milwaukee and Cincinnati, a new ballpark has not equaled more wins. Instead, these franchises have been hamstrung by bad front office decision making in the years prior to moving into a new stadium. The novelty of new retro-style amusement park stadiums in Baltimore and Cleveland gave these franchises an advantage over clubs that have been latecomers in the public stadium bonanza. For both the Indians and the Orioles, the new stadiums themselves were a draw. Even when the Orioles slipped well behind the Indians in winning percentage and in the standing, Baltimore continued to draw fans to Camden Yards, suggesting that the honeymoon effect for the Orioles franchise lingered much longer than has been the case in more modern facilities. But there is another important factor at work: both the Indians and the Orioles have been willing to spend money consistently (although the Indians, as we will see, spent their money much more wisely). Fans perceive franchise payroll as an important element in whether or not their ownership is committed to win. In the cases of Detroit, Milwaukee, Pittsburgh and Cincinnati, ownership has reduced payroll within the past year, suggesting to the fans that the public subsidization of the new ballparks has only been pocketed by the owners of these various franchises. When Pittsburgh, Detroit and Milwaukee failed to put a winning product on the field in the first year at the new facility, by the second season attendance had plummeted, helping to create a vicious cycle in which the team owners reduced payroll to compensate for the lower attendance. At the same time, new GMs with each of these franchises have concluded that it makes little sense to recommend increases in payroll until these teams can rebuild effectively for the future. As GM Dave Dombrowski has noted in Detroit: "You don't recommend adding payroll unless it makes a difference where you are in the standings." At the same time, some franchises — notably the Milwaukee Brewers — have angered fans once again by trading away their relatively young superstar, Richie Sexson, for several Arizona Diamondback bench players, a move that is in keeping with the tendency of this organization to load up on secondary veteran players whose history of mediocrity will ensure that the team will lose consistently while having one of the lowest payrolls in the game. The Reds greatly angered their fans in the first year of moving into Great American Ballpark when the ownership decided in mid season to clean house with a wholesale firing of the GM, and manager, as well as, more importantly to the fandom, the immediate trades of several popular Reds players, including Aaron Boone and Jose Guillen, in an effort to cut salary. When asked about the salary situation for 2004, as if to spit in the face of public relations, newly hired Reds GM Dan O'Brien said that payroll issues "don't pertain to the fans."

The past weighs heavily on the present. For fans of the Pirates, Tigers, Brewers and Reds, bad management decision making is most responsible for these teams' difficult position after moving into new stadiums, unable to generate the excitement among the fan base to take advantage of the potential new revenues. It is far from clear that simply spending money on notable veterans will solve any problems, though. First, each of these organizations have relatively new GMs who have the difficult task of attempting to rebuild the entire structure of the organization, meaning that attendance at the new ballparks will continue to be low as long as the rebuilding does not translate into victories. Secondly, the timing of putting a winning product on the field at the very moment that a club walks into a new stadium is exceedingly difficult and is certainly not the fault of GMs who have been recently hired to help undo the messes of their predecessors. GMs have to be unconcerned with what fans think about their initial rebuilding moves and focused instead on having a consistent long-term plan based on sound player development analysis and an ability to accurately gauge talent on the trade and free agent marketplace. The Pirates' history under GM Cam Bonifay is precisely the opposite of this approach, as the signings of veterans such as Derek Bell, Ed Sprague and Pat Meares to long-term deals hamstrung that organization with players whose statistical production indicated that they were not worth the money or the years they were given. Now new GM Dave Littlefield has to overcome not only the shortsightedness of these signings, but the extent to which poor resource allocation damaged the overall player development progress of this franchise.

With the Tigers, new GM Dave Dombrowski faces a monumental challenge due to the poor decisions of his predecessor, Randy Smith. Under Smith, the Tigers made a series of poor long-term contract decisions and even worse trades, putting the franchise in a difficult situation that will require years of serious rebuilding to improve. The 1999 signing of 30-year-old Dean Palmer to a five-year $36 million contract was a case in point, as Palmer had done little throughout his career to justify such a contract extension, especially given his low average, few walks and high strikeout totals. In 2001, the Tigers repeated the mistake, albeit arguably much worse, when they signed 31-year-old Damian Easley to a four-year $26.5 million contract. Easley had never been a full-time major league player until age 27, and he posted one very good season at age 28 before mediocre years at the ages of 29 and 30. The club continued to give contracts to old players, as illustrated by a four-year, $35 million deal with Bobby Higginson, 31. As with Palmer and Easley, Higginson was already past his prime and had started his career as a full-time player when he was already 25 years old. The organization was willing to ink Higginson to such a deal because of his career year in 2000, but all the while ignored the composite numbers that suggested that Higginson's 2000 season was an aberration, and that, at age 31, he was unlikely to approach those numbers. True to the expected statistical trend, Higginson suffered a significant dropoff in production in 2001 and 2002, leaving the Tigers saddled with yet another unproductive veteran contract that made it difficult for Dombrowski to make trades to clean house and improve the fortunes of his ball club.

The Tigers were also saddled with considerable debt upon moving into their new stadium, but then by all reports so were Cleveland and Baltimore. As the Cleveland and Baltimore cases illustrate, even with a high amount of revenue, there is no guarantee of success. Player development

PNC Park, home of the Pittsburgh Pirates. When voters rejected public financing, Pittsburgh mayor Tom Murphy cobbled together a back-door financing scheme relying on a regional board that controlled revenue from a one percent county surcharge on sales tax. The board ultimately approved, by one vote, the diversion of $143 million of sales tax money to help finance PNC Park, with the state legislature kicking in $75 million and the Pirates $44 million. Despite the gorgeous architecture of the new stadium, fan attendance has steadily declined since the first season in 2001.

and talent evaluation remain more important than revenue streams in putting a winning club on the field. If you have revenues only, but lack a sound organizational philosophy or a long-term management plan, then the results will be mediocre at best. That's the lesson that emerges when examining the different trajectories of the Indians and the Orioles, whose paths after the construction of their new ballparks diverged enough to suggest important contrasts in organizational strategy. The Indians had a long-term development plan and were consistent in its implementation, with each rung of the organization following the lead of the other. The Orioles, on the other hand, were a muddle of inconsistency, as the club downplayed the importance of player development and young talent in favor a periodic infusions of veteran players who were past their prime. Although the team was not entirely unsuccessful, as two playoff

Comerica Park, the new home of the Detroit Tigers, opened on April 11, 2000. The Tigers contributed 62 percent of the $300 million financing. Attendance figures plummeted from 2000 through 2003, indicating that the honeymoon effect of a new ballpark may be short-lived if the team is not winning. With this in mind, owner Mike Illitch gave the go-ahead to general manager Dave Dombrowski to spend money on high-priced free agents beginning with the 2004 season and extending into 2005. The architecture of the Tigers' new home favors pitching and is especially tough on right-handed power hitters, with a deep power alley in left center field.

appearances indicate, the fact that the club's fortunes vacillated from season to season while the Indians consistently won their division offers an important set of case studies for those interested in the business/organizational side of the game.

The Organizational Lessons of Cleveland and Baltimore

In eleven seasons after Camden Yards was built, the Orioles had one first-place finish and two playoff appearances. In the nine seasons after Jacobs Field was built, the Indians had six first-place finishes, six playoff appearances, and two World Series appearances. The two clubs are very comparable in resources allocated during this time, with each devoting a considerable portion of their new-found ballpark proceeds to increasing payrolls. Both clubs have consistently ranked in the top tier in the majors in payroll during this time frame, although each are now going through rebuilding phases that have meant a reduction in payroll over the past couple of seasons. If competitiveness was strictly related to money, then both clubs should have done exceedingly well. But the Indians outperformed the Orioles, which begs the question about differences in organizational strategy and player development approaches that could help us understand why some teams succeed and others fail.

In the book *Paths to Glory*, Mark Armour and Daniel Levitt develop an analysis of how great baseball teams were built, drawing upon a body of sabermetric research that can also be productively applied to the cases of Baltimore and Cleveland. Armour and Levitt examine the literature on player growth and decline in a revealing chapter that applies an "S-curve" methodology developed by a physicist to help predict how a major league player is likely to perform over the course of his career. What emerges from this exercise are several insights that can be used to help us understand the divergent paths taken by Baltimore and Cleveland during the 1990s.

First, the S-curve operates on the assumption that "many phenomena go through a life cycle: birth, growth, maturity, decline and death.... The element in common is the way in which the growth takes place; for example, things come to an end slowly and continuously, not unlike the way they came into existence.... The phases of natural growth proceed along S-curves, cascading from one to the next."[20] In the words of Theodore Modis, who developed the S-curve: "There is a promise implicit in a process of natural growth, which is guaranteed by nature: The growth cycle will not stop halfway through.... If I have the first half as a given, I can predict the future; if I am faced with the second half, I can deduce the past."[21] Armour and Levitt take this analysis of the natural growth cycle and apply it to a player's career projection. Using a basic runs created formula, the authors examine the first few years of a player's career in an attempt to gauge what that player is likely to do over the course of the remaining years of his playing time in Major League Baseball. In general, the conclusion drawn from the data examined suggests that the average career of a big-league player resembles an S-curve that has been straightened out, meaning that a player's productivity will rise in a predictable way from his earliest seasons in the big leagues until his run production reaches a peak performance around the age of 27 or 28, after which time the output plateaus and then inevitably declines. The data suggests that by knowing how well a player has performed in his earliest seasons, a general manager is in a position to predict the potential value of that player in his mid- to late career phase. The authors are able to project player performance using the S-curve method within a 10–15 percent range, with accuracy increasing with more years of data to examine.

The implications of this player projection are significant in demonstrating why Cleveland achieved a higher level of success than Baltimore after both had moved into their publicly financed stadiums. The Indians' GM, John Hart, developed a plan to sign the Indians youngest and most highly valued players to long-term contracts early in their careers — prior to their career peaks as suggested by the S-curve system. Hart's method, however, was hardly wedded to the kind of statistical methodology utilized by the sabermetric school of baseball researchers. Rather Hart relied on most heavily on tools evaluations supplied by the Indians' player development personnel and only secondarily on minor league statistics and major league performance to decide which players to offer long-term contracts. Still, whichever method is used, statistical or tools-based evaluation, the Indians' formula for success involved signing young players to contracts prior to their most productive seasons. The fact that Hart and the Indians organization chose to lock players up before they had more than two or three years of playing time meant considerable risks in projecting player performance, as the weight of minor league numbers, while valuable and insightful to a degree, are not quite as revealing as a database that includes a longer history of major league performance. Nevertheless, the organization thought the gamble was well worth the risks, given both their faith in their player development personnel and the knowledge of the trajectory of the trend of spiraling market inflation that had boosted the price for bonus signings and free agent signings in the early 1990s. The first round of signings by the Indians included 12 players who were signed to extended contracts that included club options: Sandy Alomar, Jr., Carlos Baerga, Charles Nagy, Mark Whiten, Jack Armstrong, Scott Scudder, Glenallen Hill, Dennis Cook, Steve Olin, Dave Otto, Rod Nichols, and Alex Cole. A year later Hart did the same with Albert Belle, Kenny Lofton, Paul Sorrento, Carlos Martinez, Felix Fermin, and Thomas Howard.[22] Hart admitted the organization had made some mistakes in their evaluation of Schneider, Cook, Otto, Nichols, Cole, and Martinez, "but they assured themselves of keeping the players they wanted before their salaries would escalate out of sight in the open market."[23]

GM Hart also recognized a number of spin-off benefits to signing young players to long-term deals. First, Hart devised his plan with an awareness and understanding of baseball's changing economic climate in the 1990s — as player salaries were escalating at a rapid pace in both the free agent market and in bonuses paid to high-round draft picks. Hart wanted to ease the cost burdens with a development model that locked players up at relatively low costs through the early years that they were expected to be most productive. It was Hart who also understood the importance of not allowing a single superstar to dominate a club's payroll, as the GM took advantage of internal studies that suggested a negative correlation between team winning percentage and spending more than 17 percent of a team's payroll on one superstar player. Having a core of talented players locked up freed resources for other acquisitions and prevented the club from becoming dependent on the signing of free agent players to have a shot at success. At the same time, the club could and did spend freely on the free agent market when they felt it was necessary, but having locked up a range of players at below-market costs helped make both strategies possible. Overall, the benefits of the long-term contract strategy were thought by the organization to exceed the costs, as the inevitable bad decisions on a few players were minimized by the fact that the overall payroll could be somewhat predictable and stable. Also, by signing players to long-term deals, the Indians stayed ahead of the rapid salary inflation of the mid- to late 1990s. Players signed to long-term deals were both easier to keep if they played well and easier to trade if the club was disappointed in their performance.

Several factors contributed to the rapid salary inflation of the 1990s. The first was the spiraling bonus payments to amateur draft picks that made first-round picks more prohibitive for low-revenue clubs. "First-round bonus prices jumped 40 percent in 1990, 44 percent in 1991 and 35 percent in 1992."[24] This escalation of the costs of first-round picks meant an end to the stable and relatively stagnant player bonuses that had been a staple of the amateur draft from its inception in 1965 through

1991. The decision of big-revenue teams to open their pocketbooks to their first-round draft choices set a precedent that was very difficult for low-revenue teams to follow. Over the course of the decade, low-revenue clubs found that they had to settle for less with their first-round selections, fearing that selecting their first choice would almost assuredly be equivalent to not having a pick at all, as skyrocketing bonus demands were not likely to be met for amateur athletes who were increasingly represented by agents who sought to demand what had become fair market value for their clients' services. The Indians could certainly afford these bonus payments, and not only that, their stadium revenues allowed them the luxury of locking up players to long-term deals, which given their economic status was both good baseball decision making and wise economics. However, other clubs without new stadiums who were already playing in low-revenue markets saw their position decline relative to the Indians and the Orioles.

Another aspect of salary inflation was escalating player salaries, fueled by free agency and arbitration. "Overall, major league pay climbed 42.5 percent in two years to $851,000 by 1991, then jumped to over $1 million the next season."[25] From 1995 to 1999, mean player salaries escalated from just over $1 million to $1.4 million.[26] As we have explored elsewhere in this book, there was a skyrocketing growth of national media revenue, shared equally among clubs, between 1971 and 1990 that kept pace with the salary growth during that time. From 1971 to 1990, national television money had gone up 1,742 percent while player salaries had risen 1,741 percent.[27] That trend contributed to the golden age of baseball competitiveness, as the steady infusion of shared national TV money lessened payroll disparities. By 1990, though, the limitations of this trend were becoming obvious: sagging national television ratings, reduced advertising revenue, and lower rights fees. CBS claimed losses of $100 million on its 1990 pact in which it committed $265 million a year. ESPN also found its 1990 revenues slashed and "opted not to pick up the 1994-95 seasons, preferring a $13 million contract buyout to more rights fees."[28]

On top of the above trends, the owners' collusion payouts from the concerted effort to depress player salaries during the 1980s costs Major League Baseball the equivalent of $270 million in losses, as the owners were found by the courts to be guilty of artificially depressing player salaries by agreeing not to sign prominent free agents, a practice that was engineered by the commissioner with the strong cooperation, support and encouragement of the baseball owners. The fact that baseball lost so much money in an ill conceived and illegal scheme that sought to deny free agents any semblance of a free market put low-revenue teams in more serious financial jeopardy during the 1990s than should have been the case. If the owners truly wanted competitive balance, then they could have worked more productively to share revenue among themselves, but instead chose a strategy that involved attempting to defeat the players union by undermining the system of free agency. By the 1990s, the money lost to the owners as a result of collusion coincided with a drying up of national media revenue and, most disastrously, another attempt to defeat the players' union in the 1994 labor negotiations. The last effort meant that the national media contracts were in further decline, as the owners erased potential national media revenue from 1994 that was lost to the players' strike and the subsequent lockout. The low-revenue clubs, especially those without new ballparks, suffered in comparison to the Indians and the Orioles. The widening gap between the rich and poor clubs in the 1990s was not simply preordained, but reflected a failed strategy on the part of the owners, whose efforts to take money from the players ultimately cost the very low-revenue teams that they claimed to be defending. Absent a creative strategy of pooling existing resources (and there were plenty to go around), the owners helped allow the financial gap to get worse and the high-revenue clubs to dictate the terms of bonus payments, free agent signings, and one-sided trades that allowed the rich to get richer during the late 1990s.

Both Cleveland and Baltimore were certainly beneficiaries of the changing economic environment, as their new stadiums ensured that they had the revenue to compete. Still, their experiences diverged enough to suggest that a new ballpark would never be sufficient to ensure a consistently winning franchise. The Indians had a strong player development plan and economic strategy that allowed them to spend money more wisely than the Orioles in a tougher economic environment. Unlike the Orioles, the Indians had both consistency of management personnel and a lack of meddling by the ownership in baseball decision making that contributed to the longevity of their success. In fact, we can apply Henry Fetter's argument in *Taking on the Yankees* to help us understand why the Indians outperformed the Orioles in organizational strategy during the 1990s:

That a team owner must have an intense desire to win was, and is, a crucial ingredient to running a successful ball club, but it is just as important for the team's owners to step back and afford knowledgeable professionals the leeway needed to achieve the desired results. In the new organizational structure perfected by the Colonels [of the Yankees], ownership supplied the sinews of baseball battle, selected the key front-office and on-field managerial personnel, and delineated and then respected hierarchical spheres of responsibility.[29]

The Indians' ownership from 1986 through 1999 understood the importance of a strong baseball structure that would have the autonomy and the experience necessary to make decisions independent of the whims or wishes of the ownership. When Richard E. Jacobs and his brother David H. Jacobs purchased the Indians in 1986 from an ownership group led by the estate of Patrick O'Neill, the Indians were in a serious financial bind, having accumulated debt throughout the 1980s and having muddled through a series of personnel changes in the front office that precluded any stability or long-term baseball plan. In 1978, the Indians' ownership group of F.J. "Steve" O'Neill, Gabe Paul, and Patrick O'Neill purchased the club from Alva Bonda, who essentially held the club in a kind of "holding action" from 1975 through 1978 to try to move it to investors who would pledge to keep the team in Cleveland. Bonda was chief operating officer as early as 1973 before becoming owner, at the very time that the Indians' franchise was facing bankruptcy. The years of his ownership were spent refinancing debts and moving to secure a future ownership group that would provide a more viable future for the club. The team's on field performance was consistently poor, with either fourth place, fifth place or sixth place finishes being the norm throughout the decade of the 1970s. The new ownership group that took over the franchise in 1978 did not produce better results; in fact the club hit rock bottom throughout the late 1970s and into the mid–1980s, finishing in sixth place in every year from 1978 through 1985 except for two: in 1983 and 1985 the club finished in seventh place.

The ownership group of the O'Neill family and Gabe Paul pledged to keep the team in Cleveland as a precondition for their purchase of the club in 1978. However, they soon faced financial difficulties that resulted in more debt accumulation throughout their ownership tenure, which forced them to spend most of their attention looking for potential buyers for the franchise rather than building a solid baseball organization that might be able to turn the club around at less cost. The club, continuing to lose and lagging in attendance, piled up debt estimated to be over $10 million between 1981 and 1983. Not coincidentally, the new ownership group looked for buyers almost as quickly as they acquired the franchise. Complicating matters was that negotiations transferring the team to another ownership group had to be approved by as many as 54 limited partners, a convoluted ownership structure that helped to put the franchise in financial limbo and instability throughout the early 1980s. As many as three potential sales were thwarted at the last minute, as the Indians either pulled back the sale of the club for reasons that are not entirely clear, or the parties could not work out the final arrangements necessary to consummate a deal. The death of Steve O'Neill on August 23, 1983, created a more urgent need to sell the club, as well as contributing to still further changes in the revolving Indians' front office, whose own lack of stability was simply a product of a poor organizational structure led by owners preoccupied by mounting debt.

Several significant changes in the Indians' organizational structure took place after the death of O'Neill. The first was the hiring of Peter Bavasi as club president in 1986, at the behest of Patrick O'Neill, the nephew of the late owner and an increasingly influential figure in the Indians ownership hierarchy, as the O'Neill estate had maintained a 60 percent share of the franchise. The hiring of Bavasi sparked considerable controversy concerning Bavasi's motivations, as the new Indians president was previously a paid consultant for Tampa-St. Petersburg and Indianapolis interests in their efforts to obtain major league franchises. Bavasi had not held a formal position in Major League Baseball since his stint as executive vice president and then president of the Toronto Blue Jays from 1977 to 1981, after serving as an executive of the San Diego Padres from 1968 to 1977. His first moves represented a housecleaning of the Indians' front office, initially by convincing Gabe Paul to retire, though he remained a paid consultant, and by bringing on a new vice president and general manager to replace Phil Seghi, who was reassigned by the club, while at the same time overseeing the firing of Bob Quinn as vice president and director of player development and scouting.[30] Bavasi, although maintaining a good deal of control over all decision making, moved to hire two individuals that he termed "partners," but who were given a rather elaborate set of changing titles and responsibilities. The first was Dan O'Brien, who was initially labeled the "assistant to the president," and later "senior" vice president/baseball administration/player relations. The other "partner" was Joe Klein, initially given the title of "vice president/baseball operations," and then "general manager." The lack of clearly defined responsibilities of baseball front office personnel, combined with an ongoing focus by ownership on working out the financial arrangements to sell the team, prevented the Indians from developing anything resembling a cohesive or coherent player development strategy that might have been able to win more games by spending less money. Instead, getting out from underneath the mountain of debt, some inherited, others accumulated, overwhelmed the O'Neill ownership group.

The timing of the 1986 sale would ultimately work to the benefit of the future of the franchise by establishing the key ingredients for success well before a new ballpark was even more than a fanciful dream. The ownership team of brothers Richard E. Jacobs and David H. Jacobs, who would die on September 17, 1992, at age 71, quickly moved to hire a seasoned baseball management team that would be given considerable leeway in developing a longterm strategy for moving the club out of the perennial basement. The decision to hire Hank Peters, long-time baseball administrator and executive with 42 years of baseball experience, as president illustrated the baseball savvy of the new ownership tandem. Peters had been successful as executive vice president and general manager of the Orioles for 12 years. Under his leadership, the Orioles won American League pennants in 1979 and 1983 and the World Series in 1983. Peters also had longstanding ties to past Indians organizations, having served as vice president and director of player personnel during Gabe Paul's and Vernon Stouffer's ownership from 1966 to 1971.

The Indians' ownership understood the importance of establishing an organizational structure headed by experienced baseball personnel who would then be allowed to execute a long-term strategic plan for the franchise. The division of labor mirrored that of successful franchises of the past: ownership that established a payroll limit and clarified financial expectations, a president, Hank Peters, who was also general manger until 1991, who engaged in consistent communication with the ownership about short-term trades, signings, and player development but was left to his discretion in establishing the baseball philosophy that would move the franchise forward, and a subsequent general manager, John Hart, who continued to guide the franchise in a direction initially charted by Peters and his extensive array of baseball player development personnel and scouts. The fit between Peters and Hart was emblematic of the organizational cohesion of the Indians front office, which began to develop a strategic plan well before the building of Jacobs Field, but also sought, once the stadium deal had been approved, to maximize the financial advantages of the new ballpark for fielding a winning team. GM Hart had been part of Peters's organizational structure in Baltimore, as a former minor league player, manager and third base coach, whose linkages to the personnel that Peters brought with him to Baltimore proved useful in establishing the communication channels necessary to make key decisions about long-term contracts, player development strategies, and trade and free agent options. In the winter of 1991-92, Hart met with owner Richard Jacobs to develop the outlines of a salary plan that would allow the Indians to lock up their best young players through the construction and completion of Jacobs Field. It was, according to Hart, "[A plan] to build a competitive club within a fiscally responsible program, and still present a growing, stable club to the fans, which is what really counts."[31] This plan "subsequently was endorsed by other major league clubs and became a standard for the industry."[32]

The contrast with the organizational strategy, or lack thereof, of the Baltimore Orioles could not be starker. The only ingredients that the two organizations had in common were resources from a new ballpark and a willingness to spend money. Shortly after new owner Peter Angelos purchased the Orioles from Eli Jacobs for $173 million, the most ever for a professional sports franchise, in 1993, the prominent labor attorney announced his presence with a splash of free agent signings for the following season. Angelos authorized contracts for four prominent free agents for 1994, including first baseman Rafael Palmeiro, third baseman Chris Sabo, left-handed pitcher Sid Fernandez, and closer Lee Smith, all proven veterans who would prove indicative of the kind of team that Angelos preferred to field. Unlike the Indians' ownership, and unlike former Orioles owner Eli Jacobs, Angelos and members of his family would be involved in front office decisions to a degree that proved detrimental to the development of a cohesive strategic plan. There was no long-term vision of player development and of acquiring/signing young players to long-term contracts with the intention of building an baseball club that had the perpetual ability to fill in talent gaps and win year after year. Instead, Angelos insisted on emphasizing the signing of veteran free agents, both to maximize the immediate impact on attendance and to catapult the Orioles to playoff contention in the early years after Camden Yards had been built.

This focus on veteran talent to the virtual exclusion of the acquisition and development of young prospects proved frustrating to the long-established front office personnel hired by Angelos. The history of the Angelos ownership is replete with vetoes of trades orchestrated by Baltimore general managers, firings of general managers and assistant general mangers who were judged to have veered too far from Angelos's preferences, and, in 1999, the establishment of a working committee to hire the new Orioles manager, Mike Hargrove, that included a five-member search team in which Angelos's two sons, Lou and John, were represented. During the time that Hargrove was hired, the Orioles lacked a general manager or even a director of baseball operations, choosing instead a "nebulous brain trust" that seemed unclear themselves about the structure of any recognizable chain of command within the Baltimore organization. When asked by *Baltimore City Online* whom Hargrove would talk to about player moves, John Angelos, one of Angelos's sons and therefore a member of the brain trust, was rather vague: "I would imagine he'd pick up the phone and call either [Syd Thrift] or he'd call me. He could also, of course, call Mr. Angelos." The lack of a clear chain of command, and most importantly, the lack of clear communication channels, contrasted with Hargrove's experiences in Cleveland, where player acquisition strategy, including pending needs, trade options and potential free agent signings, were a regularized topic of discussion between Hargrove and GM John Hart. Hargrove recalled of his time as the Cleveland manager, where he spent most of the 1990s, "we [Cleveland] did not make a trade that I did not sign off on."

The Angelos penchant for hiring immediate family to compose committees responsible for hiring new managers indicated the extent to which he would be willing and ready to impose his own (changing) blueprint on the Orioles' personnel decisions. Prior to the 1996 season, it appeared that Angelos might be willing to delegate more authority to the veteran front office and managerial talent that he had hired. Seeking to get Baltimore beyond the mediocrity of the 1995 season, in which the club went 71–73 and finished 15 games out of first place, Angelos overhauled the organizational structure by hiring successful GM Pat Gillick, fresh off two-time major league "Executive of the Year" awards. The owner also hired Davey Johnson, impressive enough as an Oriole player to be inducted into the Baltimore Hall of Fame for his on-field accomplishments and highly successful and respected as a manager, first with the New York Mets, where he presided over two first-place finishes and three second-place finishes over six seasons, and at Cincinnati, where he led the Reds to two divisional crowns under owner Marge Schott. Once again, Angelos opened his pocketbook for the Gillick-Johnson tandem, ensuring that the Orioles would continue to rely on veteran free agent talent with the goal of becoming a championship franchise in 1996 and 1997. GM Gillick signed three veteran free agents within a one-week period in the hope of bolstering Baltimore's playoff chances in 1996, including second baseman Roberto Alomar, lefty reliever Randy Myers and versatile B.J. Surhoff, who could play the corner infield and outfield positions, as well as catch if needed. These players, mixed with the veterans already on the Orioles roster, including Cal Ripken, Mike Mussina, Rafael Palmeiro, Brady Anderson, Chris Hoiles, Scott Erickson, and Jeffrey Hammonds, suggested a very good, but aging, team that would be in a position to make the playoffs, as a wild card team in 1996 and as a divisional winner in 1997, when further player moves were orchestrated with Angelos's considerable hands-on involvement. This included an Angelos veto of a potential 1996 trade that would have sent outfielder/third baseman Bobby Bonilla and pitcher David Wells to Seattle for catcher Chris Widger and outfielder Jeromy Burnitz. Gillick felt the team needed to get younger to be in a position to better overcome the rapid decline in performance that would otherwise debilitate the organization. But Angelos simply would not allow the trading of veterans for young players, and certainly not for unproven prospects.

 The owner's consistent pattern of vetoing trades essentially undermined any semblance of a division of labor between the Baltimore front office and the ownership, a division that was largely responsible for the success of the Cleveland Indians and other franchises that historically emulated the Yankees' effective division of labor established in the 1920s. The lack of clear signals between Angelos and his general managers and managers resulted in considerable tension, controversy and ultimate firings by Angelos of those front office and managerial personnel who would not easily accept the owner's penchant for baseball decision making. By 2000, the Orioles were fielding a team that averaged 33 years of age, well beyond what the sabermetric proponents of the S-curve would suggest was optimal player performance years, with little to show in the way of sustained minor league player development. The early warnings of GM Pat Gillick about the need to make trades to replenish the barren and unproductive Oriole farm system and to provide a core of players that the team could utilize to gradually replace the aging veterans, who most assuredly would be both overpaid and in declining productivity, seemed highly prescient.

The playoff successes of 1996 and 1997 soon gave way to the mediocrity of 1998 and 1999, as the club finished 79–83 and 78–84, both extremely poor records when matched against the high payrolls of the organization. The Orioles did much less with the same amount of money that the Indians were spending, finding themselves with an older and less productive roster in which it was difficult to move contracts of high-priced veterans. Unlike the Indians, the Orioles did not lock up a range of young players with the idea of keeping those players during their most productive seasons. Instead, under Angelos's direction, the Orioles acquired veteran free agents who could and did help the club in the short run, but whose price tags soon became a burden on the organization over the long haul. At the same time, the lack of communication and clear demarcation of organizational responsibility alienated many of the best baseball minds that Angelos had hired. Before making a decision to hire Syd Thrift to take over the general manger position after the 1999 season and combining Thrift with two of Angelos's sons to make baseball decisions, Angelos had already alienated several prospective general managers with excellent track records in the front office, including Pat Gillick, who resigned after the 1998 season, increasingly tired of the contradictory signals, lack of clear communication and routine interference in front office decision making that had become a staple of Angelos's ownership style. After hiring the capable and experienced Frank Wren for the 1999 season, Angelos chose to fire him on October 7 of the same year, replacing him in the interim with the infamous five-man committee, of which Syd Thrift was part, that became the butt of behind-the-scenes jokes by other baseball executives. Jon Heyman of the *Sporting News* summarized the state of the Orioles' front office decision-making as of the winter of 1999-2000:

> The Orioles baseball decisions are now made by GM Syd Thrift and Angelos' two sons, John and Louis. Mockingly, they are referred to as "Syd and the kids." Thrift was so ill-prepared at the winter meetings

opposing general managers were shaking their heads. The kids are better known for their rotisserie playing, which might explain the real team.[33]

The Orioles, unlike the Indians, did not establish a clear separation of powers between the owner and the front office in baseball decision-making. Throughout the 1990s, when the Cleveland Indians were implementing a game plan whose parameters had been designed by many of the same front office personnel that had been hired with the change of ownership in 1986, the Baltimore Orioles lacked a coherent organizational structure. Owner Peter Angelos has remained an activist GM, blocking decisions by experienced front office personnel, establishing his sons as high-level consultants despite their lack of experience in baseball decision-making, and failing to establish a clear and consistent line of communication and delineation of responsibility between the owner and the rest of the Orioles' baseball organization. The result has been an Orioles team that has been mostly mediocre in the standings, underperforming given the fact that the team has consistently been one of the biggest spenders in the sport during Angelos's tenure. Ultimately, the club has shifted direction a bit in recent years, as the years of high payrolls and free agent signings have given way to a recognition that the club needs to devote time and resources to player development. It seemed that the team was poised to once again make a big splash on the free agent market for the 2004 season, especially with the signing of star free agent shortstop Miguel Tejada to a six-year contract potentially worth $72 million. The question becomes: Will this off-season spending spree be like the ones in 1996 and 1997 — good enough to make the club a contender for one or two seasons but at the expense of a long-term vision about how to maintain a winning franchise over the long haul? Or will the team make wise choices that reflect some of the wisdom of previous success stories, including the Indians under John Hart during the 1990s?

Conclusions: The Stadium Boom and the Lessons of the Milwaukee Brewers

The contrasting examples of the Indians and the Orioles indicate that publicly funded stadiums can provide significant sources of revenue, but that revenue is less important than the wisdom and vision of the front office in allocating the dollars in the most productive way. The Indians were able to develop an organizational game plan that allowed for the development and retention of key players in the prime of their careers to coincide with the financial resources provided by Jacobs Field. The Orioles were less successful, with Peter Angelos never having allowed the baseball organization to have the kind of independence necessary to develop a consistent organizational plan. The Orioles chose to spend their revenues on high-priced, veteran free agents whose best years were often behind them in an effort to speed their advance to the playoffs and World Series. The penchant for veteran talent over a consistent player development strategy meant that Baltimore would hover around mediocrity for much of the decade, with the exceptions of 1996 and 1997, when the club did make the playoffs with an older roster of high-priced stars.

While the difference between the Indians and the Orioles is revealing in its lessons for winning and losing in major league baseball, the most recent examples of publicly financed stadiums have given the fans little to cheer about. The Milwaukee Brewers have done nothing but continue their losing tradition after moving into the publicly financed Miller Park in 2001. Politicians and taxpayers are demanding to know why the Brewers, after having taken advantage of the new stadium revenues for three full seasons, slashed their player payroll from $52.7 million in 2002 to $40.6 million in 2003 and planned another $10 million dollars worth of cuts for the 2004 season. The Brewers' model is increasingly typical of the failure of latecomers to the publicly financed stadium game to use their newfound resources to build a winning team. Increasingly, the honeymoon effect of a new stadium on attendance only lasts one year at best, quickly evaporating if a club loses during its first season in the new facility.

The Brewers have suffered through 12 losing seasons, tying the Pittsburgh Pirates, another beneficiary of public largesse, for the longest active streak of futility in major league baseball. The fact that Miller Park did not reverse the team's losing ways is not surprising, but simply an indication that a team's fortunes are primarily tied to the strength and skills of its organizational front office personnel rather than an influx of new revenue. Still, the failure of the Brewers raises some profound questions that go beyond winning and losing to suggest fundamental flaws in the way that Major League Baseball is operating as a professional sports league. The club is reaping the benefits of a collective bargaining agreement that provided the team with $15 million in revenue sharing for the 2002 season, has been given a public subsidy of close to $400 million in the building of its new stadium, has national TV revenue of $24.4 million and local broadcast revenue of $5.9 million during that same season. Still, the franchise owners contend that the team is faced with mounting debt obligations that have been accruing throughout the 1990s and through the 2003 season, when the club saw season attendance figures drop at Miller Park for the second consecutive season. The club claims to have a debt of $110 million and to be actively looking for additional owners to help service the debt obligations. However, independent analysts accuse the team of inflating the constraints of its debt obligations, which economist Andrew Zimbalist, Jr., says is simply not an unusually high burden for a major league club. Well before campaigning for a new ballpark, the ownership group of the Brewers appeared ill equipped or unwilling to deal with the financial demands of running a major league baseball team.

The instability of the Brewers' front office has been an indication of a franchise searching for direction, yet at the same time pocketing the largesse of public financing without improving the quality of the club. With great fanfare in September 2002, the Brewers' ownership group announced the hiring of Ulice Payne, Jr., as team president, the first African American to be a major league team's top executive. Yet within a little more than one year, the Brewers' owners fired Payne, Jr., as part of a series of decisions that included cutting payroll for the 2004 season. Payne signed a confidentiality agreement that shrouds the reasons for his firing in secrecy, but sources have suggested that Payne had expressed concern about the cost-cutting direction of the Brewers' board of directors, whose chairperson was none other than Wendy Selig-Prieb, the daughter of commissioner Bud Selig. After assuming the role of commissioner in 1998, Selig placed $30 million in a blind trust that has continued making contributions to the team, including $14.2 million out of the total ownership commitment of $44 million to the club over the last six seasons to help service the club's debt. At the same time, the team has pocketed a consistently high amount of revenue sharing, including the highest total of any big-league club after the negotiated agreement with the players association launched the terms for a new revenue-sharing plan in 2003. The fact that Selig as baseball commissioner led the negotiations with the players' union in finalizing a collective bargaining agreement that disproportionately benefited his team indicates at the very least the sloppy and haphazard management style that has too often characterized baseball's governing hierarchy. At worst, the relationship between the commissioner and the Milwaukee Brewers smacks of hypocrisy and gross self-interest masquerading as "the general welfare of the game."

The politics of the financing of Miller Park should have supplied the Brewers with ample revenue to both service their debt and still have money left over to avoid slashing payroll. The Brewers owners paid just $90 million of the $400 million required to build the retractable-roof stadium, plus they managed to saddle the Miller Park stadium district with the purchase of about $41.1 million in debt. The purchase by the district of a portion of the Brewers' debt was supposedly in exchange for the Brewers being willing to provide annual maintenance for the facility. However, as Andrew Zimbalist has noted, the quid pro quo assumed that the Brewers would otherwise not be picking up the maintenance tab, thereby providing the illusion of a bargain for county officials when in effect it was an added burden on top of the costs necessary to construct the retractable roof stadium. This buyout of debt coupled with a healthy public subsidy in financing Miller Park added to the highest revenue sharing bounty in major league baseball should be giving Brewers fans some reason for optimism. Instead, the Brewers appear to be continuing their steady drumbeat of losing seasons, while claiming to be focusing on improving their farm club and mimicking the low-cost success of teams like the Minnesota Twins, whom Commissioner Selig in ultimate irony tried to contract as part of his strategy of negotiation with the players' union in the months leading up to the latest collective bargaining agreement.

The Milwaukee Brewers are the Baltimore Orioles without the money to spend, which is to say a club that has consistently ranked in the bottom third of major league baseball's payroll and has coupled that with a very poor farm system throughout the decade of the 1990s. Although the farm system appears to have rebounded a bit, the club's current strategy of cutting spending to the bone is likely going to result in more losing seasons for a city that has become the very symbol of what is wrong with the way the game of baseball is being run.

FOUR

The Globalization of Baseball: Cost Cutting and Outsourcing

Major League Baseball and all of the major league teams have increasingly relied on Latin America, especially the Dominican Republic and Venezuela, to provide a cheap source of player recruitment to fill minor league systems. During the 1980s and 1990s, major league clubs became much more aggressive about recruiting and signing Latin American players, with all teams establishing academies in the Dominican Republic and all but two having established academies in Venezuela that would house and train players as young as 14 years old (and in some cases younger), who were enlisted in the academies, not as signed players and therefore not technically employees, but were expected to participate in team-run drills and amateur games. This allowed clubs to evade the Major League Baseball requirement that foreign-born players were not eligible to be signed until they reached the age of 16, a prohibition that has routinely been violated, as virtually all the big-league clubs have commonly and knowingly signed Latin American players well in advance of their 16th birthday, by either providing or accepting a fraudulent birth certificate. Contrary to the protestations of major league clubs that it is often difficult if not impossible to verify the age of players in the Dominican Republic, the INS has documented that there are some very clear and straightforward methods that can be used to distinguish valid birth certificates from forged ones. However, it has become all too clear that most major league teams are not interested in the nuances of such distinctions,

FOUR / *The Globalization of Baseball* 121

as they have a vested interest in getting a player, however young, to sign a contract before the competition discovers him.

As Alan Klein noted in his book, *Sugarball*, the government of the Dominican Republic issued a Presidential Decree in 1984 that attempted to prevent the worst abuses of Dominican athletes that had become the norm among the small number of major league teams that had established academies in the country during the 1970s, including Pittsburgh, Toronto, Los Angeles, and San Francisco. When other clubs moved to aggressively compete with the four franchises that had already established academies, it became common practice to sign as many players as possible, some as young as thirteen, separate them from their families without any consideration of the consequences, hide the prospects from other scouts, and deny bonuses that had been promised to the players.[1] The Presidential Decree issued by Dominican president Hugo Blanco established that all scouts operating in the country had to be registered with the Dominican baseball commissioner, all minor league contracts signed in the country had to be approved by the government, no one under age seventeen could be signed to a professional contract, and English classes were compulsory for all players in the Dominican Republic.[2] There is considerable disagreement about the effectiveness of these provisions, with Klein arguing that they served "to protect young Dominican athletes from the more rapacious scouts and organizations."[3] Others, such as Angel Vargas, have argued that the laws have had little effect, as major league clubs have simply used their relationships with local talent scouts, or buscones, to contact Latin players younger than 17 and to hide them from their competition while these players are being trained and equipped in violation of the spirit, if not the letter, of Dominican law. In researching for this chapter, I have found numerous incidents, extending through the 1980s and 1990s, of major league teams having established relationships with Dominican and Venezuelan kids as young as 14 years old through the buscone system. Buscones have managed to run a profit-making enterprise in the Dominican Republic and Venezuela that involves recruiting, training and equipping players to be offered to major league clubs in violation of both Dominican law and in violation of the rules and regulations of Major League Baseball, which prohibits any MLB team from establishing formal or informal contacts with local talent scouts. In return, buscones have often taken a share of the bonuses that officially are given by major league clubs to Dominican and Venezuelan players. The system is informal enough that major league clubs can disavow any formal relationship with the local talent scouts, yet still rely on them for access to players prior to the players' eligibility for signing.

In that sense, the recruitment of players in Latin America bears some resemblance to the traditional scouting that took place in the United States before the advent of the amateur draft and the institutionalization of the drafting process expedited by the creation of the National Scouting Bureau. Just as the draft provided a regulated environment for the recruitment of players, the National Scouting Bureau provided a wide range of information on potential prospects that has been regularly made available to all major league clubs. The scouting process in Latin America, with its minimal regulation, has resulted in a cutthroat competition among major league clubs who attempt to use every advantage, including their relationships with buscones and the initiative of their local scouting staffs, to shield a prized prospect from the eyes, ears and clutches of opposing major league teams.

The teams' recruitment and treatment of these foreign players has frequently violated the laws of the Dominican Republic and Venezuela regarding terms of recruitment and working conditions, including the signing of players to English-only contracts and the signing of underage players to contracts, which are also violations of Major League Baseball's rules. Major league teams have routinely violated rules, regulations and national laws in a race to see which club could acquire the most promising collection of prospects at the cheapest possible cost. The timing of the globalization of major league baseball, which has reached its highest plateau from the 1990s to the present, coincided with escalating bonus payments to U.S.- and Canadian-born players selected in the amateur draft, who have been increasingly represented by agents who have helped protect their financial interest in dealing with major league teams. Increased recruitment also coincides with the escalating costs of free agent signings and the widening revenue gaps between the top and bottom major league clubs, as teams have scrambled to lower the costs of their operations during the heightened competition for player talent in the 1990s. In Latin America, major league teams have been able to cut costs by recruiting players in a limited regulatory environment that has allowed teams to establish a baseball academy, sign 30–40 Dominican and/or Venezuelan players, and pay the salaries of eight full-time scouts for less than the cost of a first-round U.S. amateur draft pick.

FOUR / The Globalization of Baseball

The relationship between Major League Baseball and the Dominican Republic and Venezuela has been shaped by the willingness of the commissioner's office to back away from enforcing existing regulations regarding the recruitment of foreign-born players, although recently the commissioner's office has finally begun to send personnel to the Dominican Republic and Venezuela to monitor the conditions of baseball academies and to supervise the signing of Latin players to minor league contracts. This belated posture stands in contrast to the behavior of the commissioner's office throughout the 1990s. During the decade that has seen the most significant expansion of the recruitment of low-cost Latin American talent in the history of the sport, the commissioner's office has often looked the other way as clubs made a routine practice of recruiting and signing players younger than 16 years old to play in baseball academies that were run by major league teams in the Dominican Republic and Venezuela. At the same time, the commissioner's office did nothing to establish a protocol that would ensure that major league teams provide a Spanish-language version of their contracts to their young recruits.

Throughout the 1990s, and to a large extent today, Latin American players, often lacking the formal representation of agents, have relied on "buscones," or local talent scouts, to facilitate the signing of contracts with major league teams, despite the fact that major league rules prohibit any "commission" paid by a major league team to a buscone or dirigente who represents a player in contract negotiations. Buscones are also prohibited by Major League Baseball rules from working for a particular major league club. In reality, these prohibitions have been widely ignored and major league teams commonly work with buscones in the recruiting and signing of Latin players. Unlike agents, buscones work on behalf of a Latin player only until that player signs a contract, part of the value of which is siphoned off by the buscone. The commission of the buscone is often tied to the bonus offered to the player by a major league club. Teams have routinely presented contracts to players in English-only versions whose key provisions are "translated" by the buscone to the player prior to securing the player's signature. Typically such "translations" are outright lies, quoting the player a dollar figure that is much less than the amount that is guaranteed to the player under the specific terms of the contract, whose monetary value is often tied to performance bonus requirements that the player cannot possibly meet or exceed. Buscones also have been known to provide one salary figure for the recruited player that is considerably below the salary figure provided by the major league team, with the buscone then pocketing the difference as part of his "commission." This too is a blatant violation of Major League Baseball rules and the laws of the Dominican Republic and Venezuela, yet the practice has become a common tactic in the unregulated environment of the recruitment of Latin American ballplayers. But it is not only buscones who engage in these practices, as major league teams routinely rely on such scouts to secure players at cheap rates, often with team officials being well aware of the methods that are being used to sign such players. At other times, team officials bypass the buscone system and sign players directly, using many of the same tactics of the buscone in providing English-only contracts, verbally overstating the value of the actual contract, and not informing the player about the myriad of performance clauses that will in most instances make the contract worth considerably less than the team implies.

What explains the timing of the explosion of academies run by major league teams to train Latin players? Certainly the escalating costs of signing amateur draft picks in the U.S. was one important factor. The legal structure of the amateur draft has provided a process that has served to protect the interests of amateur players in the U.S., Canada and Puerto Rico by establishing a set of rules, regulations and procedures that govern the selection of such talent. For exam-

Left: Miguel Tejada, superstar shortstop from Bani, Dominican Republic. The Oakland Athletics signed Tejada at the age of 17 for $2000, cheap even by the low rates paid to players in the Dominican. Like other young Latin prospects, he had no agent and did not understand the terms of his English-language contract. (The $2000 that it took to sign Tejada pales in comparison to the $1.2 million offered to teammate Ben Grieve.) Tejada's success, unfortunately, is a rare exception to the rule for foreign-born athletes, as between 90 and 95 percent of them are released while in the minor leagues, according to MLB statistics.

ple, Major League Rule (MLR) 4(e) mandates that "major league teams send to their draftees written notice that they have been drafted, a copy of relevant MLRs that affect the drafting of players, and copies of completed and executed Major League Uniform Player Contracts. If the MLB Commissioner determines that a major league team violates any of these MLRs, then the player becomes a free agent and can sign with any other major league team. The MLR ensures that the draftee is fully informed about his status and about the contractual documents that will determine his relationship with the major league team."[4]

In contrast, the unregulated environment of Latin American recruitment helps to perpetuate what some have termed a "wild west" atmosphere in recruiting and signing players, driven by economic considerations that have allowed teams to staff their minor league system with higher percentages of athletes that are recruited and signed in foreign countries, with the Dominican Republic and Venezuela being the most important source of the growing foreign talent base. In 1990, only about 25 percent of players on minor league rosters were foreign born; by 2000 that figure was 40 percent, and today foreign-born talent exceeds 50 percent of all players signed to professional contracts in the minor leagues. Also, today over 80 percent of all foreign-born players signed to minor league contracts come from either the Dominican Republic or Venezuela. At the major league level, about 15 percent of players signed to contracts were from Latin America in 1990; by 2000 that figure had increased to 25 percent and is steadily climbing as this book goes to press. The cost-cutting mechanisms of this system involve more than just low signing bonuses. Major league teams also cut costs by underfinancing their baseball academies, ensuring that several academies during the 1990s were operated on shoestring budgets that included the following typical conditions: unsafe playing surfaces, crime-ridden facilities for players, lack of adequate sanitation services, poorly maintained housing, poorly trained medical staff, insufficient food and nutrition, lack of serious educational activities, lack of consistent and adequate supplies of clean water."[5]

Major League Baseball has looked the other way, declining to monitor the conditions surrounding the recruitment of Latin American athletes and failing to establish a clear regulatory framework and enforcement bureaucracy that could check some of the most serious violations of Major League Baseball rules. As recently as 2000, scouts were saying off the record that more than half of Latin American signings violated the

16-year-old age requirement of Major League Baseball. Former Los Angeles Dodgers manager Tom Lasorda, after the Dodgers were penalized by the illegal signing of Adrian Beltre at age 15, said that he did not doubt that the practice was widespread and that the Dodgers were simply doing what other teams routinely practice. The decision of Major League Baseball to leave the Latin American player market virtually unregulated and unpoliced is a product of their focus on globalization as a way to grow the game's revenues. The commissioner's office has thus far emphasized the globalization of the sport as a way to generate revenues and lower costs for the game and for major league teams. The establishment of an organized and regulated structure for player recruitment in Latin America, including the implementation of a worldwide draft, has most recently been pushed by the commissioner's office as a way to help deal with systematic violations of Major League Baseball rules regarding foreign-based recruitment. Still, such a draft has not materialized, and it is very unclear whether the installation of such a draft would improve the bargaining position or the representation of Latin American players in the signing process, let alone the conditions of the team-owned academies in which the youngest Latin American players are trained to weed out future minor leaguers from the players left behind. Thus far, the development of a regulated and negotiated system that helps protect the rights of foreign players exists only as part of formal agreements between Major League Baseball and the Japanese Professional Baseball League, as well as agreements between Major League Baseball and the Mexican Professional League regarding the terms of player recruitment. These agreements provide a process that major league teams have to go through to acquire players from the Japanese League and the Mexican League, thereby making the acquisition of these players significantly different from the relatively unregulated environment of scouting and recruitment in Latin America.

The MLB-Japanese baseball agreement requires that any major

Opposite: Adrian Beltre of the Dominican Republic. On December 21, 1999, commissioner Bud Selig fined the Los Angeles Dodgers an undisclosed amount for signing Beltre to a professional contract prior to his 16th birthday, a violation of the rules of Major League Baseball. According to Selig, the Dodgers admitted that they purposely falsified Beltre's birthdate to sign him as a 15 year old. Beltre's request for free agency was denied because Beltre did not notify the league about this issue within the required one-year period. Responding to the controversy, former Dodgers manager Tom Lasorda was quoted as saying that it was quite routine for teams to sign underage Latin players.

FOUR / *The Globalization of Baseball*

league baseball team that is interested in a Japanese player must first go to the MLB commissioner's office. The commissioner's office then contacts the Japanese baseball commissioner to determine if the Japanese player is available. In cases where there is no approval needed from the Japanese club, the major league team is free to begin negotiating with that player. In cases where the major league club needs the approval of the Japanese team to negotiate with the player, the MLB Commissioner notifies all major league teams of the player's potential availability. This process then triggers a bidding competition among interested major league clubs for the right to negotiate with the Japanese player. Each major league club interested in the Japanese player submits a monetary bid to the team controlling his services, and the highest bid, as long as it is approved by the Japanese team, guarantees only the right to negotiate with the player, not the right to sign the player. The major league club then has thirty days to reach an agreement with the player, after which "the duty to compensate the Japanese club and the negotiating rights with the player both terminate."[6]

The rules and regulations governing the negotiating rights of major league teams for Japanese players stand in stark contrast to the unregulated environment of recruitment in Latin America. First, the integrity of the Japanese baseball league is protected by regulations that require the active involvement of the Japanese commissioner's office and the approval of the Japanese team prior to any negotiation process with a major league baseball club. Second, the conditions of any negotiations provide monetary compensation to the Japanese team that loses a player to Major League Baseball. The exceptions are Japanese players who qualify as 10-year free agents and thereby have earned the status of being able to negotiate a contract with a major league club without approval from their former Japanese club or from the Japanese commissioner's office. Of course, the process is more costly for major league teams, which have to spend considerable sums to the Japanese club just for the rights to negotiate with a player, and, assuming that the player in question signs a contract with the major league team, that team is saddled with the expenses of both the negotiation rights and the value of the player's contract. Thus the institutionalized framework of the U.S.–Japanese baseball arrangement is a game that only revenue-rich major league clubs can play, potentially contributing to a widening of the already large payroll discrepancy in major league baseball.

The institutionalized arrangement of signing foreign-born players extends to the Mexican League, although the rules and regulations of the negotiating process are less structured than they are between the Japanese League and MLB. First of all, major league baseball teams do not deal with the Mexican League commissioner's office, but instead are free to negotiate directly with Mexican teams in making arrangements or agreements for the signing of players. Still, the process involves restrictions regarding the eligibility of Mexican players for MLB contracts and as such provides some protection for the Mexican teams to ensure that those clubs don't simply operate as extensions of the MLB farm system. As a result of this system, there are a much smaller number of Mexican players in the major leagues compared especially to the Dominican Republic and Venezuela.

Major league clubs' use of Latin America for the acquisition of cheap talent is a long-established practice that did not begin with the surge in Latin American signings in the 1990s. A variety of baseball historians have documented the history of major league clubs' recruitment practices in Latin America from the early part of the 20th century, replete with examples of the "boatload mentality" recruiting practices that have continued to the present day. The difference between the past and the decade of the 1990s is one of intensity and degrees of recruitment efforts. During the '90s, the commissioner's office embarked on a most ambitious effort to globalize the sport by signing merchandising and licensing agreements with 109 countries and television rights fees with over 60 countries. The widespread marketing of the sport developed alongside the decision of major league teams to establish academies in the Dominican Republic and Venezuela. Such a globalization strategy evolved in the '90s as a response to the rising costs incurred by major league baseball in the aftermath of its failed collusion strategy under commissioner Peter Ueberroth, escalating bonus payments to amateur draft picks, a decline in national television revenue that widened the gap between rich and poor franchises, and the fallout from the 1994 strike and 1995 lockout that resulted in a further escalation of costs for the sport.

Explaining Major League Baseball's Globalization Strategy

By the mid- to late 1990s, major league baseball was pursuing an active strategy of globalization that involved concerted efforts to promote, market and sell major league baseball merchandise and memorabilia. The commissioner's office throughout the decade of the 1990s developed a strategy to establish foreign offices devoted to market development in large-revenue cities such as London, Sydney and Toronto, ignoring cities such as Caracas where the effort was focused on the recruitment of players rather than the selling of merchandise.[7] Major league games were broadcast in 215 countries and territories by either U.S.–based media companies such as ESPN or foreign media companies. The commissioner's office developed a marketing strategy that focused on developing a synergy between Japanese and South Korean players and the selling of broadcast rights in those markets. "During the 1997 season, for example, each game pitched by South Korean Chan Ho Park for the Los Angeles Dodgers was broadcast live in South Korea. In 1998, Korean baseball fans could tune in to more than 100 games, including live telecasts of Park's games, the All-Star Game, and the World Series. Japanese interest in the success of Ichiro Suzuki of the Seattle Mariners in 2001 illustrates powerfully the connection between MLB international broadcasting and foreign players in the major leagues."[8]

The commissioner's office decision to pursue an aggressive globalization strategy during the 1990s is closely linked to mounting financial obligations in the early part of the decade, due in large part to reductions in national television money that had played a major role in promoting greater competitive balance during the 1980s. At the close of the 1990 season, CBS claimed loses of $100 million as the fall World Series proved to be a ratings disaster for the network. In 1991, CBS announced a $169 million quarterly loss from its baseball deal. After 1992, "ESPN opted not to pick up the 1994–95 seasons, preferring a $13 million contract buyout to more rights fees."[9] Nielson surveys showed a one-quarter drop-off in baseball viewership from 1989 to 1992, while professional football rose 16 percent and pro basketball by 31 percent.[10] The prospective lowering of national television revenue would hurt the small-market clubs the most, especially absent any stadium deals to generate short-term revenue from other sources. The confrontations between the owners and players made the revenue situation much worse for the small-market clubs, especially the owners' aggressive and failed efforts to impose a salary cap that precipitated the 1994 strike and the 1995 lockout. By 1994, "the value of baseball's new national television contract fell by over 50 percent."[11] That proved devastating to clubs that were unable to gen-

FOUR / *The Globalization of Baseball* 131

erate lucrative local television contracts. As recently as 1990, 40 percent of average team revenue came from the distribution of national television revenues, as each team received about $19 million from major league baseball's central fund. When this revenue declined dramatically by 1994, there was a corresponding rise in revenue inequality between the top and bottom major league clubs.

The strategy of the commissioner's office was to try to take revenues away from the players by forcing the Players Association to agree to a salary cap or some form of strong limitations on rising player salaries. But that strategy has cost the owners much more revenue and has eventually pushed major league baseball toward revenue solutions that do not involve trying to defeat the Players Association. Still, the long-term costs of this confrontational approach should not be underestimated, especially the lost national television revenues of the mid-1990s or, before that, the costly failure of collusion, which burdened the owners with a hefty $280 million settlement with the Players Association, paid in lieu of taking the matter to federal court, which Ueberroth and hard-line owners preferred. The price tag for collusion was $10 million per team, and the industry's first installment came on January 2, 1991, with subsequent $40 million payments on July 15, September 15, November 15, 1991, and April 15, 1992.[12] These costs made a significant dent in the money that small-market teams could have used to defray the lack of solid local television deals. At the start of the 1992 season, four clubs, Seattle, Kansas City, St. Louis, and Milwaukee, began the season without any firm local television deals and were further burdened by the costs of the collusion payouts, which hit clubs equally regardless of existing revenue streams.

The growing gap between the haves and have-nots of major league baseball was further exacerbated by the escalating prices for first-round bonus payments for amateur draft picks, which increased by 40 percent in 1990, 44 percent in 1991, and 35 percent in 1992. The commissioner's office responded to this trend with a policy that attempted to allow drafting clubs to retain exclusive rights to high school picks for five years. The policy failed to hold up in court after being challenged by agent Scott Boras and the Players Association. The rush by major league teams to expand recruitment to the low-cost environment of Latin America is in part a product of the escalating bonus payments for amateur draft picks. As noted in a previous chapter, the rising bonus payments broke a trend of relatively stagnant bonus payments that lasted from the origins of the draft in 1965 to 1990. The reasons for the escalation in bonus payments in the 1990s include a better representation of amateur draft picks by agents intent on winning higher payments for their clients and a willingness of large-revenue clubs to break ranks and offer higher signing bonuses to early-round picks. This trend, coupled with the reductions in national television revenues and the success of some franchises (but not others) in securing stadium deals, put pressure on franchises to find creative ways to cut costs by recruiting in the loosely regulated and low-cost environment of Latin America. Such efforts were even more crucial for small-revenue franchises who could not take advantage of the high-priced negotiations to secure the best first-round draft picks, or could not afford the expensive and highly regulated option of trying to buy Japanese talent.

However, despite the potential benefits of Latin American recruitment for small-revenue franchises, the reality of competing with large revenue franchises for Dominican and Venezuelan talent has bid up the purchase price for the top-tier talent available in the Latin American market. Small-revenue teams cannot win bidding wars for non-drafted Latin American talent any more than they can pay the escalating costs for first- and second-round draft picks. With this in mind, Major League Baseball, led by executive vice president of operations Sandy Alderson, has proposed a worldwide amateur draft with the intention of providing a regulatory framework that would theoretically allow the teams that rank lowest in the standings to secure exclusive negotiating rights for the top picks available in the Dominican Republic and Venezuela. However, it is difficult to imagine that such a global draft could avoid the escalating bonus payments that have long prevented low-revenue clubs from securing their first choice in the U.S. amateur draft.

At its inception in 1965, and through 1991, the amateur draft did succeed in achieving Major League Baseball's goal of holding down bonus payments, as discussed as some length in chapter two. However, the explosion of bonus payments throughout the 1990s and the turn of the millennium has been one of the trends creating a greater gap between large-revenue and small-revenue teams in terms of access to affordable talent. Still, executives within Major League Baseball think that the development of a worldwide draft could contribute to lower-cost recruitment of foreign talent that would benefit a wider range of teams. According to Alderson, a worldwide draft would give more leverage to major league teams in negotiating with top Dominican and Venezuelan prospects. Unlike amateur picks from the United States, impoverished foreign-born players and their families would be reluctant to hold out for an entire year and take the risk of re-entering the draft for a potentially higher bonus payment. According to this line of thinking, the implementation of a worldwide draft would institutionalize a negotiating process that would minimize bidding wars and make foreign talent, especially top-tier talent, more affordable to a wide range of clubs. The next section of the chapter examines some of the issues surrounding the concept of a worldwide draft, including its current status and the possible impact it might have on the structural inequalities that exist in Major League Baseball, as well as the impact it might have on the choices available to Latin American players attempting to play professional baseball.

The Prospect of a Worldwide Draft

The Collective Bargaining Agreement of August 30, 2002, signed by Major League Baseball (MLB) and the Major League Baseball Players Association (MLBPA), included an attachment letter from MLB's Rob Manfred to union president Donald Fehr in which the two negotiators agreed in principle to the concept of a worldwide draft. However, the attachment letter was rushed and provided no details of how such a draft would be implemented. In principle, both parties agreed only to expand the First-Year Player Draft to cover all eligible players worldwide, and that the draft should have between 20 and 38 rounds. The rest of the details were left to a special World-Wide Draft Subcommittee of MLB and MLBPA representatives, who were to negotiate a final agreement. So far the subcommittee has yet to produce a regulatory framework for a worldwide draft, meaning that the current rules governing the amateur draft have remained in effect and so far a worldwide amateur draft is no closer than it was at the conclusion of the latest Collective Bargaining Agreement in 2002.

The difficult issues yet to be determined include the number of rounds; the age of draft eligibility for players from countries without organized high school baseball; and the desirability of maintaining or developing baseball academies in such countries. In addition, the subcommittee must decide whether bad teams should get proportionately more draft picks; whether clubs who fail to sign a drafted player should receive some type of compensation; and whether the current system of compensation for clubs that lose free agents with draft picks should be maintained. The fact that these issues have yet to be resolved is due to several factors, including the technical complexity surrounding the creation of a worldwide draft, disagreements between the owners and the players regarding how such a draft will proceed, and uncertainty regarding the likely effects of such a draft on a whole host of issues ranging from impact on competitive balance to bargaining rights for Latin players. Due to the complexity of the issue and its secondary status compared to other more pressing economic concerns, MLB did not make such a draft a priority in its latest CBA with the players association. Still, the issue of a worldwide draft may one day gain momentum, so it's worth exploring the potential ramifications of such a draft for the issue of competitive balance and the likely impact on the status of Latin American recruits.

Although most owners, according to Alderson, are now on board in supporting the concept of a worldwide draft, there is mixed opinion about how effective it would be in dispersing foreign talent more evenly among major league teams. Some low-revenue clubs that have been utilizing the "wild west" environment of recruitment in Latin America to their advantage, including executives and scouting personnel for the Houston Astros, are skeptical about the advantages of a global draft. "Right now, you can sign 10 players for $2,000 each and, with development, one or two might make it to the big leagues," one scouting director said. "You make what by comparison are modest investments in scouting and development and it pays off. I'm not sure I like a system that takes that away."[13] The current environment encourages clubs to utilize their own academies and their own local talent scouts to recruit, train, and possibly sign Dominican and Venezuelan ballplayers before other clubs gain knowledge of their efforts. The environment is the closest baseball has come to mimicking the traditional scouting in the U.S. that took place in the decades prior to the amateur draft of 1965. Low-revenue clubs such as Houston and Montreal have benefited from aggressive scouting in Latin America and have produced more major league talent from their recruitment efforts over the past two decades than the New York Yankees. The problem for low-revenue clubs has not been being unable to compete with the high-revenue teams for Latin talent.

Instead, the problem often is holding onto that talent as these players mature and become eligible for arbitration and free agency, an issue that a worldwide draft would not address.

Regarding which teams have fared best under the current system, we devised a simple methodology to gauge which clubs have produced the most premium major league talent in signing nondrafted free agents from the Dominican Republic and Venezuela. We used Bill James' Win Shares point system to evaluate the contributions of Latin American players signed within the past two decades by major league teams. James devised Win Shares as an all-inclusive sabermetric category to measure the offensive and defensive contributions of major league players on a per-season basis, with players scoring a 20 and above having achieved exceptional or star status in a given season and with players scoring a 10–19 having achieved an average to good performance in a single season. To simplify our approach, we gave a major league club credit if they signed a nondrafted free agent from Latin America who went on to produce at least a 10 Win Share in two of three major league baseball seasons (2001, 2002, 2003). For purposes of this study, we omit considerations of whether or not that player remained with the club that signed him (the overwhelming majority did not). Instead, we assume that in many cases the signing club, even if not able or willing to retain the player, was able to use his trade value to obtain something in return.

If it is true that the large-revenue clubs have been able to outbid their counterparts in recruiting talent from Latin America, then we would expect to find this reflected in the numbers. That is, teams such as the Yankees should have scored much better than teams such as the Astros and the Expos. The Astros easily outdistanced all other clubs in their recruitment efforts, both in numbers of major league players recruited (five) who made average or above-average contributions in at least two of three seasons from 2001 to 2003. Houston established the first academy in Venezuela, and their early efforts have paid consistent dividends, including the signing of premier players such as Bobby Abreu, Freddy Garcia, Richard Hidalgo, Carlos Guillen, and Melvin Mora, the five players whose Win Shares scores qualified them for inclusion in this study. In addition, the Astros also signed two of the top pitching prospects from Venezuela, Wilfredo Rodriquez and Carlos E. Hernandez, putting Houston at the top of major league organizations increasingly relying on nondrafted free agents from Venezuela to fill slots in their minor league systems. During the 1990s, there was a dramatic increase in Venezuelan talent in professional baseball, with an increase from 250 in 1992 to 714 by 1999. Between 1990 and 2000, the number of Venezuelans playing in the big leagues rose from 55 to over 110.[14]

The Expos finished second to Houston in their overall recruitment efforts from Venezuela and the Dominican Republic, with the likes of Vladimir Guerrero, Ugueth Urbina, Orlando Cabrera and Miguel Batista totaling a collective Win Shares score of 201 over the three-year span. The Expos had produced enough young talent by 1994 that they had the best record in baseball at the time of the players' strike. In fact, the owners' effort to force the players' union to accept a salary cap ultimately did irreparable harm to the small-revenue clubs, especially Montreal, which was damaged by a reduction in national television revenue that followed 1994 and the subsequent revenue losses precipitated by the owners' lockout in 1995, with each of these developments creating a growing dependence of franchises throughout the 1990s on local sources of revenue. A worldwide draft would not only fail to address the larger issues of inequities in market structure, but would simply be a repeat of a flawed strategy on the part of owners to try to reduce bonuses paid to a handful of Latin American players as a supposed way of leveling the playing field for small-revenue clubs.

Would the worldwide draft really aid small-market clubs? There are several compelling reasons to suggest that such a draft would, at best, do little in the way of improving competitive balance. At worst, the worldwide draft could simply make it more difficult for enterprising clubs such as the Astros and Expos to effectively recruit talent from Latin America. Under the current rules, low-revenue clubs have an incentive to take risks on several low-cost prospects from Latin America, and organizations such as Houston and Montreal have been utilizing strategies of recruiting more Latin American prospects than their richer counterparts, who have other options of getting high-ceiling talent by either turning to the higher-priced markets of Japan and South Korea, cutting deals with Mexican League teams with which they have a working relationship, or simply electing to spend more money on free agent talent in the U.S., an option which low-revenue teams simply do not enjoy. Under a global draft, teams such as the Astros would be limited to selecting a Latin prospect only once among 30 draft picks, thereby diluting an advantage that the club now enjoys.

FOUR / *The Globalization of Baseball*   137

    At the same time, it is doubtful, given the recent trends in the amateur draft, that bonus payments to top-tier Latin players would be reduced by a worldwide draft. More likely, the worldwide draft would allow agents to play a larger role in the selection process. Agents would establish relationships with Latin players by encouraging them to fulfill a basic requirement endemic to any drafting process that would be established: registration for the draft to protect their eligibility. At the same time, an equivalent of the National Scouting Bureau would likely be established internationally to make information available to all teams regarding who the top prospects are and where those prospects are ranked in terms of projectable major league performance. The result would likely be a drafting process that increases bonuses paid to Latin players identified by the scouting bureau (and/or hyped by agents) as having the most potential to contribute to a major league organization. There would be low-cost incentives for more teams to participate in the draft, but there would also be fewer advantages for small-revenue clubs that have historically scouted well and have spent resources in identifying and developing Latin American talent.

    By standardizing the drafting process, the differentiation in terms of skill and luck in recruiting talent would be replaced by a process that limits the number of top prospects that can be taken by individual major league teams from the region. At the same time, due to the wealth of information that would be standardized and provided to all teams, the bonus payments to the top players would certainly have a good chance of either staying the same or increasing. This would potentially be very good for the Latin players who have been labeled the best prospects in the system, and the worldwide draft might be worth defending on that basis alone (more on that argument later in the chapter). However, it is difficult to imagine the draft having any appreciable positive effect on competitive balance. Some owners clearly prefer the worldwide draft for the same reason that they initially supported the amateur draft in the U.S. in 1965: as a way to increase leverage over Latin players who would then be unable to enter bidding wars for their services. However, the owners are likely to fail to keep bonus payments down to top-tier Latin talent, for the simple reason that agents are now much more prevalent in the process of athlete recruitment than was the case in the early decades of the U.S. draft. In fact, it was player agents who tested the rules of the amateur draft in the early 1990s and secured huge signing bonuses for players who had not been properly offered contracts by the teams that drafted them, helping to usher in a following decade of spiraling bonus payments. These bonus payments are not going to disappear because of a worldwide draft, but are likely to be institutionalized in a manner that allows high-revenue clubs to sign more players for larger amounts of money than might have been the case without a worldwide draft, most likely through taking advantage of another owner proposal that would allow for the trading of draft picks selected in the first two rounds. This ability to trade picks, which has already been endorsed by the MLBPA, would place immediate financial pressure on low-revenue clubs to sell their slots for cash, further undermining the competitive balance that the worldwide draft was supposed to combat. At any rate, the owners' driving motive in promoting a worldwide draft — depressing bonuses and salaries to Latin players — is not a worthy one on its own terms in its negative impact for Latin prospects and would likely be undercut anyway by the institutionalization of Latin recruitment promoted by the draft.

Another goal of Major League Baseball is to use the worldwide draft to restructure the entire drafting process, with the goal of giving more leverage to teams and less leverage to players signed in the amateur draft. As such, the owners have floated another proposal to the players' union which has rightly been firmly rejected by the MLBPA: restricting eligibility for amateur draft picks to a 0, 2, 4 formula in which players would be eligible for the draft after high school (0), after two years of junior college (2), or after four years of college (4). The union has, understandably, expressed opposition to this proposed change, which would give MLB teams more leverage over amateur draft picks in the negotiation over bonus payments. An ongoing battle between MLB and the MLBPA is likely to emerge over how much time a foreign-born athlete would have to accept an offer from a major league club without being declared ineligible for the draft for an entire year, a provision that could be harmful to the Latin athlete and his family, as a lost year of eligibility in an environment of dire poverty is then viewed as "leverage" by major league baseball. Assuming that MLB was able to get a six-week window approved as part of a worldwide draft regulatory structure, it would not help competitive equality or small-revenue clubs, but it might do more to help the position of agents who would increasingly be utilizing their own firms to run player academies. Agents would have little trouble advising a Latin prospect to reject the contract offer of a major league team that in the agent's estimation was offering too little. That waiting process would not necessarily benefit the Latin player, but could all too easily result in the agent's firm, and the agent himself, pocketing a larger percentage of any future bonus the player received, in exchange for recouping the expenses incurred by the agent in continuing to allow the firm to utilize and train on facilities owned by the agent's firm. This process would be equivalent to indentured servitude and would not be that different from the exploitative processes utilized by major league teams and buscones in the present unstructured environment. However, a worldwide draft might simply shift the profits of such a system away from teams and buscones and toward agents and their firms, thereby continuing to place Latin athletes in the same precarious position they are in now without a worldwide draft. According to one prominent agent: "I guarantee you that if it's implemented, our agency will be one of the first to start a big, first-class academy in the Dominican Republic to recruit players. I'm sure there will be plenty of teams willing to sell their academies. I don't see much reason why they would need them."[15] *Baseball America* writer David Rawnsley concludes, "It's unlikely Major League Baseball wants a talent pool and development program controlled by agents, yet no one disputes that this would happen with a worldwide draft."[16]

Globalization and the Latin Player: Prospects for Reform

Thus far we've examined the possible impact of a worldwide draft on competitive balance in Major League Baseball, as well as the goals of the commissioner's office in supporting a worldwide draft. The conclusions suggest that a worldwide draft would do little to improve competitive balance in the sport, as such a draft would simply institutionalize the shift of power to agents, which could then continue to drive up bonuses paid to the top Latin athletes, while leaving the rest of the unrepresented athletes, selected lower in the draft or excluded entirely from the draft, to fend for themselves. For the Latin player, with the exception of those at the very top of the drafting pyramid, there is little reason to think that a worldwide draft would improve their current bargaining position. Such a draft, as proposed by the commissioner's office, would be implemented solely in an attempt (likely unsuccessful, in our view) to rein in bonuses to top Latin players while doing nothing to regulate the often illegal practices that undermine the welfare of the vast majority of Latin recruits. Thus the worldwide draft, absent a larger regulatory framework, would fail in its goals of improving competitive balance and also in its ability to address the inequalities in power and resources that have lead to persistent abuses in the recruiting process.

As documented in a wide range of studies dealing with the process of recruitment of Latin athletes by major league baseball teams, the Latin player is often given either misleading or false information prior to the signing of a contract with a big-league club regarding the terms of the contractual arrangement. At the same time, copies of contracts are sometimes not provided in Spanish, a tactic that allows the major league team to conceal the "fine print" details of the contract from the player, which prevents the player from fully understanding the implications of signing the contract. The intervention of the buscone, or local talent scout, often puts the player in a more tenuous situation, as the buscone is interested in maximizing his own percentage of any monetary deal between the player and the major league club. Although major league rules technically prohibit the use of buscones in the process of player recruitment and signing, clubs typically rely on their services to help them find and secure players in the cutthroat, unregulated environment of Latin American recruitment. A buscone will often demand a sizeable fraction of any signing bonus paid by the team to the player, or will, as intermediary, not reveal the full worth of the player's contractual deal, with the intent of keeping an undisclosed fraction of the bonus for himself.

This system benefits the Houstons and Montreals of the baseball world, but such an unregulated system preys on the fears and powerlessness of Latin athletes who are struggling to remove themselves from domestic poverty. The establishment of a governance structure that would provide both a set of rules and regulations governing the recruitment process and a regulatory body that could enforce these rules and regulations would be a first step toward giving Latin athletes more leverage and equity in the bargaining process. The existence of a regulatory structure that governs player recruitment in Japan and Mexico contrasts starkly with the lack of any structure governing player recruitment in the rest of Latin America and the Caribbean. Owners have conceived the worldwide draft as a tool that they hope will increase their leverage further in the recruitment of Latin athletes, while deliberately sidestepping the routine violation of existing rules governing the signing of players from the region. Major League Baseball has over the years implemented rules governing the recruitment process in the Dominican Republic and Venezuela that are habitually ignored by major league clubs, who see little disincentive for noncompliance, absent any regulatory agency that can enforce these rules. At the same time, major league teams routinely ignore Venezuelan and Dominican laws in the recruitment of baseball players.

Nothing better illustrates the existing power dynamics between major league clubs and the countries of Latin America than the refusal of the New York Yankees to acknowledge that Venezuelan labor law applied to their operations in Venezuela. In December of 2000 a Venezuelan labor law court found that the Yankees violated Venezuelan labor laws by improperly terminating the employment of pitching coach Winston Acosta, who had been employed by the team at its Venezuelan academy. According to an account provided by Arturo Guevara and David Fidler, "The New York Yankees had employed Acosta as a pitching coach from January 1, 1992, until July 13, 1999, when the Yankees fired him. During his employment with the Yankees, Acosta earned approximately $1,000 per month. Acosta began litigating against the Yankees on July 27, 1999."[17]

Venezuelan court authorities twice notified the Yankees of the pending lawsuit and of their responsibility under the Venezuelan Civil Code to appear in Venezuelan court to contest Acosta's allegations. The Yankees simply refused to acknowledge the legitimacy of these court proceedings and did not send any representative to appear before the Venezuelan labor court in charge of adjudicating the case. According to Venezuelan law, a failure of a defendant to appear in court is equivalent to automatic acceptance of the plaintiff's allegations as proven. Therefore the Venezuelan labor court ordered the Yankees to pay Acosta a total award of $6,865.30, which is what the former pitching coach was demanding a fair and just compensation for the Yankees' premature dismissal of his services under Venezuelan labor law. To this day, the Yankees have not bothered to respond to this lawsuit or to pay the amount awarded by the Venezuelan court. However, the club did shut down its Venezuelan baseball academy in the aftermath of this verdict, indicating that they were prepared to divest from the country rather than abide by the country's labor laws. The Oakland A's and the Texas Rangers also closed their Venezuelan academies for the same reasons: unwillingness to be exposed to Venezuelan labor laws.

The move of three baseball teams to divest their organizations from Venezuela in the aftermath of attempted enforcement of labor laws is due to the asymmetry of power and resources between Major League Baseball and Latin American countries. If Latin athletes are to be afforded even minimal levels of protection in this relationship, equivalent to athletes recruited from Canada, Puerto Rico, Japan and Mexico, the governments of Venezuela and the Dominican Republic must cooperate in penalizing major league clubs that violate labor laws in one country while continuing to maintain full academies and operations in the other. Efforts to foster cooperation will not be easy, given the cultural, social, economic and political differences between these two countries, but could be encouraged by aggressive involvement and leadership by prominent Latin American athletes, as well as associations including the Venezuelan Professional Baseball Association, led by Angel Vargas. Vargas has commented on the resource difficulties that make it difficult for his association to go much beyond its current role in facilitating and supervising Venezuelan professional leagues, but he has also recognized the importance of pursuing a "globalization of labor" strategy in improving the bargaining position of Latin athletes recruited from countries such as Venezuela and the Dominican Republic.[18]

A cooperative relationship between the Venezuelan and Dominican governments, given that the majority of Latin athletes are recruited from these countries, would help to increase the costs for Major League clubs who choose to divest from one of the two countries in favor of maintaining its presence in the other country. If such a cooperative relationship had existed in the aftermath of the Venezuelan court decision against the Yankees, the Dominican Republic might have been prepared to take a range of actions, including denying academies to teams that divested from Venezuela for the purpose of avoiding the implications of Venezuelan labor law, or supporting the Venezuelan government in their efforts to collect the court-ordered damages from the Yankees.Given the myriad of economic, social and political problems that Latin American countries face, it might be asking a lot to focus attention on the abuses of power by Major League Baseball teams. However, even if the Venezuelan and Dominican governments began to raise these issues in a concerted way, cooperating with international non-governmental human rights organizations and prominent Latin athletes, they might succeed in putting more pressure on the Yankees and other clubs that have evaded Latin American labor laws.

There is evidence that focusing the spotlight on the abuses by Major League teams in the recruitment of Latin athletes has already had some positive effects in prompting Major League Baseball to finally begin monitoring the rules and regulations governing player recruitment in the Dominican Republic and Venezuela. After two decades of complete inaction in establishing any office in these countries, Major League Baseball finally opened an office in the Dominican Republic on December 5, 2000, from which a new administrator for Latin America would oversee MLB operations in the Dominican Republic and Venezuela. Rafael Perez was named the new Latin American administrator, appointed by the commissioner's office and entrusted with overseeing the monitoring of player signings by major league teams in Latin America. The duties included identifying and investigating illegal signings; insuring compliance with the 16-year-old rule in the Dominican Republic and other Latin American countries; and interacting with and instructing scouts in the Dominican Republic and Latin America to ensure that they understand the signing rules; inspecting academies in the Dominican Republic and Venezuela to ensure compliance with the standards adopted by Major League Baseball; and making recommendations with respect to necessary improvements that may be required in the academies located in the Dominican Republic and Venezuela.[19]

The jury is still out regarding how effective or serious Major League Baseball has become in monitoring the most serious violations of their own rules in Latin America, and their presence does nothing to address the systematic ability of teams to evade the law in Latin countries, as the Yankees did in Venezuela. Still, the establishment of such an office is an important, if belated, first step in a process that could lead to greater regulation and protection of player rights in countries where they have routinely been ignored and/or shunted aside. For Major League Baseball, the Dominican Republic and Venezuela have served as cheap recruiting grounds to staff their minor league systems at low costs, while keeping players in the dark about their own contract status and the specific terms of their signing bonuses. Authors Arturo Marcano Guevara and David Fidler have documented the numerous examples of double standards in the recruiting of Latin American players compared to players from

Canada, Puerto Rico and Japan. The double standards identified by the authors include the following:

1. Major league teams are prohibited from signing high school players in the United States, Puerto Rico, and Canada during the period of their eligibility to participate in high school athletics. Major League Baseball accords high school students in Latin American countries no equivalent protection.
2. Major league teams are prohibited from signing players in colleges in the United States, Puerto Rico, and Canada except under specific conditions. No similar protection applies in Latin American countries.
3. Major league teams sign cannot sign players playing in American Legion youth baseball. Major League Baseball does not accord the same protection to players playing for Latin youth leagues.
4. Major league rules prohibit major league teams from trying to influence a student to withdraw from high school or college. Major league teams are, however, free to try to influence Latin children and young men to leave school to play professional baseball.
5. Major league rules closely regulate when tryouts for high school, college, junior college, and American Legion players may be held. Latin players are not accorded equivalent protections in connection with tryouts.
6. Major league rules require major league teams to provide drafted players with a) written notice of their selection; b) a copy of the Major League Rule on contracts; and c) copies of the Minor League Uniform Player Contract completed by the major league team. No Major League Rule exists on tendering contracts to Latin minor league players.
7. If a major league team violates the above-mentioned contract tendering rules, the player automatically becomes a free agent. Latin minor league players are not similarly protected in the tendering process.
8. Major league teams must translate into Spanish major league rules on misconduct (e.g. betting on games) and post such translations in the dugout. Major League Baseball does not, however, have a rule mandating that teams translate the Minor League Uniform Player Contract and other important documents into Spanish for use with Latin minor league players.

FOUR / *The Globalization of Baseball* 145

9. Under major league rules, major league teams bear the responsibility for determining whether a player is eligible to sign. In Latin America, major league teams are not under an express mandate to determine whether a player meets the criteria of the 16-year-old rule; all the teams must do is send documents on proof of age.
10. Under major league rules, a player gets credited with a year of minor league service for each championship season in which the player was on the active or disabled list of a minor league club. However, a player's time on the active or disabled list of a minor league club in a minor league outside the United States or Canada does not count toward minor league service.
11. Major league rules contain detailed quality standards that apply to minor league facilities in the United States and Canada. These detailed quality standards are not applied to minor league facilities of major league teams in Latin American countries.
12. If a major league team violates the Major League Rules in signing a player, the contract shall be declared null and void and the player is a free agent. In Latin America, if a major league team violates the 16-year-old rule, the contract is not automatically null and void because the commissioner has discretion whether to so declare.[20]

The establishment of a permanent MLB office in the Dominican Republic does not seem to have altered the existence of institutionalized double standards as outlined above in the recruitment of Latin athletes. The commissioner's office, for example, still does not require that major league teams provide Latin players with contracts that they can read. The office has instead begun making available Spanish translation of contracts to scouts, who then are trusted to provide such contracts to players. The lack of monitoring of this process, and the lack of a provision of a regulatory framework that would hold teams accountable for failure to provide clear contractual terms to Latin players, still does not exist. At the present time, there is simply little or no incentive for Major League Baseball to take more than token action to address the serious inequities that deny Latin recruits the same institutional rights that exist to protect players in Puerto Rico, Canada, and Japan.

What is ultimately needed is counter-pressure on Major League Baseball to provide Latin players with the range of protections that they need to be on a level playing field with recruits from other markets in the world. The most obvious possibility would be the creation of a Latin Players Association that could serve as a vehicle to began pressuring Major League Baseball to provide a regulatory framework for recruitment of Latin players that would offer these players rights that could not simply be dismissed at the whim of major league teams or the commissioners office. Such a players' association is not likely to emerge from the current Major League Baseball Players Association, which has been unresponsive to moving beyond protecting the fortunes of existing major league baseball players. Nor is it likely to come from Latin associations such as the Venezuelan players' association led by Angel Vargas. These Latin associations have limited resources and would not be in a financial position to oversee the tremendous task of building a players union that could start defending the rights of Latin athletes in Venezuela and the Dominican Republic. Instead, the most likely financial support for such an association would be Latin major league stars or former stars, who have the respect of their fellow countrymen necessary to bridge political divisions within their home countries and who have the financial resources necessary to contribute to the building of a Latin players' union. As Guevara and Fidler have noted, former Latin players understand the extent to which Latin athletes are exploited in the recruitment process and the need for serious changes in the way that Major League Baseball regulates this process.

Former major leaguer Tony Fernandez, from the Dominican Republic, has spoken about the need for Latin players to have legal and political support from those veteran major leaguers who have the resources and the inclination to step forward:

> There are a lot of players who are afraid to talk in relation to the way they have been exploited or what they have been subjected to as a minority by MLB. Some of us, the players who have been around for many years and have reached the top are in a better position than the rest of the players from Latin America, and it is these players who have the responsibility of being the voice of all the rest of the players.[21]

Chico Carrasquel, a legendary Latin star, agreed with Fernandez about Latin star players playing a leadership role in protecting the interests of Latin players who are recruited by MLB teams:

> Today, the Latino superstars have the ability to tackle the problems MLB teams cause in our countries. Confronting these problems will

not be easy for Latino players. Many are very grateful for the opportunity that the major leagues have given them to escape poverty and provide a good life for their families. But perhaps the time has come for all of us to confront our responsibilities.[22]

In short, the globalization of baseball raises serious long-term questions about labor relationships between MLB teams and Latin athletes who are subjected to a set of standards that differ significantly from the recruitment process that has been institutionalized in North America and Japan. While the commissioner's office has tended to support a pattern of recruitment in the Dominican Republic and Venezuela that has kept costs exceedingly low for major league teams, the countering pressures to provide a more regulated and fair bargaining relationship between the Latin athlete and major league clubs continues to increase. Major league baseball has responded to these pressures by establishing an office in the Dominican Republic, but whether or not that office exists merely to pacify critics or to institutionalize a set of protections for Latin athletes remains to be seen.

FIVE

The Politics and Economics of Expansion

The decision by baseball owners to add four new franchises during the 1990s contradicted claims that the sport was in serious financial crisis. The competition for new franchises indicated that the market for Major League Baseball remained much larger than the 26 clubs that comprised the big leagues at the start of the decade. Also, the fact that Major League Baseball was able to attract several competing bidders despite an all-time high expansion fee of $95 million (required for the Florida Marlins and Colorado Rockies, who began play in 1993), suggested that owning a Major League Baseball club was considered a winning proposition by wealthy investors in several prospective big-league cities. During the expansion process, Major League Baseball delayed, cajoled and forced the bidders for franchises to play by its tightly restricted ground rules. The fact that several cities had been clamoring to join the big-league circuit for the better part of the decade prior to the 1990s expansion, and that the U.S. Senate had established a task force as early as November 4, 1987, with the goal of six new major league teams by the year 2000, served as a launching pad for getting the commissioner of Major League Baseball to begin discussing the logistics of expansion. However, the goals of Major League Baseball were clear from the outset of this process: to delay and limit expansion so as to maintain a high level of competition for any potential new franchises, thereby driving up entrance fees and terms that competing bidders would have to satisfy, while maintaining sufficient "franchise scarcity" to utilize threats of franchise relocation to prod cities, counties and states to finance new ballparks.

FIVE / The Politics and Economics of Expansion

In keeping with these goals, Major League Baseball proceeded slowly with expansion by adding only two franchises at the beginning of the decade, over the objections of the Senate task force that pressed MLB to add six new franchises at one time. Commissioners Peter Ueberroth, Bart Giamatti, and Fay Vincent were most concerned about forestalling any attempt by the Senate task force to lobby for legislation that would threaten baseball's antitrust exemption. The willingness of the commissioner's office to meet with the Senate task force should not be confused with an embrace of expansion, which baseball owners have been very reluctant to undertake unless prodded with threats from Congress targeting the antitrust exemption. The ability of baseball to operate as a cartel free from antitrust law has long hinged on the 1922 Supreme Court decision that has yet to be overturned by subsequent court rulings, as the courts have chosen to defer the entire matter of the legality of the exemption to Congress, which periodically flexes its muscle to suggest that the exemption might be in danger whenever Major League Baseball runs afoul of a powerful senator or representative. Commissioner Bart Giamatti, who followed Pete Ueberroth and preceded Fay Vincent in addressing the Senate task force, emphasized the importance of the antitrust exemption to Major League Baseball by trying to convince senators that such an exemption served their own interests by protecting small-market franchises who would otherwise be much more likely to lose their teams to relocation. Giamatti insisted that it was only the antitrust exemption that stood in the way of small-market teams such as the Pirates moving to a more profitable environment, as without the exemption the commissioner's office would not be able to stop owners from behaving like their football counterparts, who can more easily move their teams.

Despite Giamatti's appeal to the "best interests" of the senators, the commissioners' office values the antitrust exemption for a host of different reasons. First, the exemption allows Major League Baseball to exercise greater limitations and control over the entire market structure of the sport, including the minor league structure, which, if subject to antitrust law, might well go the way of the dinosaur, as major league teams would likely not be able to maintain their existing relationships with minor league affiliates. Secondly, the commissioner's office can utilize the exemption from the antitrust law to control the entry and exit of franchises in a manner designed to maximize pressure on states and localities to publicly finance stadiums. Major League Baseball has used its own discretion in deciding whether or not to authorize its owners to sell or move teams, often relying on the threat of relocation to see if the price of keeping the team in its current location exceeds the price of relocating the club to a city that is offering specific amenities to attract a wayward franchise. By keeping cities, counties and states locked in a perpetual bidding war, Major League Baseball has often been able to extract more public subsidies than it could have if it had no control over the location and number of franchises. Most often, the threat of relocation is simply a tool, seldom utilized but available, that is used to extract an expenditure of greater public resources for an existing owner. By keeping franchises scarce and the threat of relocation a realistic possibility, the commissioner's office increases its leverage over the allocation of future revenues for the sport.

That analysis provides a partial, but incomplete, picture of the politics of expansion of the 1990s. The decision by baseball owners to award franchises to Denver, Miami, Phoenix and Tampa Bay was influenced by a convergence of factors, only one of which was the suggestion of concerted Senate action that could have threatened the elimination of the antitrust exemption and thereby the market privileges that baseball has taken for granted for much of its existence. The other factors included political mobilization by cities and ownership groups that had long lobbied for inclusion in baseball's exclusive club and along the way had established an important connection to baseball's power brokers, giving them an edge in the politics of expansion. The fact that Major League Baseball was in the midst of paying an extensive amount of legal damages for ownership collusion during the mid- to late 1980s to keep player salaries low was another factor that helped lead to the first round of expansion. Put simply, baseball owners were looking for an easy way to acquire a quick cash flow to help compensate teams for the costs of their earlier sins. That helps explain the high price of expansion for the Colorado Rockies and the Florida Marlins, whose owners were expected to pay $95 million just for the privilege of owning a Major League Baseball team. At the same time, the existing owners, fearing a precipitous decline in national television revenue by 1993, were unwilling to share any central revenue funds with the new expansion clubs during their first year of operation, leaving those clubs even more financially strapped and handicapped in the beginning of organizational building. Also, by making the terms for expansion so onerous and by limiting the expansion

FIVE / *The Politics and Economics of Expansion* 151

pool to two new teams scheduled to start play in 1993, major league baseball indicated its intention to carefully control the process, while maximizing its short-term revenues and leaving the left-out cities continuing to hunger for baseball at some later date, when they too would be willing to pay a prime rate just to have the privilege of being a member of this exclusive club.

Given these financial constraints, and given also the history of expansion teams. experiencing close to a decade of utter futility before fielding a playoff-ready squad, the success of the Florida Marlins in winning two World Series is worth examining in more detail, as the ups and downs of this franchise contribute added nuance to the themes raised in this book. How were the Marlins able to capture two titles in their first eleven years? At the same time, why has the franchise operated like Jekyll and Hyde, complete with the most thorough dismantling in Major League Baseball history following its first championship of 1997, only to be rescued from near oblivion to win yet another championship (under their third owner in franchise history), in 2003? How did the Marlins and the Rockies approach their expansion drafts of 2002? What were the organizational approaches that the Marlins used to win in 1997? Was it simply a case of buying the World Series for one year, or was more at work?

The debate over the Marlins' success in 1997 and (by a very different route) in 2003 touches on all the major themes raised in this book: the importance of revenues and free agency versus player development in building a winning franchise; the politics of stadium revenues, including how those revenues have been utilized by Marlins' owners and executives, as well as the ongoing push for a new stadium for the team; and the extent to which the Marlins' quick success in winning a World Series in five years, only to be eclipsed by the expansion Arizona Diamondbacks, heralds a new environment in which expansion franchises can win quickly, in contrast to the less competitive decades of the past. The common wisdom prior to the 1993 expansion, now challenged by the recent successes of the Marlins and the Diamondbacks, was that expansion teams would flounder for seven or more years and that the best path to sustained success was exemplified by the long-term developmental approach of the Toronto Blue Jays, rather than the veteran-laden approach followed by the California Angels. Have the Marlins and Diamondbacks successfully refuted these earlier case studies of how to be successful? If so, their player development and player acquisition strategies deserve close scrutiny in comparison with their earlier expansion brethren. At the same time, given the framework of this book, we will also examine the changing competitive structure of Major League Baseball and explore the extent to which the more competitive environment of recent decades has contributed to the early World Series titles of Florida and Arizona.

We begin by providing a brief history of the politics of expansion, followed by an examination of the political process that led Major League Baseball to expand by two additional teams in 1993 and by two more teams in 1998, when the Diamondbacks were joined by the Tampa Bay Devil Rays. The politics of expansion have involved national, regional and local coalitions of political and economic elites who exerted pressure on Major League Baseball through local initiatives, congressional committees, and the development of important contacts between prospective team owners and members of Major League Baseball's expansion committees, which have often been initially established as a delaying tactic to forestall congressional action limiting, amending or eliminating the antitrust exemption. Over time, Major League Baseball's expansion committees have taken on a life of their own, responding to pressure from organized coalitions of city officials, congressional representatives and senators, and prospective team owners to begin the process of awarding franchises to those cities deemed most worthy by Major League Baseball. The criteria used by Major League Baseball's expansion committees have involved maximizing the short-term value of the expansion franchises to the existing major league teams by charging an expansion fee, to be divided evenly among the MLB clubs, and, in the expansion of 1991, by denying the new entrants any revenues from national television package for their first year of existence. The next section looks more closely at the history of the politics of expansion and then examines the particular reasons for the selection of Colorado and Florida as the first two expansion teams of the 1990s.

The History of Expansion and the Birth of the Rockies and Marlins

How and why did Major League Baseball award franchises to the Colorado Rockies and the Florida Marlins in 1991, with both organizations fielding major league teams by 1993? Major League Baseball expan-

FIVE / *The Politics and Economics of Expansion* 153

sion has typically come on the heels of actions by Congress to investigate or vote on the antitrust exemption enjoyed by Major League Baseball. Congressman Emanuel Celler of New York established a congressional subcommittee on monopoly power that examined the implications of the antitrust exemption for U.S. cities and for U.S. consumers. Celler's report was released in 1952, although hearings began in 1951, and Congress would periodically subject the antitrust exemption to further scrutiny and discussion throughout the 1950s. A key player on the subcommittee was Los Angeles congressman Patrick Hillings, who led the challenge to baseball's restrictions on rewarding and relocating franchises.[1] In the same year, Major League Baseball responded with a report by National League president Ford Frick that examined the potential of the Pacific Coast for baseball expansion. The following year baseball eased its restrictions on franchise shifts by dropping its longstanding requirement for a unanimous vote in both leagues, substituting the less onerous criteria of a vote by the affected league. The decision of Major League Baseball to allow as many as four franchises to relocate during the 1950s succeeded in sidelining any serious effort by Congress to remove the antitrust exemption during the decade, despite the formation of numerous subcommittees that periodically reviewed the exemption. At the same time, Major League Baseball remained in firm control of the allocation and relocation of franchises, playing off city against city in the process of moving baseball teams further west, although baseball was not at all in control of the timing of expansion, as the commissioner's office found itself responding to political pressure in a rather haphazard way in order to fend off periodic threats to the antitrust exemption.

All the major league cities that lost a team during the 1950s had been two-team markets at least, and in the case of New York, which lost two of its three major league teams with the move of the Brooklyn Dodgers and New York Giants to Los Angeles and San Francisco, respectively, the commissioner's office eventually moved to counter any Congressional backlash by New York congressmen by placing an expansion team in New York. MLB allowed the entry of the New York Mets and the Houston Colt 45's as part of a two-team National League expansion in 1962, an expansion prompted as a compromise solution to the Continental League's threatened incursion into Major League Baseball territory. This round of expansion followed the 1961 entry of two American League clubs, the Minnesota Twins and the Los Angeles Angels. The expansion process, in part haphazard, in part dependent on political connections of the aspiring ownership groups and in part a reaction to congressional threats to revoke the antitrust exemption, would be mirrored with later expansion projects. In particular, the expansion process has on several occasions been dictated by whether or not a city abandoned by Major League Baseball could plausibly threaten legal action against Major League Baseball for having relocated a franchise to a competing metropolitan area.

Most of the time, relocation has been a threat employed by MLB to support an owner's effort to gain political leverage in ongoing stadium/lease discussions. But when such leverage could not be achieved, MLB sometimes allowed owners to move their club to a new location, especially from small markets whose prospects for revenue generation were judged by MLB to be inadequate. Thus MLB allowed Milwaukee's team to move to Atlanta in 1966 after dipping to a season-low attendance of about half a million in Milwaukee in 1965. Five years later MLB gave Milwaukee another team when the Seattle Pilots lasted only one year after they could muster only 700,000 fans during the 1969 season and subsequently filed for bankruptcy. The Pilots' move to Milwaukee brought big-league baseball back to that small market in 1970. The Pilots were able to move into the stadium that had previously been home to the Milwaukee Braves, and they were welcomed by a longtime civic association led by Bud Selig committed to bringing big-league baseball back to Milwaukee. Similarly, the ability of Kansas City to secure an expansion team in 1969 was facilitated by the existence of a baseball stadium (not to mention millionaire owner Ewing Kauffman) that had been vacated by the departing Kansas City Athletics just two years earlier. In addition, powerful politicians such as Missouri senator Stuart Symington threatened to begin initiatives in Congress to rally opposition to baseball's exemption from antitrust status unless baseball moved to place a new team in Kansas City to replace the departed Athletics. The awarding of an expansion franchise to Kansas City was also aided by the pledge of American League president Joe Cronin to find another team for the city after the league allowed owner Charlie Finley to move the franchise in 1967. This conflux of political circumstances allowed Kansas City to secure a franchise in a short two-year time frame after having lost the Athletics to Oakland. As part of the same agreement that created the Kansas City Royals, Major League Baseball awarded a franchise to the Seattle Pilots.

FIVE / The Politics and Economics of Expansion

The brief financial history of the Pilots provides a capsule illustration of the politics, pitfalls and pratfalls of the expansion process. In awarding Seattle a franchise, the league secured a working agreement with the new ownership that minor league Sicks Stadium would be renovated and upgraded to meet major league specifications until a new ballpark could be financed. The league also made the franchise conditional on voter approval in Seattle of a $40 million bond issue for building a domed stadium and on the owners of the Pilots paying the Pacific Coast League $300,000 in indemnities for encroaching on its territory. None of these conditions were entirely fulfilled, as the agreement fell apart due to infighting between the ownership group and Seattle mayor Floyd Miller about who was responsible for the delays in renovations to Sicks Stadium, and the mayor threatening to evict the team from the city-managed stadium unless the renovations were completed. Seattle voters eventually approved the bond issue, but not until the franchise had already left town amidst controversy surrounding the escalating cost projections for the stadium, which doubled from $40 to $80 million. The ownership group of William Daley, chairman of the Reading Railroad, and Pacific Coast League president Dewey Soriano, along with brothers Max and Milton, failed repeatedly to provide needed capital to this upstart franchise and eventually looked to sell the team, with Soriano declaring bankruptcy to facilitate the sale of the club to Milwaukee.[2]

Major League Baseball worked behind to scenes to find local buyers to prevent the franchise from being moved, but when no local buyers materialized, MLB eventually allowed the Pilots' owners to sell to a group of Milwaukee investors. The relocation of the club to Milwaukee produced local injunctions and lawsuits filed by Seattle and the state of Washington totaling $32.5 million against Major League Baseball, although court decisions would ultimately uphold the sale of the team. Of greater long-term concern to Major League Baseball, Washington's U.S. senators, Warren Magnusson and Henry Jackson, called for a congressional investigation of baseball's antitrust exemption, but were appeased by baseball's pledge to put a franchise back in Seattle during the 1970s. The creation of the Seattle Mariners rested on the time-tested tradition of lawsuits against Major League Baseball and congressional maneuvers to investigate baseball's antitrust exemption, the same set of circumstances that spawned other expansion clubs. The Toronto Blue Jays were born as an expansion team the same year as the Seattle Mariners, with an ownership group in place that had attempted to purchase the San Francisco Giants for $13.5 million, only to be put on hold by a court injunction obtained by San Francisco mayor George Moscone that delayed the sale long enough for Bob Lurie to buy the Giants and keep them in San Francisco. With pressure from the state of Washington to put another team in Seattle, Major League Baseball decided in 1977 to simultaneously expand to Toronto, a move facilitated by the city's 1971 expansion of the Canadian National Exhibition Stadium for baseball use, and by the allure of the large and untapped Toronto market.[3]

The expansion fever cooled in the 1980s, but during that decade both Denver and Miami would be laying the groundwork for their successful applications for major league franchises in 1991, with the Colorado Rockies and the Florida Marlins to begin major league games in 1993. As early as 1984, the mayor of Denver, Federico Pena, created the Denver Baseball Commission, a "blue-ribbon panel with a paid staff, a permanent office, and a $75,000 seed grant from AT&T."[4] The commission held its first event in the spring of 1984 with the Denver Baseball Symposium, "which brought the two league presidents and a dozen other baseball executives to Denver for a tour of the city and a lavish banquet."[5] The purpose of the Denver Baseball Committee (DBC) was to serve as a lobbying arm to convince Major League Baseball of the wisdom of placing an expansion team in Denver.

The DBC sent a delegation to baseball's winter meetings in 1984, along with other expansion hopefuls who had been promised a confidential meeting (no leaks to the press allowed) with baseball commissioner Peter Ueberroth, who then proceeded to address hopefuls from Denver, Washington, D.C., St. Petersburg, Buffalo, and Indianapolis about the topic of expansion. Ueberroth, while insisting that the meeting remain secret, gave no promises to any of the hopefuls that expansion would occur any time soon. Instead, the aim of the MLB leadership seemed to be to keep the expansion ball afloat solely to help existing franchises use the threat of relocation to secure publicly financed stadiums or better lease terms at their current homes. Ueberroth made clear to those expansion aspirants that MLB would call the shots, that expansion would occur under terms established by MLB, and that cities would only hurt themselves by being too aggressive in pursuing a franchise beyond the timetable that would be established by the league itself. Undeterred, the DBC showcased Denver's potential as a major league baseball city by utilizing a renovated Mile High Stadium to host two exhibition games between the Cubs and the Mariners in the spring of 1985. Despite the positive reaction of George Argyros, owner of the Mariners, who along with the Cubs' ownership benefited by pocketing $130,000 from the 76,000 fans that attended the two exhibition games, MLB would not contact Denver about the topic of expansion until October of 1985, when the DBC received a letter from deputy commissioner Ed Durso that outlined the very stringent criteria that MLB had established for the awarding of an expansion franchise. The commissioner's office insisted that any expansion club must have a local owner in place with a net worth of $100 million or more, who was willing to commit his entire net worth to baseball; a baseball-only stadium with natural grass, luxury boxes, a state-of-the art video scoreboard; a "compliant local government, one that understands it must minimize or eliminate political pressures ... and tax disincentives," and a "minimum 10,000 season tickets for the first five years, guaranteed."[6]

Under the direction of commissioner Peter Ueberroth, baseball created an expansion committee in 1985 that offered invitations to 13 city delegations, including one from Denver, to discuss the criteria and expectations established by major league baseball for the next round of expansion. As Ueberroth led the first set of meetings on November 7 and 8 of 1985, it became apparent to all the expansion hopefuls that Major League Baseball was not seriously entertaining expansion any time soon. The meetings were a combination of delaying tactics and hard-sell warnings by the commissioner that Major League Baseball, not the expansion hopefuls, would dictate the terms of expansion, and that those terms would be extremely difficult and costly to meet. The ground rules for the first November meetings epitomized Ueberroth's approach, as the rules for attendees "were strict, arbitrary and ... kept changing."[7] The Denver Baseball Commission had prepared a video for the meeting, only to be told at the last minute that the video would not be allowed. Ueberroth also informed the expansion hopefuls that they would not be welcomed at baseball's winter meetings, and that if they had anything to say, "they should say it right now."[8] After Ueberroth resigned from the commissioner's office in 1989 amidst the scandal surrounding the owners' collusion and was replaced by Bart Giamatti, nothing had been accomplished by the expansion committee. The committee had only served to inflict frustration on those expansion-hopeful cities that had endured repeated cancellation of previously scheduled meetings, lack of clarity on whether and when expansion would occur, and a general dissatisfaction with Major League Baseball regarding the entire process.

For the Denver Baseball Commission, the best leverage appeared to be congressional assistance, especially the leadership of Senator Tim Wirth, who began a Senate task force in 1987 with the goal of expediting the expansion process by putting some political pressure on Major League Baseball. The official name of the task force was the Senate Task Force on the Expansion of Major League Baseball, with its proclaimed goal to have six new major league teams by the year 2000. The commissioner's office, first under Ueberroth, then under Giamatti, and then, after Giamatti's death in 1989, under Fay Vincent, initially treated the task force with the same delaying tactics and lack of commitment that had long frustrated the expansion-hopeful city delegations. On November 6, 1987, Ueberroth skipped the first meeting of the Senate task force, sending his assistant instead. When Ueberroth did arrive, he told the senators in no uncertain terms that Major League Baseball, not some group of Senators, would determine the pace and scope of expansion, then refused to attend another meeting until June 22 of 1988.

Ultimately, the most important factor to get the attention of the commissioner was the involvement of a larger body of powerful senators in the baseball task force, especially those senators who could lead a threat to baseball's antitrust exemption. These included Howard Metzenbaum of Ohio, who was hoping to help Columbus land a major league team and also happened to be chairman of the Antitrust, Monopoly and Business Rights Subcommittee of the Senate Judiciary Committee; and Dennis DeConcini of Arizona, the ranking Democrat behind Metzenbaum on that committee.[9] This array of a growing list of potentially powerful Senators to the baseball task force suggested that Congress was getting prepared to undertake a more detailed examination of baseball's antitrust exemption, a position articulated by Republican Senator John Warner of Virginia, who warned baseball that "it better get its act together, because if Congress gets into the batter's box, we'll hit the ball and we have no idea where it will go."[10] With that added pressure, Ueberroth quickly agreed to attend another session with the Senate task force, and this time the tone was much more cordial, although once again noncommital. It would take a letter from Senator Tim Werth to Commissioner Fay Vincent on March 1, 1990, to finally push baseball into establishing a firm timetable and schedule regarding expansion. The letter was a strong appeal by

Werth and fellow senators for the establishment of a professional baseball team in Denver and had been signed by senators from the entire Western Plains and Rocky Mountains region, which amounted to 19 senators overall, about 20 percent of the Senate, and "all of them united behind Denver" as one of the next expansion franchises.[11] That letter provided more than enough clarity for baseball owners, who understood that the pressure for expansion was building enough political momentum to potentially threaten baseball's antitrust exemption unless the commissioner's office acted quickly.

Under the brief tenure of Commissioner Bart Giamatti, and later followed by Fay Vincent, baseball owners developed a strategy for pursuing expansion that would serve to limit the number of teams to two, thereby continuing to limit the number of baseball teams in a fashion designed to maximize the advantages of baseball's cartel structure. By refusing to allow six new clubs to enter the majors at one time, baseball would preserve the threat of relocation of existing teams to those markets that failed to win a franchise in 1991. Secondly, baseball owners insisted that the new expansion clubs pay a hefty fee of $95 million, which would provide a short-term band-aid to help pay for the collusion damages that baseball owners owed the players for colluding to artificially depress free agent salaries in the mid- to late 1980s. Baseball owners also moved to ensure that the new expansion teams would not take any of the national television revenue distributed among major league franchises in their first seasons of operation, 1993, with the owners anticipating (correctly) that there would be a significant drop in the terms of the next national television contract. As usual, the politics of expansion precluded any serious long-term planning by Major League Baseball on the purposes, effects and costs/benefits of expansion to the game itself. Instead, the commissioner's office acted only when threatened with the removal of the antitrust exemption, and then only on terms that maximized the short-term benefits of expansion for the existing major league owners. Still, the fact that there were so many cities, politicians and wealthy investors ready to compete on the terms established by major league baseball showed very clearly why the antitrust exemption worked to perpetuate an artificial scarcity of franchises that the lords of major league baseball could use to their advantage during the expansion process.

Under the leadership of baseball commissioner Fay Vincent, the owners strategized that the choice of two cities, rather than the six being pushed for by the Senate task force, would allow them to divide and conquer the disparate personalities on the task force pushing for expansion. By selecting two of the expansion hopefuls, some senators would be appeased while others would be frustrated, but that would make it more difficult for the Senators to coalesce around an immediate challenge to the antitrust exemption. Since the task force was not pushing for a team in Washington, D.C., baseball owners knew that they could take advantage of the divisions that existed on the task force, with some senators pushing for a team in Florida, some wanting a team in Denver, some in New York, some in California, some in Tennessee and some in Ohio. As one baseball executive put it: "I never was really worried about the Senate task force when it was obvious they weren't pushing for a team in Washington. There were just inherent conflicts among all of them as to where these teams would go."[12]

In addition to the political concerns of the baseball establishment about limiting the expansion teams, Commissioner Giamatti noted another reason for limiting expansion: to guard carefully against any dilution of talent in the major leagues. In fact, it has been a truism among baseball insiders, sportswriters and fans that expansion is especially pernicious in its dilution of pitching talent, resulting in an increase in offense that is the product of the subpar pitchers who are needed to fill expansion rosters. This point has been refuted by statistical analysis of the effects of expansion, as documented by the work of Greg Spira of *Baseball Prospectus*. According to Spira, in the expansion years 1961 and 1962, there was no jump in offensive levels; in the 1969 expansion, there was a dramatic increase in offense, but this can best be accounted for by the lowering of the mound and the shrinking of the strike zone. In the American League expansion of 1977, there was a significant increase in offense levels, but the National League, which did not have expansion, experienced an increase almost as large; in the National League expansion of 1993 the offensive jump was due mostly to the addition of thin air in Denver. And the offense of 1998 did not increase notably over the offensive levels achieved in 1997.[13] At the same time, the pool of available major leaguers has substantially increased over the decades, first with the breaking down of the barrier of segregation, and most recently with the rapid globalization of the game and the increased recruitment in the Dominican Republic, Venezuela, Japan, and South Korea. Taken together, these arguments weaken the position of the commissioner's office that expansion weakens the game, although there is some truth to the notion that expansion promotes greater extremes in performance, accentuated by the number of players playing highly above or highly below the mean. At the same time, as Giamatti himself noted to the expansion task force, the process of development in baseball is slower than in other sports and requires attention to minor league development, which expansion might well try to circumvent because of the need for more players at the big-league level. Still, it is hard to deny that the pool of potential major league players, due to integration and globalization, is greater than at any time in the game's history.

Given that baseball was adamant about limiting expansion to two teams, instead of six, that would begin play in 1993, what explains the awarding of franchises to Denver and South Florida? In the case of Denver, political leadership played a crucial role in getting the city on the map of expansion hopefuls, including the leading role of Mayor Federico Pena in creating the Denver Baseball Commission and U.S. Senator Tim Wirth in pushing Major League Baseball toward expansion. Ultimately, the Rockies would not have been formed without political leadership in Denver helping to bring together an investment coalition that went through several transformations before being able to satisfy the payments and capital guarantees sought by Major League Baseball. The importance of political leadership is especially noteworthy in explaining the extremely favorable lease terms secured by the Rockies at their publicly financed Coors Stadium, where they played after their first seasons at Mile High Stadium. The state legislature of Colorado authorized the creation of the Denver Metropolitan Stadium District as early as 1989 to oversee financing of a new park for the Rockies and at the same time approved legislation authorizing a referendum that would ask voters to approve a sales tax to help finance the construction of the new facility. Ironically, the sales tax was approved in the six-county area surrounding Denver, but not in Denver itself!

The Denver Metropolitan Stadium District then succumbed to political pressure from the mayor's office and from the newly formed ownership group to go well beyond the intent of their legislative mandate in offering a lease agreement that was highly favorable to the team. The district agreed to pay the entire cost of construction of the stadium, not 50 percent, which was the goal of the legislation that created the stadium district. At the same time, the district allowed the team to capture all of the stadium revenues, including concessions, parking, novelties, luxury boxes, and free rent until the year 2000, when the district would get 2.5 percent of the owners' net taxable income.[14] This easily represented the best lease agreement in professional baseball and was a leading reason for Denver ultimately being awarded a major league team. That the district authority had circumvented the intent of the legislation authorizing its creation by denying taxpayers any public monies generated by the new stadium only made Denver more attractive to Major League Baseball.

While Denver got their expansion club with a good deal of political lobbying, legislation, and taxpayer support, the choice of South Florida as the second expansion club was almost solely the result of the deep pockets of Wayne Huizenga and his political connection to the baseball establishment via his president of baseball operations, Carl Barger, who had been a longtime executive in the game, most recently the president of the Pittsburgh Pirates. The fact that Huizenga had purchased controlling interest in Joe Robbie Stadium, and that the stadium was constructed as a multipurpose facility with the idea of attracting a professional baseball club, also proved important in landing a big-league team. Huizenga surpassed all the Major League Baseball requirements for owning a club: he made clear his ability and intentions to pay all the upfront costs, including the $95 million expansion fee, by selling stock and not by borrowing; the renovations to make Joe Robbie stadium baseball-ready were accomplished courtesy of a sales tax break passed by the state legislature; and the insider connection to baseball's expansion committee was there in the presence of Carl Barger. At the time, Huizenga purchased 50 percent of Joe Robbie Stadium and signed a working agreement with the Robbie estate to "use their best efforts to support the decision of major league baseball to award a franchise to South Florida."[15] The South Florida market also proved to generate lucrative media revenues (consistently in the top third of Major League Baseball under Huizenga, but devalued in the latter sale of the team to John Henry, who was convinced by Huizenga to accept a 10-year agreement with Huizenga-owned Sports Channel, which locked the Marlins into a rate that was well below what the team should have been earning).

Huizenga was shrewd enough to be very conservative when estimating revenues and expenditures before the owners' expansion committee, as the Marlins have had to grapple with lease terms that were not favorable compared to other major league teams due to the debt still owed to stadium lenders. The overall value of the deal for Huizenga hinged on several factors: 1) the likely appreciation of the asset, which would easily offset the high entrance fee demanded by major league baseball; 2) Huizenga made the Marlins part of Huizenga Holdings, thereby allowing the owner to shuffle profits and losses in a way that maximized tax writeoffs; 3) Huizenga was able to use the Marlins to enrich the value of Sports Channel, on which most of the Marlins' games would air and which he would purchase and later sell at an appreciated price. As it turns out, Huizenga also bet on higher attendance for Marlins games than actually materialized and was part of a group of hard-line owners that lost the battle with the players' union during the strike of 1994 and the lockout of early 1995. He also lost his bid to secure public financing for a new Marlins stadium, so he chose to sell the team after his IRS tax writeoffs of the value of player salaries expired after the first five years of ownership. Nonetheless, Huizenga always saw the Marlins as an investment to make money, with no notion of any concept of public trust in owning a baseball team that is supported by the larger South Florida community. He made decisions with an eye to the bottom line and got out of the sport when he was not doing as well as he had projected.

Wayne Huizenga, owner of the Florida Marlins 1993–1998. After dramatically expanding payroll to help win a World Series in 1997, Huizenga slashed it the next year. He also demanded significant player concessions in contract negotiations. When he failed to get his way during the collective bargaining agreement of 1996, he sought public support for a new baseball-only facility in South Florida. After failing to secure a second tax rebate for the Marlins toward renovating Pro Player Stadium, Huizenga decided to sell the club. His stadium lease agreement with the next owner, John Henry, gave the Marlins the worst lease terms in Major League Baseball — an agreement that plagues the third owner, Jeffrey Loria, to this day.

To summarize, Huizenga managed to convince Major League

Baseball owners to award him a franchise in South Florida through a combination of showcasing his immense wealth, his connections to the baseball ownership/executive fraternity through team president Carl Barger, and the failure of Tampa Bay/St. Petersburg, which had been the favorite to land a franchise, to maintain a financial commitment from key owners during the selection process. Tampa Bay politicos had been pushing for an expansion team for over a decade, going so far as to secure a taxpayer-financed domed stadium valued at over $234 million, and securing a tentative working arrangement with principal investors the Kohl brothers, Sydney, Allen and Herbert, who had pledged a $50 million cash commitment to help put a baseball team in Tampa Bay. Herbert Kohl also owned the Milwaukee Bucks, and the baseball expansion committee was impressed by word of his initial commitment. At the same time, Tampa Bay had been crudely used in the past by franchises such as the Oakland A's and the Chicago White Sox, who both had threatened to move their franchises to Tampa Bay, only to renege at the last minute in favor of staying in their existing locations. The A's used the threat of relocation to Tampa Bay to negotiate more favorable lease terms with Oakland mayor Lionel Wilson in 1984, ultimately reneging on an oral arrangement to sell the A's to Tampa Bay businessman Frank Morsani. The White Sox used the threat of relocation to Tampa Bay to secure favorable terms on a 30-year lease extended by the Illinois legislature in 1988, as well as funds committed by the legislature toward the construction of a new stadium for the White Sox . The fact that Tampa Bay both had a baseball stadium that had been completed and had been targets of relocation threats from other markets increased its profile on baseball's expansion radar screen. However, the deal breaker was the withdrawal of the Kohls' financial backing, which left the Tampa Bay coalition without a solid ownership group that could suitably impress the owners' expansion committee. Tampa Bay businessman Frank Morsani battled Major League Baseball for over one decade (with an out-of-court settlement reached in 2003) over the failure of Major League Baseball to place a team in the Tampa market. Morsani's legal action threatened to raise the issue of baseball's exemption from the antitrust laws, with Morsani claiming that MLB had violated trade laws and interfered with private commerce in a manner inconsistent with federal law. With legal action pending, Major League Baseball did award a franchise to Tampa in 1994, although not to Morsani, who continued to press his lawsuit. The commissioner's office deemed Morsani's suit serious enough to negotiate an out-of-court settlement of undisclosed terms in 2003.[16]

The awarding of franchises to Denver and South Florida was consistent with past expansion trends. Major League Baseball's choise of these locations was due not to careful long-term planning and thoughtful reflection, but instead to the immediate political threats that the league faced from the U.S. Senate if expansion did not occur within a certain time frame. The fact that a powerful Colorado senator, Tim Wirth, was involved in the Senate efforts to press the league on expansion worked in Colorado's favor, as well as political lobbying in the Colorado legislature that secured authorization for a county referendum that would ultimately approve a sales tax for a new stadium. The successful lobbying efforts of the long-organized Denver Baseball Commission, as well as support from Denver's mayor, helped exert enough political pressure on the Denver Stadium Authority to secure a dream lease for the prospective team, one in which taxpayers would get virtually nothing while the team would secure 100 percent of all notable revenue streams. In the case of the Marlins, Wayne Huizenga impressed the owners' expansion committee with his oral presentation and his wallet, winning out over other cities such as Tampa Bay due to the difference in financial commitment to the franchise. The size of the South Florida market, ranking in the top half of MLB franchises, also proved a strong selling point.

With the expansion process as political background, what about the baseball decisions made by Florida and Colorado? In particular, why and how have the Marlins managed to capture two World Series titles in their 11-year existence while the Rockies have made one lone playoff appearance? Does the Marlins' success tell us something about the economics of the game in the 1990s and at the turn of the millennium? Or are the failings of the South Florida franchise more revealing in that Florida became the first World Series team since the 1915 Philadelphia Athletics to get rid of all of their star players? Indeed, the dismantling of the Florida Marlins even dwarfs the dismemberment of Connie Mack's A's and has led some observers to equate the Marlins' disparate ups and downs with the poor state of baseball economics in the present day. The next sections examine the Marlins' success and failures and locats these in the context of organizational decision making as well as the economics of the sport.

The Marlins' Organizational Cohesion

Both the Marlins and Rockies entered Major League Baseball almost two years before the teams played their first major league games in 1993. The MLB expansion committee awarded the expansion franchises to Denver and South Florida on July 5, after the owners had signed off on the committees recommendations for the two expansion teams. The expansion committee had actually announced its selections of Denver and Miami as early as June 10, but the owners delayed approving the new clubs for about one month. The reason for the delay: a squabble between the National and American Leagues over whether or not the lofty expansion fees would be shared by the two leagues, or would go exclusively to the league acquiring the two new teams, as had been past practice. The American League owners argued that they deserved a cut of the expansion fees, given the unprecedented practice of allowing the Marlins and the Rockies to make selections from the rosters of both National and American League clubs. In the past, the expansion teams drafted from the rosters of the league that they were joining. In 1992, the year of the Rockies' and Marlins' expansion draft, the new clubs would be allowed to draft in three rounds, with one selection from all 26 teams in the both the first and second rounds, and with 20 selections (12 from the NL and 8 from the AL) in the third and final round. In the first round, all 26 non-expansion clubs would be able to protect 15 players from the draft throughout their entire organization, with most single-A players not eligible. In the second round, the NL teams would be allowed to protect three more players and the AL teams four additional players. In the third round, the draft would last for only 20 selections and would include all 12 NL teams but only 8 AL clubs. Given this dynamic, the American League teams wanted the expansion fees to be split, while the NL clubs wanted all of the expansion fees for their teams. The compromise solution, forged by commissioner Fay Vincent and reluctantly agreed to by the warring parties, involved giving $12.4 million to each NL team and $3 million to each AL team.

Once these details were worked out, the ground was established for the Marlins and Rockies to begin their organizational building blocks, starting with front office hires and extending to managers, coaches, player development positions, and scouts. In comparison with earlier expansion clubs, what were the advantages and disadvantages faced by these fledg-

FIVE / The Politics and Economics of Expansion

ling organizations in putting together a winning baseball team? First, the disadvantages involved a hefty expansion fee of $95 million, which forced each team to commit huge capital outlays at the outset of the expansion approval process, potentially reducing the expenditures on major league–ready players. Secondly, neither of the expansion teams would be allowed a cut of the national television revenues for 1993, their first year of play, and after that year, as documented elsewhere in this book, the national television pie would actually decrease during the mid–1990s over what had been a relatively lucrative central fund from the 1980s through the early 1990s. Therefore, these expansion teams were entering major league baseball at the very time that the distribution of shared revenue was tapering off, due in part to the long-term effects of the 1994 strike and 1995 lockout.

Despite these financial limitations, the new ownership groups were able to compensate quite effectively due to a different set of circumstances. For Denver, the ownership group was the beneficiary of the best lease arrangement in baseball, courtesy of the Denver Metropolitan Stadium District. The guarantee of pocketing 100 percent of the revenues from all the revenue streams generated by the new facility meant that the Rockies would be able to spend money quickly and be active players on the free agent market in just a few short years after their creation. The Rockies also compensated for being in a smaller media market than South Florida by selling more tickets, as the club consistently enjoyed sellout crowds during much of the 1990s, buttressed by a large season ticket base. The Marlins' lease arrangement was not as favorable, but owner Wayne Huizenga was by all accounts one of the richest owners in sports, who managed to consolidate his ownership of the Marlins with his larger entity, Huizenga Holdings, which maximized the writeoff potential for the expenses incurred by the baseball side of the operation. When Huizenga claimed to be losing $30 million on the team during the 1997 World Series run, he conveniently ignored the revenue generated by the stadium, which he also owned, even if some of the stadium money was going to pay off debts that had been incurred by the Robbie estate to finance the building of the facility. At the same time, Huizenga benefited from owning a team in one of the larger media markets in the nation, although his dual ownership of Sports Channel ultimately served to lower the true value of the team's television rights, as Huizenga did what numerous owners have done: sell the Marlins' television rights to Sports

Channel at a bargain price, thereby using the team to inflate the value of Sports Channel. In addition, Huizenga owned a team in a state that had no state income tax, meaning that his overall tax burden was lowered, and meaning that big-league players found South Florida quite attractive as a tax haven and year-round living environment.

Both franchises were able to compensate for a high expansion fee and for the absence of shared national television revenue in their first year, as well as a less lucrative shared national television pie during subsequent seasons. On the baseball side, no teams in the history of major league expansion would be able to choose from such an extensive array of big-league players from both leagues. In addition, no previous expansion teams were given as much time to prepare for the expansion draft as were the Marlins and the Rockies. The difference between baseball in the free agent and pre-free agent eras also helps account for additional advantages for these clubs over their pre-free agent expansion brethren. In the free agent era, a wealthy owner of an expansion team would have more options to field a winner, as players could not be locked up in perpetuity by the dominant major league clubs, but were able to jockey their services to the highest bidders. The increased movement of star players from team to team by the mid–1990s gave both Colorado and Florida a chance to add marquee talent to the prospects that they were collecting. Although player movement in the pre–free agent era differed little from the free agent period, by 1995 there was an important difference: more star players were changing teams. At the same time, by the 1990s the amateur draft had become an expensive item for franchises struggling to meet their bottom line payroll demands. Teams with wealthy owners, such as the Marlins' Wayne Huizenga, or favorable leases, such as the Colorado Rockies, enjoyed an advantage in being able to sign their amateur draft picks.

All these structural advantages enjoyed by the Marlins and Rockies over their expansion predecessors fails to explain why the Marlins were able to set an expansion record by winning a World Series in only their fifth year of existence as a major league team. The place to start is the careful organizational planning that the Marlins started no less than three days after being officially awarded a franchise. In contrast to the Rockies, who focused more of their early efforts at organization building on the business side of the ledger, the Marlins were quick to have their key front office positions filled shortly after the expansion draft. First, Wayne

Huizenga offered Carl Barger the job of executive president of baseball operations on July 8, 1991, just three days after the franchise winners had been announced. Barger came to the position with considerable experience as president of the Pittsburgh Pirates, and in fact he did not officially resign his Pirates position until August 2, 1991. Having helped to build the successful Pirates club of the early 1990s, Barger had the experience and connections necessary to design a stable and coherent front office, coherent because its leading parts all came from the Montreal Expos, led by general manager Dave Dombrowski.

By November, 1991, with opening day a year and a half away, Dombrowski had already filled the key slots in the Marlins' front office by taking 14 former Expos, composing almost a third of the Marlins' baseball staff. These included scouting director Gary Hughes, farm director John Boles, assistant general manager Frank Wren, senior adviser Whitey Lockman, director of Latin American operations Angel Vasquez, and associate scouting director of international operations Orrin Freeman. By contrast, Colorado Rockies GM Bob Gebhard was only just beginning to focus his full-time effort on the Rockies, as he had elected to finish the 1991 season as assistant GM to Andy MacPhail in Minnesota. Gebhard had less money to work with than Dombrowski, had less discretion in spending his money, and lagged behind his counterpart in putting together the Rockies' front office. By November, 1991, Gebhard's most significant hire was scouting director Pat Daugherty, who was the organization's second choice behind Frank Wren, and who had very limited administrative experience, having earned his reputation as a field scout.

Henry Fetter, in his recent book, *Taking on the Yankees*, argues that organizational coherence, continuity and skill are the most important ingredients in explaining the relative success and failure of franchises.[17] In particular, Fetter emphasizes the importance of a clearly demarcated separation between the business side of a ball club: owner and president, and the baseball side, general manager, director of player development, scouts, etc., in predicting whether or not a club will succeed. The willingness of owners and presidents of franchises to grant wide discretionary authority to the general manager, who is then responsible for baseball decisions without persistent meddling by the business side of the club, is therefore an important predictor of future success, according to Fetter. By this measure, the Marlins, and later the Diamondbacks, had a strong, coherent and stable organization through their first five years of existence, with Dombrowski and his front office given wide discretionary authority over the baseball side of the operation, with no interference by Huizenga and the team presidents to override baseball decisions. Huizenga established the spending parameters, but did not interfere with the choices made by Dombrowski to allocate franchise resources.

In contrast, the cumbersome organizational structure of the Rockies was a noticeable contrast, with the franchise jointly operated by three managing partners: John Antonnuci, whose title was chairman and chief executive officer; Steve Ehrhart, president and chief operating officer; and Mickey Monus. In addition, the lawyer Paul Jacobs was up near the top of the Rockies' organizational chart as executive vice president and general counsel. This cumbersome organizational flow chart often made decision making more difficult for Gebhard, who had to work through a disparate set of officials to get confirmation on key decisions. Whereas Dombrowski had a pipeline directly to one man, Wayne Huizenga, Gebhard had to navigate a more complex bureaucracy to get approval for deals that involved the expenditure of baseball revenue. To make matters more difficult, Gebhard had less discretion than Dombrowski and a smaller initial budget.

Despite this, the Rockies did succeed in making the playoffs in their second year of existence, but their overall trajectory was not one of steady improvement, as was the case with the Marlins, but instead reflected considerable ups and downs, parallel with changes in the ownership structure and the front office. By January 1993, the Rockies restructured their front office. Jerry McMorris became chairman, president and CEO; Oren Benton and Charles Monfort became vice chairmen. Florida never experienced these sorts of structural changes during their first five years, allowing Dombrowski to work with the same owner the entire time and with many of the same front office personnel. As a result, the Marlins were able to implement a steady and consistent plan that built methodically on an analysis of the successes and failures of the previous season. The Rockies never developed such a coherent plan and had the added difficulty of working to build a team in the difficult environment of Coors Field, where the light air has wreaked havoc with pitching staffs and made long-term planning more problematic for this franchise. As of this date, the team is still working on another in a series of statistical formulas to help determine how to build a winning club in the unique environs of Coors Field, the publicly financed stadium that the team has called home since

1995. Contrast this with the Marlins' pitching-friendly environment of Pro Player Stadium, which has been much more conducive to developing young arms and for allowing the Marlins to build a team around pitching and defense. Statistical studies undertaken by *Baseball Prospectus* suggest that the best place to build a new franchise is in a pitching-friendly home park, which helps to compensate for the inevitably weak pitching that new franchises must endure at the start of their existence.

The Marlins' continuity of front office personnel should not be confused with the implementation of a steady plan that fell in lockstep from the day of the expansion draft until the World Series championship of 1997. Instead, the Marlins' organizational continuity proved to be most important in allowing the team to consistently access the organization's strengths and weaknesses which allowed for steady improvement from 1993, their first year of existence, to 1997, their championship season, and to change plans according to each periodic reassessment. Dombrowski began the building process with an expansion draft philosophy of taking the best player available, while also conceding to the realities of having to put a big-league team on the field that would be remotely competitive in the first couple of seasons. Most of the expansion draft picks of both the Marlins and the Rockies did not have long big-league careers. Instead, the value of a pick was often measured in how that pick could be used in a trade to acquire a star player who would provide an anchor for the big-league club for years to come. Dombrowski recognized at the outset of the Marlins' existence that if the club could establish a core of star-caliber players over the first few years, through a combination of player development, trades and free agent acquisitions, then it would be much easier to replace those players who were well below average at their positions in building a winning team. On the other hand, if the Marlins had chosen to try to compete sooner by adding a wide range of serviceable, but mediocre big-league talent, then they would likely have been mired in a perpetual cycle of losing, never having the opportunity to improve.

One past mistake of expansion clubs, which Dombrowski had studied closely, could be labeled the California Angels model of the 1960s, a club that succeeded in achieving mediocrity quicker than any other expansion club, but could never improve on that mediocrity. This is because teams with average talent across the board are not skilled enough to win a championship and are also hard pressed to trade for missing pieces that might make them better over the long run. Dombrowski was able to steadily improve the club by acquiring a core of star talent through a triad of prospect development, trades and free agent acquisitions prior to the 1996 season, when the club continued its steady climb to respectability, finishing the season with an 80–82 record. By 1996, Dombrowski and his staff had already identified the key ingredients necessary to make the team able to compete for a championship and correctly estimated the amount of payroll additions that would be necessary to make the Marlins playoff competitive in 1997.

The first key piece to the Marlins' puzzle was acquired early in their history, from a trade with San Diego that netted superstar outfielder Gary Sheffield for three Marlins prospects, including their second expansion draft pick, Jesus Martinez, and their fourth expansion pick, Trevor Hoffman. The deal epitomized Dombrowski's early philosophy of acquiring high-ceiling young talent capable of anchoring the club when it became more competitive and his willingness to utilize the best prospect acquired in the expansion draft to trade for such talent. The Marlins also attempted to bolster their pitching through the acquisition of 20-year-old Kurt Miller and 23-year-old Robb Nen from the Rangers for pitching prospect Chris Carpenter. As is typical with the acquisition of young pitchers, so much is hit and miss, and few pitching prospects ever pan out. While Miller never reached his potential, Nen became a key ingredient and a star closer of the 1997 championship club.

It was in the pitching department that Dombrowski relied heavily on the free agent market, signing left-hander Al Leiter and right-hander Kevin Brown after the 1995 season. At that point, Dombrowski and his staff had concluded that the club was farther along in its hitting than its pitching. The Marlins turned out to be right about the high-ceiling potential of both Leiter and Brown. But most importantly, given that the Marlins were still on a limited budget, they signed these pitchers before they had demonstrated their ace potential. The Marlins' scouting department deserves credit in correctly identifying that Brown and Leiter were undervalued in the free agent market. At the same time, the club made an effort to improve the other serious weakness of the team: defense and overall productivity in center field. To replace the under-performing Chuck Carr, the Marlins signed free agent Devon White prior to the 1996 season. These player moves were an attempt to identify and improve upon the weaknesses that had prevented the team from approaching a .500 record through their first three years of existence. As of 1996, Dombrowski was guided by an organizational philosophy that sought incremental improvement, especially since the club had finished the 1995 campaign with a 67–76 record, although the team scored and allowed an equal number of runs, suggesting that they were closer to a .500 club as early as 1995.

The Lessons of the Marlins' 1997 World Series Championship

The confluence of circumstances that led the Marlins to dramatically increase their payroll prior to the championship season in 1997 deserves some discussion. Many accounts of the 1997 championship concluded erroneously that the Marlins had "bought the World Series" with the acquisition of several high-priced free agents. Indeed, the club did go on an unprecedented spending spree, offering a combined $89 million spread over the next several years to sign Bobby Bonilla, Moises Alou, Alex Fernandez, Dennis Cook, Jim Eisenreich and John Cangelosi, all of whom would prove to be key component parts to the team's success in winning the World Series. Owner Wayne Huizenga authorized such a payroll increase after posing the question to Dombrowski and team president Don Smiley regarding how much the club would need to spend to compete for a championship. What is often missed in the analysis of the Marlins is how prescient Dombrowski's numbers turned out to be. The general manager had concluded, based on the near-.500 record of 1996, that the team could potentially win a championship if some additional parts were added, and the payroll increased from $32 million to $47 million. As it turns out, the club actually spent more than $47 million, making additional acquisitions prior to and during the season that elevated their payroll past the $53 million mark.[18]

Still, Dombrowski's calculations that the team was capable of winning it all if the right free agent acquisitions were made illustrates the importance of careful organizational planning and steady team improvement prior to the 1997 season that laid the groundwork for the championship. Without the move toward .500 in 1996, and the winning record during the second half of the 1996 season, when the team played at a 41–35 clip after the firing of manager Rene Lachemann and the hiring of manager John Boles, the organization's free agent spending spree would not have allowed the team to compete for a championship. In baseball, even star players are unable to add more than six to eight wins to a team's performance beyond what would have been possible had their positions been filled by below-average talent. The additions of Bonilla, Alou, and Fernandez, all keys to the team's success in 1997, would not have made the Marlins a contender without an already established mix of star players that had been developed in the minor league system or had been acquired in trades. The key to sound organizational leadership is in knowing when an addition of payroll can help your club reach the next level of performance. The Marlins' organization, benefiting from strong continuity in scouting, player development personnel, and ownership, and benefiting from a careful division of labor in which the owner and the business side of the front office did not interfere in baseball decisions, were able to make the choices necessary to give their club a chance to win in 1997. The fact that they did win clearly proves their combination of astute baseball knowledge and some degree of luck, as the baseball playoff structure allows a club that did not play the best during the season to win the prize in October.

The Marlins' success in 1997 reinforces our analysis presented in chapter two, which concluded that a winning formula in baseball is contingent on a mixture of strong player development skills, acquisition of key players in trades, and expeditious use of the free agent market. Certainly, there is some overlap between all of these ingredients and a large payroll, but the slow nature of the player development process in baseball, and the inherent difficulties in gauging pitching talent — which is woefully unpredictable, leading some observers to suggest that there is no such thing as a pitching prospect — help to level the playing field in ways that a cursory examination of payrolls cannot appreciate. In short, it is not possible to simply buy a pennant. Money is one factor of several, and that fact helps temper the monetary advantages of teams such as the Yankees with an awareness that high spending does not automatically guarantee success. What is true historically is that there is a statistically significant correlation between higher payrolls and winning percentage throughout baseball history. Equally true is that this correlation has mattered less overall in the era of free agency, especially the golden age of competitiveness during the 1980s and the first half of the 1990s. Once again, after the latest collective bargaining agreement, there appears to have been a return to the very recent golden age of competi-

FIVE / *The Politics and Economics of Expansion* 175

tiveness that we've documented here, a point that we'll return to in the postscript. The Marlins' success is illustrative of the overall pattern of winning franchises in baseball history: the triad of player development, successful trades and free agent acquisitions were all in place, a necessary mix for clubs that are contending for titles in the sport.

The Marlins' formula for completing the triad can easily be glimpsed through the following lists, which document the three-pronged route to the championship season of 1997:

Minor League Talent/Player Development: Edgar Renteria, Charles Johnson, Tony Saunders, Livan Hernandez, Felix Heredia, Vic Darensbourg.
Trades: Robb Nen, Jay Powell, Gary Sheffield, Jeff Conine, Kurt Abbott, Craig Counsell, Ed Vosberg, Darren Daulton.
1995 Free Agents: Al Leiter, Kevin Brown, Devon White.
1996 Free Agents: Alex Fernandez, Dennis Cook, Moises Alou, Bobby Bonilla.

These lists suggest that the Marlins utilized a balanced mix of the triad in their assemblage of the 1997 World Series team. Note that the 1995 free agents are grouped separately due to the fact that they were relative bargain in the free agent market. The Marlins spent $4.5 million for Kevin Brown and $2.9 million for Al Leiter. Their salaries were low enough to allow plenty of other clubs to vie for their services, including the long-suffering Chicago Cubs and Boston Red Sox, but these franchises simply chose not to pursue these starting pitchers. The presence of a solid foundation through bargain free agent signing, as well as a farm system that has been known for producing both quality pitching prospects and solid middle infielders, allowed the Marlins to spend money in a productive fashion in the winter of 1996.

Just how did the Marlins' payroll compare to other clubs in the 1997 season? If we examine the end-of-the-year payroll figures, the Marlins narrowly edged the Braves in total payroll, spending $53,490,000 compared to Atlanta's $52,171,000. However, the payroll discrepancy between the top National League team and the rest of the league, with the exceptions of Pittsburgh and Montreal, was within a ratio that was not very extreme compared to later seasons. Four National League clubs had payrolls in the $40 million range, certainly close enough to be comparable to the Marlins' top NL payroll, yet only one of those teams, the San Francisco Giants, made the playoffs. The St. Louis Cardinals, despite having the third highest payroll in the NL at approximately $48 million, finished well below .500 in the Central Division, while the Houston Astros won the division with a $34 million payroll. The Pittsburgh Pirates, the team with the lowest payroll in baseball, just over $12 million, finished in second place in the NL Central.

Table 10
NL Team Payrolls, 1997

Team	Payroll	Season Record
Florida	$53,490,000	90–72
Atlanta	$52,171,000	101–61
Los Angeles	$48,385,304	88–74
St. Louis	$48,274,167	73–89
San Francisco	$44,121,713	90–72
Colorado	$41,567,334	83–79
New York	$39,881,500	88–74
Cincinnati	$36,881,500	76–86
Houston	$34,182,500	84–78
San Diego	$31,713,672	76–86
Chicago	$30,816,000	68–94
Philadelphia	$30,681,500	68–94
Montreal	$18,460,500	78–84
Pittsburgh	$12,174,166	79–83

The Marlins' championship season in 1997 illustrates the simple-mindedness of attributing World Series victories to team payroll, as the above payroll data suggests. The Marlins' success also tells us something about the precision of team accounting when it comes to projected attendance. In a preseason discussion of the consequences of increasing the team payroll from $32 million to the $50 million range, Huizenga asked team president Don Smiley to project both attendance and financial "losses" that would be a consequence of the payroll spike. Smiley projected average attendance of just under 30,000 per game, which turned out to be exactly what the team drew at the box office, with a final average attendance of slightly over 29,000 per contest. Smiley also projected losses of $30 million, which did not include the estimated $38 million in revenue generated at Pro Player Stadium from parking, concessions, advertising, naming rights, luxury suites and club seats. The careful separation between the Marlins' revenue and the revenue from the stadium allowed Huizenga to claim significant losses for tax purposes. In addition, the Marlins won the championship in their fifth year of existence, which allowed the Marlins owner to take advantage of an IRS tax code provision that allows clubs to deduct up to 50 percent of the value of player salaries through the first five years of ownership. Also Huizenga was able to increase the value of his Sports Channel cable network by undervaluing Marlins television rights. The numerous mechanisms for turning losses into profits were well tested formulas in the world of professional sports, but Huizenga was still convinced that the Marlins were a long-term losing proposition for an owner who clearly hoped to make more money from owning a baseball team. He gambled unsuccessfully on positive political fallout from the Marlins' off-season spending spree, hoping to secure a second state sales tax subsidy of $60 million for further renovations to Pro Player Stadium, which would help defray the expenses of increasing the Marlins' payroll and test the political waters for a later push for a publicly financed stadium. But Florida taxpayers opposed to a second tax break for Pro Player Stadium contacted state senators and representatives, who then killed the measure prior to the start of the 1997 season. Huizenga concluded that he did not have the political clout to secure public financing for a new stadium, and therefore had decided before the curtain even rose on the 1997 season to sell the team to a local buyer.

From Champion to Loser to Champion Again

Huizenga's decision to sell the team did not preempt needed additions to the Marlins' roster during their championship run. It did, however, put Marlins employees on notice that they might not have jobs following the 1997 campaign. As part of the preparations for the sale of the club following the 1997 season, Huizenga ordered team president Don Smiley and general manager Dave Dombrowski to slash payroll by trading all but the least expensive Marlins players in the off season and/or by the beginning of the 1998 season. This fire sale represented the most extensive ever undertaken by a World Series champion, as the Marlins' front office proceeded to eliminate any vestige of the roster that defeated the Cleveland Indians in a dramatic seven-game championship series. The cumulative payroll slashing reduced about $40 million from the $53 million World Series payroll, after all the high- to moderately priced players disappeared from the Marlins' roster in a record-setting time frame. The team's fall from World Series champion to one of the worst clubs to don major league uniforms was evident when the Marlins posted a record of 54–108 in the 1998 season.

After the 1998 season, Huizenga completed the sale of the team to commodities trader John Henry. The terms of the sale left the team with the worst lease in baseball. Huizenga still owns Pro Player Stadium (now Dolphins Stadium), and he negotiated very favorable terms in his sale of the club that allowed him to pocket 30 percent of the net revenue from the sale of food, beverages and souvenirs, 62.5 percent of the parking revenues and all of the revenues from the luxury suites. Meanwhile the Marlins agreed to pay rent and the cost of stadium ushers, custodians, ticket takers and security. Huizenga also negotiated an agreement that required the Marlins to maintain a 10-year contract with Sports Channel, a deal that undervalued the television rights of the club but allowed Huizenga to ensure a higher price for Sports Channel, which he then proceeded to sell.

The worst lease in baseball would seem to have precluded the Marlins from going to the World Series again, if there were a simple equation between team spending and team success. But the story of the Marlins' resurgence to win the 2003 World Series defied the standard arguments about low-payroll clubs having no chance on baseball's uneven playing field. To make matters more absurd: the Marlins defeated the New York Yankees, whose payroll advantages towered above all big-league competitors. The Yankees began the season with a payroll of just over $149 million, while the Marlins started the season with a payroll of just over $48 million. By the time the teams met in the Fall Classic, the Yankees had a payroll of $164 million, compared to the Marlins' $54 million. The Yankees payroll easily ranked first in the majors, while Florida's ranked 21st and seventh among the eight playoff teams of 2003. The season marked the second consecutive year that three relatively low-spending teams made the playoffs, as the Marlins were joined in 2003 by the Minnesota Twins, whose $57 million payroll ranked 19th, and the Oakland A's, whose $50 million payroll ranked 25th. The A's had made the playoffs for the fourth consecutive year, despite ranking near the bottom each season in payroll, and the Twins had made the postseason for the second year in a row. In 2002, the World Series champion Anaheim Angels ranked 16th at $62 million in payroll. The Diamondbacks had a high payroll in 2001, when they defeated the New York Yankees, but were distinguished by having eclipsed the Marlins' record for an expansion team winning the World Series. The D-Backs won the Series in just their fourth year of existence.

What does the Marlins' 2003 success tell us about present competitiveness trends? First, the implications are very hopeful, given that they reinforce the central point made in chapter two that money is simply one factor among three in determining competitiveness and that franchises can overcome their relatively low payrolls (and in the Marlins' case, a horrible stadium lease) with sound player development strategies and productive trades. The Marlins, ironically, made it to the World Series quicker than they probably would have without the fire sale ordered by Huizenga. Dombrowski's trades netted key components of the Marlins' 2003 success, including third baseman Mike Lowell and first baseman Derek Lee. The fact that the Marlins' new owner, John Henry, was committed to player development and to signing top young prospects helped to net first-round draft pick Josh Beckett in 1999, the year of the first amateur draft under Henry's ownershihp, and to secure the signing of top Venezuelan prospect Miguel Cabrera in July of 1999. Henry's most sensible move may have been to work hard to ensure the continuity of the Marlins' front office by persuading GM Dave Dombrowski to stay with the organization. This allowed the organization to move forward with a continuity of leadership that made astute evaluations in the decision to make Luis Castillo and Alex Gonzalez, both Marlins farm products, key ingredients to the rebuilding of the franchise. Dombrowki led the Marlins' organization in a renewed emphasis on player development and trades for young players, such as Arizona's Brad Penny, to dramatically improve the Marlins from a league-worst 54–108 record in 1998 to a respectable 79–82 in 2000. However, the Marlins slid back during the final year of the Henry/Dombrowski organizational tandem, with the team posting a 76–86 record in 2001.

The 2001 season marked a financial crisis for the organization, as Henry labored under the terrible lease agreement that he had signed with Huizenga and repeatedly failed to secure public financing for a retractable-roof stadium. Henry spent millions on lobbyists, but showed little political skill in navigating the layers of government necessary for a publicly financed stadium. The team first unveiled their plan for a tax on the cruise line industry in Miami-Dade County to finance a new Marlins stadium, without a careful analysis of the political clout of the industry at the highest levels of state government and without an adequate base of political support for such a tax from Miami-Dade County and city officials. The team then embarked on a complicated, three-tiered plan to finance a stadium with a combination of Dade County, city of Miami, and state legislative dollars. The plan initially got bogged down, and delayed for months, with an insistence by the Marlins on a stadium site, Bicentennial Park, that proved to be too controversial for city officials to approve. By the time another site was chosen, considerable time had been lost. Although the club had secured support for funding from the county and the city, the effort to secure a state legislative sales tax break was ultimately defeated by the decision of the state Senate president to block the legislation from reaching the floor of the Senate.

At the same time, the Marlins were on a list of possible contraction candidates when Major League Baseball decided to use the threat of contraction in the collective bargaining agreement with the players' association. Although Montreal and Minnesota were the ultimate targets of threatened contraction, Henry had clearly tired of what he perceived to be the financial futility of continuing to run the South Florida franchise. Prodded by fellow owners to consider jumping ship and going to another franchise after the failure of the latest stadium deal in March of 2001, Henry got his opportunity in a three-way ownership swap engineered by Major League Baseball. Under the terms of the agreement, Henry would become part of an ownership group that would bid for the rights to purchase the Boston Red Sox. At the same time, the commissioner's office would give the go-ahead to Jeffrey Loria, majority owner of the Montreal Expos, to begin negotiating the purchase of the Florida Marlins prior to the 2002 season. Major League Baseball would then own the Expos, with the 29 baseball owners being responsible for paying for the running of the Montreal franchise until a buyer could be found.

The ownership swap placed the Marlins in an apparently desperate position, as Jeffrey Loria had to confront a South Florida market whose fan base had plummeted to new lows in his first year of ownership. Loria himself had to purchase a block of tickets in 2002 on the final day of the season just to prevent his Marlins from posting a worse attendance total than his former franchise, the Montreal Expos. The fact that Loria inherited the worst lease in baseball from John Henry made matters even more difficult. The new ownership barely got their feet wet in 2002, as it took time simply to consolidate economic relationships with advertisers to

FIVE / *The Politics and Economics of Expansion* 181

begin stadium promotions and a newspaper and television ad campaign. When stadium promotional giveaways did not start until June and advertising was slow to nonexistent, conspiracy talk began to emerge in South Florida, with some local commentators suggesting that the Loria ownership was simply performing a holding operation for Major League Baseball until the team could be relocated. In the face of all of this, the Marlins' front office spoke time and again of their intentions to keep the team in South Florida, with Loria declaring, "We're in this for the long haul."

Given this context, along with a massive change of organizational personnel from GM Dombrowski, who fled to Detroit, to new GM Larry Beinfest, who had relatively limited experience as a GM and was brought along by Loria from Montreal, the state of the Marlins' organization was repeatedly described by baseball insiders as dismal. Veteran baseball writer Mike Berardino of the *Sun-Sentinel* even penned a featured article for *Baseball America* with the title "Hung Out to Dry," describing the general animosity harbored by longtime baseball scouts for the way that Jeffrey Loria and his team president/stepson David Samson had run the baseball operation in Montreal. In the view of many scouts and longtime baseball insiders, Loria and Samson were a combination of arrogance and incompetence. Clearly, the new ownership had a long way to go, and no one could possibly have predicted the success with which they would turn around the fortunes of the Marlins' franchise in just their second year of ownership.

In fact, a careful examination of the talent added to the organization by new GM Larry Beinfest, compared to what had already been added by Dombrowski, shows that the Marlins' success in 2003 was equally attributable to both organizations. If anything, the Marlins' World Series championship demonstrated that two heads were literally better than one, or in this case, two organizations. The key to Beinfest's move in the off season of 2002 was an ability to sort out which players the club should retain and which players the club needed to move. In a complicated deal with Colorado, the Marlins managed to unload the expensive contracts of Preston Wilson and Charles Johnson and in turn acquired the speedy presence of leadoff man Juan Pierre, who would be important to the team's success. Although the team had to agree to take on the salary of pitcher Mike Hampton in the deal, who subsequently was shipped to Atlanta, the savings allowed the Marlins to add more pieces to the roster. This included trading for veteran left-handed starter Mark Redman, who also proved a valuable addition by Beinfest. And as a last-minute show of support from ownership for the job Beinfest was doing in rebuilding the team, Jeffrey Loria authorized the use of "special money" to sign free agent Pudge Rodriguez to a one-year, $10 million deal, with the money to be spread out over the next three seasons. Trades made by Beinfest during the 2002 season, including the multiplayer swap that sent outfielder Clif Floyd to Montreal and brought Carl Pavano to the Marlins, turned out to be crucial to the team's success, although this deal was roundly criticized in the South Florida press. As the following table indicates, Beinfest's trades netted considerable value in accounting for the world championship of the Marlins in 2003. The table uses the sabermetric statistical category "value over replacement player," abbreviated as VORP, to examine the contributions of players signed, traded for or drafted by Beinfest, whose acquisitions are designation by an asterisk after the player's names. All other players were acquired by Dombrowski. The table is the work of *Baseball Prospectus* author Dayn Perry.

Table 11
Beinfest's Trades

Player	VORP	Player	VORP
Mike Lowell	48.9	Brad Penny	0.5
Ivan Rodriguez*	46.3	Josh Beckett	0.2
Derrek Lee	45.0	Tommy Phelps*	0.0
Luis Castillo	39.2	Allan Levrault*	-0.3
Juan Pierre*	32.6	Justin Wayne*	-0.3
Alex Gonzalez	24.9	Tim Spooneybarger*	-0.4
Juan Encarnacion*	12.1	Mike Mordecai*	-1.0
Miguel Cabrera	11.9	Mike Redmond	-1.2
Ramon Castro	6.9	Chad Allen*	-1.3
Dontrelle Willis*	6.7	Michael Tejera	-1.4
Brian Banks	3.4	Carl Pavano*	-1.9
Todd Hollandsworth*	2.2	Gerald Williams*	-4.2
Jeff Conine*	2.0	Andy Fox	-5.7
Rick Helling*	1.0	Mark Redman*	-7.7
A.J. Burnett	0.6		
Lenny Harris*	0.6	Total	259.6

Some notes on the above data: Multi-team players have only their Marlins contributions listed above; the pitcher numbers you see are for their contributions at the plate only.

According to Dayn Perry, "of the 259.6 VORP runs tallied by the Marlins offense last season, Beinfesters contributed 86.4 of those runs, or 33.3 percent of the total."

Now for the pitchers...

Table 12
Beinfest's Pitcher Trades

Player	VORP	Player	VORP
Dontrelle Willis*	36.5	Tim Spooneybarger	4.2
Mark Redman*	33.2	Juan Alvarez*	3.1
Josh Beckett	32.2	Toby Borland*	2.9
Brad Penny	22.0	A.J. Burnett	0.7
Carl Pavano*	21.8	Nate Bump	0.7
Ugueth Urbina	17.7	Justin Wayne*	-4.0
Braden Looper	14.8	Armando Almanza	-7.4
Chad Fox*	9.6	Blaine Neal	-7.9
Rick Helling*	9.2	Kevin Olsen	-11.4
Tommy Phelps*	5.8	Vladimir Nunez	-15.4
Allen Levrault	4.9		
Michael Tejera	4.5	Total	177.5

According to Dayn Perry, "Marlin pitchers posted an aggregate VORP of 177.5; the Beinfesters totaled 118.1, which is 66.5 percent of the team's total pitching VORP runs."

Also from Perry: "Beinfest's additions contributed 46.8 percent of the Marlins' VORP total. Considering he was hired in early 2002, that's a fairly impressive percentage. There's no removing Dombrowski's fingerprints from the incumbent world champs, but Beinfest had much to do with their success. In particular, his additions to the pitching staff—particularly his trades for Willis and Redman—were a serious boon to the team's fortunes in 2003."

Also from Perry: "In terms of salary, the Beinfesters were paid a total of $20,859,426 in 2003, while Dombrowski's charges made a total of $27,590,574. Bringing VORP into the calculus, the Beinfesters were paid $102,002.08 per run of VORP, and the Dombrowskiites' tab ran $118,618.12 per run of VORP. On the surface, it may appear that Beinfest has netted more bang for his buck, but keep in mind that all of Dombrowski's contracts were handed out back in the days of the uncorrected/non-collusive market, and that many of those players carry more service time."[19]

The combination of two organizational styles helped the Marlins win the World Series in 2003, as the Henry/Dombrowski tandem did not succeed in making the necessary additions for the Marlins to compete in their final year of this organization, but the moves of Dombrowski did lay a solid foundation for GM Beinfest, who was able to make the correct evaluations regarding which of Dombrowski's players to hold and which to trade. Clearly, the success of such a club, with the worst stadium lease in baseball, the threat of contraction/relocation alienating local fans to the point where average attendance dipped to an all-time low in 2002, and the wholesale changing of organizations in 2002, demonstrates that money is one limb of the triad of success in baseball planning, and that with good player development, trades and selective free agency, teams can win within a low budget. The Marlins' success also does not stand alone among recent trends in the sport. As we've indicated, the proliferation of low-payroll entries into baseball's playoffs from 2001 to the present suggests that the sport may be headed back to the golden age of competitiveness enjoyed from the 1980s through 1993, when an unprecedented wide range of clubs made the playoffs. The next section explores the larger competitive context of the Marlins' World Series triumph.

The Current State of Competitiveness: The Marlins and Beyond

The Marlins captured their 2003 championship in the context of a 2001–2006 agreement with Fox Television Network that increased Major League Baseball's revenues by 45 percent over the previous payment for the same package, and another television, radio and internet deal with ESPN that increased revenues from ESPN by an even greater margin.[20] This book has argued that one of the most important factors in explaining baseball's golden age of competitiveness during the 1980s through 1993 was the escalation of national television revenue during this time frame. After 1993, the money available from national television decreased from its previous rate as a result of an unprecedented agreement with ABC and NBC that based revenues on advertising sales. The fluctuations in national television revenue go a long way toward explaining the difference in competitiveness over these two earlier periods. With increases in national television money that were unprecedented during the 1980s came competitiveness trends that were also unprecedented, trends that lasted through the early 1990s. Conversely, when national television money dramatically declined from 1994 through 2000, baseball experienced a significant reduction of competitiveness, if measured by the range of payroll teams making the playoffs during this time period, as well as using our competitiveness index developed in this book.

Put simply, if you were a baseball fan in the mid-to-late 1990s, you would have been able to predict the vast majority of the teams that made the playoffs by examining their payroll expenditures. This contrasted with the period from 1981 through 1993, when all 12 National League teams finished first at least once, and 11 of 14 American League teams finished in first place. Nothing else so clearly explains the golden age of competitiveness than the dramatic increases in national television revenue during this time, which was the most important component of Major League Baseball's central fund that was distributed equally to all teams. The increases in the revenues of the central fund during the 1980s helped to offset the increased monies that some teams were able to pocket from large-market local television deals.

Now, just as a wider range of teams have been making the playoffs from 2001 to 2004, there is a correlation between the increased competitiveness of recent years and an increased distribution of revenue from the central fund, most of it explained by the negotiation of a more favorable television deal with Fox and ESPN. Also, Major League Baseball has a new collective bargaining agreement agreed to by owners and players during the 2002 season, whose terms also have impacted the amount of money that gets distributed to teams. Although there are numerous flaws in the revenue-sharing aspects of the latest collective bargaining agreement, the agreement has increased the amount of money available to mid- and small-revenue clubs in a manner that is worth noting. Taken together, the increases in the national television money and the changes in the distribution of revenue authorized by the latest collective bargaining agreement suggests that baseball has moved beyond the period of the late 1990s and into a new era of increased competitiveness. However, the flaws in the revenue sharing aspects of the CBA may undermine its positive effects over the long run, and we will explore the implications of these flaws later in this section.

For now, let's examine the changes in revenue sharing that have taken effect with the 2003 season, when the Marlins stunned the baseball universe by capturing the World Series with a payroll three times lower than their opponent, the New York Yankees. Prior to the 2002 collective bargaining agreement, Major League Baseball had a more modest revenue sharing plan with a different structure than the one currently in place. Under the previous revenue-sharing agreement from 1995 to 2001, the owners contributed 20 percent of their local revenue to the revenue-sharing pool, after deducting ballpark expenses. The pool was then redistributed, with 75 percent going to all 30 teams and 25 percent to only those teams with local revenue below the major league average. The distributional effects of this revenue sharing system is noted in Table 13 below, with dollars that were spent by teams in revenue sharing placed in parenthesis. Following the revenue-sharing figures, Table 14 is provided to indicate the market size of the clubs giving and receiving revenue sharing.

There are three serious flaws with the previous revenue sharing scheme that are replicated in the new revenue-sharing formula. The first

Table 13
Distributional Effects of Revenue Sharing System

Team	Income from baseball operations	2001 revenue sharing	Income from baseball operations after revenue sharing
Milwaukee Brewers	$14,385,000	$1,744,000	$16,129,000
Seattle Mariners	$34,266,000	($18,791,000)	$15,475,000
New York Yankees	$40,859,000	($26,540,000)	$14,319,000
San Francisco Giants	$19,000,000	($6,308,000)	$12,892,000
Detroit Tigers	$533,000	$5,127,000	$5,660,000
Oakland Athletics	($7,113,000)	$10,520,000	$3,407,000
Cincinnati Reds	($11,056,000)	$13,404,000	$2,348,000
Minnesota Twins	($18,533,000)	$19,089,000	$536,000
Anaheim Angels	($9,569,000)	$9,594,000	$25,000
Kansas City Royals	($16,134,000)	$15,997,000	($137,000)
Pittsburgh Pirates	($2,984,000)	$1,782,000	($1,202,000)
Chicago Cubs	$4,797,000	($6,568,000)	($1,771,000)
Baltimore Orioles	$1,460,000	($6,807,000)	($5,347,000)
St. Louis Cardinals	$1,869,000	($8,229,000)	($6,360,000)
Houston Astros	($1,214,000)	($5,185,000)	($6,399,000)
New York Mets	$8,292,000	($15,669,000)	($7,377,000)
San Diego Padres	($16,151,000)	$8,668,000	($7,483,000)
Philadelphia Phillies	($20,865,000)	$11,752,000	($9,113,000)
Florida Marlins	($27,741,000)	$18,561,000	($9,180,000)
Colorado Rockies	($3,415,000)	($6,029,000)	($9,444,000)
Chicago White Sox	($5,687,000)	($4,201,000)	($9,888,000)
Montreal Expos	($38,519,000)	$28,517,000	($10,002,000)
Tampa Bay Devil Rays	($22,843,000)	$12,384,000	($10,459,000)
Cleveland Indians	$1,881,000	($13,254,000)	($11,373,000)
Boston Red Sox	$2,712,000	($16,438,000)	($13,726,000)
Texas Rangers	($15,689,000)	($8,744,000)	($24,433,000)
Atlanta Braves	($14,380,000)	($10,647,000)	($25,007,000)
Arizona Diamondbacks	($32,152,000)	($4,432,000)	($36,584,000)
Toronto Blue Jays	($52,927,000)	$9,830,000	($43,097,000)
Los Angeles Dodgers	($45,343,000)	($9,107,000)	($54,450,000)
Net Operating Loss			($232,241,000)

Table 14
Market Size and Revenue Sharing

Team	Local revenue	Metropolitan population	Per capita local revenue	Revenue sharing
Milwaukee Brewers	$88,949,000	1,689,592	$52.65	$1,744,000
Seattle Mariners	$178,033,000	3,554,760	$50.08	($18,791,000)
Cleveland Indians	$137,841,000	2,945,831	$46.79	($11,373,000)
Colorado Rockies	$107,412,000	2,581,506	$41.60	($6,029,000)
St. Louis Cardinals	$108,058,000	2,603,607	$41.50	($8,229,000)
San Francisco Giants	$145,894,000	3,519,861	$41.45	($6,308,000)
Pittsburgh Pirates	$84,305,000	2,358,695	$35.74	$1,782,000
Arizona Diamondbacks	$106,653,000	3,251,876	$32.80	($4,432,000)
Atlanta Braves	$122,450,000	4,112,198	$29.78	($10,647,000)
Boston Red Sox	$152,581,000	5,819,100	$26.22	($16,438,000)
Tampa Bay Devil Rays	$62,337,000	2,395,997	$26.02	$12,384,000
Cincinnati Reds	$46,486,000	1,979,202	$23.49	$13,404,000
Chicago Cubs	$105,373,000	4,578,770	$23.01	($6,568,000)
Kansas City Royals	$39,295,000	1,776,062	$22.12	$15,997,000
Houston Astros	$100,228,000	4,669,571	$21.46	($5,185,000)
Texas Rangers	$110,509,000	5,221,801	$21.16	($8,744,000)
New York Yankees	$217,807,000	10,599,933	$20.55	($26,540,000)
San Diego Padres	$55,321,000	2,813,333	$19.66	$8,668,000
Chicago White Sox	$87,281,000	4,578,770	$19.06	($4,201,000)
Detroit Tigers	$82,390,000	5,456,428	$15.10	$5,127,000
New York Mets	$158,230,000	10,599,933	$14.93	($15,669,000)
Los Angeles Dodgers	$119,206,000	8,186,823	$14.56	($9,107,000)
Oakland Athletics	$51,068,000	3,519,861	$14.51	$10,520,000
Baltimore Orioles	$103,901,000	7,608,070	$13.66	($6,807,000)
Toronto Blue Jays	$54,078,000	4,763,200	$11.35	$9,830,000
Minnesota Twins	$31,865,000	2,968,906	$10.73	$19,089,000
Florida Marlins	$36,146,000	3,876,380	$9.32	$18,561,000
Philadelphia Phillies	$57,114,000	6,188,463	$9.23	$11,752,000
Anaheim Angels	$67,330,000	8,186,823	$8.22	$9,954,000
Montreal Expos	$9,770,000	3,474,900	$2.81	$28,517,000
Average	$94,264,000	4,529,342	$23.99	

Source: Doug Pappas, *Baseball Prospectus*

is that the determination of whether a franchise is a giver or receiver of revenues is determined strictly by how much local revenue has been generated in the previous season, not by actual market size. Therefore large-market franchises such as the Philadelphia Phillies and the Toronto Blue Jays qualify for revenue sharing under this system. Secondly, the system encourages franchises that are mid- or small-market to lose just enough money to be eligible for revenue-sharing funds, that is to be a receiver rather than a giver. Finally, the revenue-sharing system allows teams to count ballpark expenses against their overall local revenues. This is a potentially serious loophole that has been retained in the current revenue sharing formula and could well be utilized by franchises such as the Yankees, who are now suggesting that they will pay almost all of the cost of a new ballpark for themselves, estimated at $700 million. This would take a significant bite out of the revenue-sharing pie.

The new revenue-sharing system operates differently from the old system in several ways, although it suffers from the same systemic flaws noted above. First, the new revenue-sharing formula increases the amount of local revenue that all teams must contribute to the pool to 34 percent, payable to a fund that is divided equally among all major league teams. Once again, as with the old agreement, ballpark expenses are allowed to be deducted from local revenues when calculating the amount that a team owes in revenue sharing. Secondly, the new agreement provides for a central fund component that adds another $72.2 million to the central fund, taken annually from richer teams and distributed to poorer teams. This component is to be 60 percent funded in 2003, 80 percent in 2004, and 100 percent in 2005-06. At the same time, there is a luxury tax included in the latest CBA, with terms that have thus far affected the Yankees and seemed to be designed with the New York club in mind. This is reasonable, as the Yankees' market advantages tower above their competitors, and that will be the case unless baseball ever realizes the potential value in locating at least one more team in the New York/New Jersey market. The luxury tax threshold was established at payrolls above $117 million in 2003, $120.5 million in 2004, $128 million in 2005, and $136.5 million in 2006. The tax rate will range from 17.5 percent to 40 percent, depending on the year and the number of times the team exceeds the threshold. Luxury tax revenues will be used to fund player benefits and player development programs.

Overall, the new revenue sharing from 2003 through 2006 is expected to transfer about $1 billion in money from high- to low-revenue teams

FIVE | *The Politics and Economics of Expansion*   189

over a four-year time frame. Over the short-term, despite the structural problems with the agreement noted above, the transfer of money to clubs such as the Twins and Marlins, who are respectively small-market in the case of the Twins and suffer from the worst lease in baseball in the case of the Marlins, is bound to improve the competitivness of these low-revenue franchises, provided that they are run as well as they have been in recent years. In fact, it is hard to imagine that the Marlins would have won the World Series in 2003 without the help of the new national television contract that has provided more money to all franchises and without the help of the new CBA that continues to transfer more than $20 million in revenue sharing straight to the Marlins' front office. This has helped the new owner of the team, Jeffrey Loria, compensate for the poor stadium lease agreement that he inherited from previous owner John Henry.

Still, there is a serious loophole in the current revenue-sharing scheme, beyond the structural problems of not including market size in the revenue distribution equation. That is the ability of major league clubs to count stadium expenses against local revenues in a manner that could significantly reduce the contribution of rich, large-market clubs like the Yankees to the revenue-sharing pool. According to Neil deMause, who has followed the economics of stadium financing closely, Steinbrenner's newfound willingness to pay the entire $750 million cost for a new Yankees stadium is directly related to the clause in the latest collective bargaining agreement, specifically Article XXIV, Section A (5) that allows teams to deduct the "Stadium Operations Expenses of each club, as reported on an annual basis in the Club's FIQ [Financial Information Questionnaire]." DeMause argues that Major League Baseball has been allowing teams to count stadium construction costs as "stadium operation expenses," claiming these expenses as a deduction against revenue sharing. DeMause calculates that, under this allowance, the Yankees would be able to shift the burden of their stadium debt to the other 29 teams, reducing their annual revenue-sharing obligations by approximately $15.6 million a year until the $300 million of stadium debt is paid.[21]

The ability of the richest club with the biggest market advantage in baseball to shift its revenue-sharing burden to the other 29 teams would greatly weaken the contribution of revenue-sharing to greater competitive balance. If the Yankees move forward and utilize stadium debt as a way to reduce their revenue-sharing commitment, such a maneuver could well invite a serious internal backlash among small-revenue teams when the current collective bargaining agreement expires after the 2006 season. Yankees owner George Steinbrenner's lone vote against the current collective bargaining agreement demonstrates the divisions between baseball's largest-market franchise and the other owners. There is a possibility that Steinbrenner and other high-revenue owners could join forces prior to the next collective bargaining agreement in an effort to significantly lower their future revenue-sharing burden, or to render any future burden less meaningful by retention of such clauses as the stadium debt allowance. The extent to which small-market franchises may insist on a tougher revenue-sharing arrangement will likely hinge on how well they are faring under the current economic system.

The last strike and lockout of 1994/95 occurred in the context of dramatically reduced national television revenues, which put more financial pressure on small-revenue owners to take a hard-line stand for a salary cap. The current national television contract is by comparison quite generous and has arguably led to a period of relative tranquility and greater competitiveness than in the mid-to-late 1990s. But this contract expires in 2006, at the very time that a new collective bargaining agreement will have to be hashed out with the players' association. The terms of the new national television contract will likely have a bearing on the position of the owners, especially the small- and mid-revenue owners, as to whether or not to take a hard line in pressing for more revenue sharing. The players' association will also have to assess whether or not the new system has been good for aggregate player interests. In any case, despite the improvements in baseball competitiveness, there are many unanswered questions as the sport moves farther into the new millennium.

Notes

Introduction

1. For a good recent account of this period, see Robert Burk, *Never Just a Game: Players, Owners and American Baseball to 1920*. Chapel Hill: University of North Carolina Press, 1994.
2. Leonard Koppett, *Koppett's Concise History of Major League Baseball*. Philadelphia: Temple University Press, 1998, 401.

Chapter One

1. For an overview of the appreciation of baseball franchises and a comparison with other sports leagues, see Soonhwan Lee and Hyosung Chun, "Economic Values of Professional Sports Franchises in the United States," *The Sport Journal*, vol. 5, no. 3, fall 2002.
2. "The Report of the Independent Members of the Commissioner's Blue Ribbon Panel on Baseball Economics." New York: Major League Baseball, July 2000.
3. Doug Pappas, "Overview of Collective Bargaining Agreement," *Baseball Prospectus* (website), June 3–11, 2003.
4. For an analysis of these contracts, see Paul Staudohar, "Baseball Negotiations: A New Agreement," *Monthly Labor Review*, December 2002, pp. 16–17.
5. Rodney Fort, "Revenue Disparity and Competitive Balance in Major League Baseball," Statement for the Senate Subcommittee on Antitrust, November 17, 2000.
6. Andrew Zimbalist, *Baseball and Billions*. New York: Basic Books, 1992, 96.
7. Jules Tygiel, *Past Time: Baseball as History*, New York: Oxford University Press, 2000, 165–197, for a detailed examination of the shifting geography of baseball in the 1950s.
8. See Robert Burk, *Never Just a Game*. Chapel Hill: University of North Carolina Press, 1994, for the most complete dissection of the historical origins of baseball's minor league system.
9. For the best and most comprehensive recent account of the owners-players history during the pre- and post-free agency period, see Charles Korr, *The End of Baseball as We Knew It: The Players Union, 1960–1981*. Chicago: University of Illinois, 2002.
10. Robert Burk, *Much More Than a Game: Players, Owners and American Baseball Since 1921*. Chapel Hill: University of North Carolina Press, 2001, 55.
11. Neil Sullivan, *The Minors*. New York: St. Martin's Press, 1990, 237.
12. Zimbalist, *op. cit.*, 109–110.
13. Tygiel, *op. cit.*, 167.
14. Burk, *Much More Than a Game*, 109.
15. Donald Dewey and Nicholas Aco-

cella, *Ball Clubs*. New York: HarperCollins, 1993, 380.
16. Zimbalist, *op. cit.*, 48.
17. Bill James, *The New Bill James Historical Abstract*. New York: St. Martin's Press, 2001, p. 311.
18. Tygiel, *op. cit.*, 200.
19. Doug Pappas, "The Numbers: Part I: Gate Receipts," *Baseball Prospectus* (website), December 7, 2001.
20. Ronald Cox and Daniel Skidmore-Hess, "Baseball Competitiveness in the Free Agency Era." *Nine: A Journal of Baseball History and Culture*, vol. 11, no. 1, fall 2002, 59–68.
21. Roger Angell, *Late Innings*, New York: Ballantine Books, 1982, 21.
22. Bob Costas, *Fair Ball*. New York: Broadway Books, 2001, 3.
23. Leonard Koppett, *Koppett's Concise History of Major League Baseball*. Philadelphia: Temple University Press, 1998, 385.
24. Costas, *op. cit.*, 71–76.
25. Michael Ozanian, *Wall Street Journal*, D12, July 17, 2002.
26. Bill James, *op. cit.*, 325.

Chapter Two

1. Ronald W. Cox and Daniel Skidmore-Hess, "Baseball Competitiveness in the Free Agency Era." *Nine: The Journal of Baseball History and Culture*, vol. 11, no. 1, fall 2002, 59–68.
2. Rodney Fort, "Revenue Disparity and Competitive Balance in Major League Baseball." Statement for the Senate Subcommittee on Antitrust, November 17, 2000, 12.
3. Jules Tygiel, *Past Time, op. cit.*, 148.
4. *Ibid.*
5. *Ibid.*, 154.
6. Leonard Koppett, *Concise History of Major League Baseball, op. cit.*, 158.
7. John Heylar, *Lords of the Realm*. New York: Ballantine Books, 1994, 390–391.
8. Andrew Zimbalist, *Baseball and Billions, op. cit.*, 150.

9. Soonhwan Lee and Hyosung Chun, "Economic Values of Professional Sports Franchises in the United States," *The Sport Journal*. New York: Sage, 1998, 5.
10. Rodney Fort, *op. cit.*, 12.
11. Keith Sherony, Michael Haupert, and Glenn Knowles, "Competitive Balance in Major League Baseball," *Nine: The Journal of Baseball History and Culture*, vol. 9, 1–2, 226.
12. Doug Pappas, "The Numbers, Part II: Local Media Revenues," *Baseball Prospectus* (website), December 12, 2001.
13. Doug Pappas, "MLB's Greatest Lie Yet," Doug Pappas Website, December 5, 2001.
14. Andrew Zimbalist, *May the Best Team Win*. Washington, D.C.: Brookings Institute, 2003, 57.
15. *Ibid.*, 58.
16. *Ibid.*, 59.
17. Zimbalist, "Baseball By the Numbers," *New York Times Magazine*, March 31, 2002.
18. *Ibid.*
19. Doug Pappas, "The Numbers: Part 8: MLB vs. Forbes." *Baseball Prospectus* (website), April 3, 2002.
20. Dennis Zimmerman, "The Baseball Strike and Federal Policy: An Economic Analysis." Washington, D.C.: Congressional Research Service, February 24, 1995, 7.
21. Alan Simpson, "The Amateur Draft," *Total Baseball Encyclopedia*, 6th ed. New York: Total Sports, 1991, 579.
22. *Ibid.*
23. *Ibid.*, 580.
24. *Ibid.*

Chapter Three

1. Andrew Zimbalist, *May the Best Team Win, op. cit.*, 46.
2. Zimbalist, *Baseball and Billions, op. cit.*, 50.
3. Katherine Willers, "The Determinants of Attendance of Major League Baseball Games from 1989 to 1999 and the

Implications of the 1994 Labor Strike," B.A. thesis, Department of Economics, Cornell University, 2001.

4. Joanna Cagan and Neil deMause, *Field of Schemes*. Monroe, Maine: Common Courage Press, 1998, 13.

5. Bruce Hamilton and Peter Kahn, "Baltimore's Camden Yards Ballparks," in Roger G. Noll and Andrew Zimbalist, *Sports, Jobs and Taxes: The Economic Impact of Sports Teams and Stadiums*. Washington, D.C.: Brookings, 1998, 259.

6. *Ibid.*, 260.

7. Cagan and deMause, *op. cit.*, 12.

8. *Ibid.*, 25.

9. Zimbalist, *May the Best Team Win*, *op. cit.*, 126.

10. *Ibid.*

11. *Ibid.*

12. Hamilton and Kahn, *op. cit.*, 261.

13. Ziona Austrian and Mark S. Rosentraub, "Cleveland's Gateway to the Future," in Roger G. Noll and Andrew Zimbalist, *Sports, Jobs and Taxes: The Economic Impact of Sports Teams and Stadiums*. Washington, D.C.: Brookings, 1998, 358.

14. Mark Rosentraub, *Major League Losers*. New York: Basic Books, 1997, 258–259.

15. *Ibid.*, 262.

16. *Ibid.*, 265.

17. Cagan, deMause, *op. cit.*, 23.

18. Rosentraub, *op. cit.*, 266.

19. *Ibid.*, 253.

20. Mark Armour and Daniel Levitt, *Paths to Glory*. Washington: Brassey's Inc., 2003, 205.

21. *Ibid.*

22. Russell Schneider, *The Cleveland Indians Encyclopedia*. New York: Sports Publishing, 2001, 368.

23. *Ibid.*

24. Robert Burk, *Much More Than a Game*. Chapel Hill: University of North Carolina Press, 2001, 274.

25. *Ibid.*

26. *Ibid.*, 309.

27. *Ibid.*, 274.

28. *Ibid.*, 276.

29. *Ibid.*

30. Henry Fetter, *Taking on the Yankees*. New York: W.W. Norton, 2003, 31.

31. Schneider, *op. cit.*, 356.

32. *Ibid.*, 368.

33. *Ibid.*

34. Jon Heyman, *The Sporting News*. June 19, 2000.

Chapter Four

1. Alan Klein, *Sugarball*. New Haven: Yale University Press, 1991, 43.

2. *Ibid.*

3. *Ibid.*

4. Arturo J. Marcano Guevara and David Fidler, *Stealing Lives*. Bloomington: Indiana University Press, 26.

5. Angel Vargas, "The Globalization of Baseball: A Latin American Perspective," *Indiana Journal of Legal Studies*, August 8, 2001, 6.

6. Guevara and Fidler, 29.

7. *Ibid.*, 16.

8. *Ibid.*

9. Robert Burk, *Much More Than a Game*. Chapel Hill: University of North Carolina Press, 2001, 276.

10. *Ibid.*, 275–276.

11. Paul D. Staudohar, "Baseball Negotiations: A New Agreement," *Monthly Labor Review*, December 2002, 17.

12. Burk, *op. cit.*, 274.

13. Milton Jamail, *Baseball America*, Feb. 4, 2001, 10.

14. David Rawnsley, *Baseball America*, Feb. 19–March 4, 2001, 17.

15. *Ibid.*

16. *Ibid.*

17. Guevara and Fidler, *op. cit.*, 190.

18. Vargas, *op. cit.*

19. Guevara and Fidler, *op. cit.*

20. *Ibid.*, 175–177.

21. *Ibid.*, 192.

22. *Ibid.*, 193.

Chapter Five

1. Jules Tygiel, *Past Time*. New York: Oxford University Press, 2000, 169.

2. Donald Dewey and Nicholas Acocella, *Ball Clubs*. New York: HarperCollins, 1996, 542.
3. *Ibid.*, 562.
4. David Whitford, *Playing Hardball*. New York: Doubleday, 1993, 31.
5. *Ibid.*
6. *Ibid.*, 35.
7. *Ibid.*, 36.
8. *Ibid.*, 37.
9. *Ibid.*, 69.
10. *Ibid.*, 68–69.
11. *Ibid.*, 86.
12. *Ibid.*, 79.
13. Greg Spira, "The Offensive Explosion That Wasn't," June 12, 1998, Baseballprospectus.com.
14. Whitford, *op. cit.*, 125.
15. *Ibid.*, 161.
16. For good background, see Paul Pederson, *Build It and They Will Come*. Stuart, Florida: Florida Sports Press, 1997.
17. Henry Fetter, *Taking on the Yankees*. New York: W.W. Norton, 2003.
18. For further elaboration, see Ronald W. Cox, "Did the Marlins Buy the 1997 Championship?" in *From McGillicuddy to McGwire: Baseball in Florida and the Caribbean*. Cleveland: SABR, 2000.
19. Dayn Perry, "Tip of the Cap to Beinfest," *Can of Corn*, Feb. 5, 2004, Baseballprospectus.com.
20. Paul Staudohar, "Baseball Negotiations: A New Agreement," *Monthly Labor Review*. December 2002, 16.
21. Neil deMause, "The Evil Empire Strikes Back," August 1, 2004, Baseballprospectus.com.

Bibliography

Angel, Roger. *Late Innings*. New York: Ballantine Books, 1982.
Armour, Mark, and Daniel Levitt. *Paths to Glory*. Washington: Brassey's, 2003.
Austrian, Ziona, and Mark S. Rosentraub. "Cleveland's Gateway to the Future." In Roger G. Noll and Andrew Zimbalist, eds., *Sports, Jobs and Taxes: The Economic Impact of Sports Teams and Stadiums*. Washington, D.C.: Brookings Institution, 1998.
Burk, Robert. *Much More Than a Game: Players, Owners and American Baseball Since 1921*. Chapel Hill: University of North Carolina Press, 2001.
_____. *Never Just a Game: Players, Owners and American Baseball to 1920*. Chapel Hill: University of North Carolina Press, 1994.
Cagan, Joanna, and Neil deMause. *Field of Schemes*. Monroe, Maine: Common Courage Press, 1998.
Costas, Bob. *Fair Ball*. New York: Broadway Books, 2001.
Cox, Ronald W. "Did the Marlins Buy the 1997 Championship?" In *From McGillicuddy to McGwire: Baseball in Florida and the Caribbean*. Cleveland: SABR, 2000, 6–7.
_____, and Daniel Skidmore-Hess. "Baseball Competitiveness in the Free Agency Era." *Nine: A Journal of Baseball History and Culture*, vol. 11, no. 1, fall 2002.
Dewey, Donald, and Nicholas Acocella. *Ball Clubs*. New York: HarperCollins, 1993.
Fetter, Henry. *Taking on the Yankees*. New York: W.W. Norton, 2003.
Fort, Rodney. "Revenue Disparity and Competitive Balance in Major League Baseball." Statement for the Senate Subcommittee on Antitrust, November 17, 2000.
Guevara, Arturo J. Marcano, and David Fidler. *Stealing Lives: The Globalization of Baseball and the Tragic Story of Alexis Quiroz*. Bloomington: Indiana University Press, 2003.
Hamilton, Bruce, and Peter Kahn. "Baltimore's Camden Yards Ballparks." In Roger G. Noll and Andrew Zimbalist, eds., *Sports, Jobs and Taxes: The Economic Impact of Sports Teams and Stadiums*. Washington, D.C.: Brookings Institution, 1998.
Heylar, John. *Lords of the Realm*. New York: Ballantine Books, 1994.
James, Bill. *The New Bill James Historical Abstract*. New York: St. Martin's Press, 2001.
Klein, Alan. *Sugarball*. New Haven: Yale University Press, 1991.
Koppett, Leonard. *Koppett's Concise History of Major League Baseball*. Philadelphia: Temple University Press, 1998.

Korr, Charles. *The End of Baseball as We Knew It: The Player's Union, 1960–1981.* Chicago: University of Illinois Press, 2002.

Lee, Soonhwan, and Hyosung Chun. "Economic Values of Professional Sports Franchises in the United States." *The Sport Journal (Part One),* vol. 5, no. 3, fall 2002.

Pappas, Doug. "The Numbers (Part One): Gate Receipts." BaseballProspectus.com, December 7, 2001.

———. "The Numbers (Part Two): Local Media Revenues." BaseballProspectus.com, December 12, 2001.

———. "The Numbers (Part Eight): MLB vs. Forbes." BaseballProspectus.com, April 3, 2002.

———. "Overview of Collective Bargaining Agreement." BaseballProspectus.com, June 3–11, 2003.

Pederson, Paul. *Build It and They Will Come.* Stuart, Florida: Florida Sports Press, 1997.

Perry, Dayn. "Tip of the Cap to Beinfest." *Can of Corn,* BaseballProspectus.com, Feb. 5, 2004.

"The Report of the Independent Members of the Commissioner's Blue Ribbon Panel on Baseball Economics." New York: Major League Baseball, July 2000.

Rosentraub, Mark. *Major League Losers.* New York: Basic Books, 1997.

Schneider, Russell. *The Cleveland Indians Encyclopedia.* New York: Sports Publishing, 2001.

Sherony, Keith, Michael Haupert and Glenn Knowles. "Competitive Balance in Major League Baseball." *Nine: The Journal of Baseball History and Culture,* vol. 9, nos 1–2.

Simpson, Alan. "The Amateur Draft." In John Thorn, Pete Palmer, Michael Gershman, David Pietrusza, eds., *Total Baseball Encyclopedia,* 6th ed. New York: Total Sports, 1991, 578–585.

Spira, Greg. "The Offensive Explosion That Wasn't." BaseballProspectus.com, June 12, 1998.

Staudohar, Paul. "Baseball Negotiations: A New Agreement." *Monthly Labor Review,* December 2002.

Sullivan, Neil. *The Minors.* New York: St. Martin's Press, 1990.

Tygiel, Jules. *Past Time: Baseball as History.* New York: Oxford University Press, 2000.

Vargas, Angel. "The Globalization of Baseball: A Latin American Perspective." *Indiana Journal of Legal Studies,* August 8, 2001.

Whitford, David. *Playing Hardball.* New York: Doubleday, 1993.

Willers, Katherine. "The Determinants of Attendance of Major League Baseball Games from 1989 to 1999 and the Implications of the 1994 Labor Strike." B.A. thesis, Department of Economics, Cornell University, 2001.

Zimbalist, Andrew. *Baseball and Billions.* New York: Basic Books, 1992.

———. "Baseball by the Numbers." *New York Times Magazine,* March 31, 2002.

———. *May the Best Team Win.* Washington, D.C.: Brookings Institution, 2003.

Zimmerman, Dennis. "The Baseball Strike and Federal Policy: An Economic Analysis." Washington, D.C.: Congressional Research Service, February 24, 1995.

Index

Numbers in **_bold italics_** refer to photographs.

AA Toledo 22
ABC TV 17, 54, 184
Abreu, Bobby 135
academies *see* minor leagues
Acocella, Nicholas 25
Acosta, Winston 141–142
Alderson, Sandy 66, 132–133, 134
Alomar, Roberto 114
Alomar, Sandy, Jr. 105
Alou, Moises 173, 174
amateur players draft: bonus payments 64–65, 106–107, 131–132, 137–138; cost of 168; creation of 63–65; eligibility for 138; long range affects 79; Major League Rule (MLR) 4(e) 125; *see also* worldwide amateur draft
American League 14, 16, 111, 153, 166
Anaheim Angels 178
Anderson, Brady 114
Angell, Roger 31
Angelos, John 113
Angelos, Lou 113
Angelos, Peter 86, 89, 112–116, 117
antitrust exemption: and congress 29, 149–150, 154, 155, 158–159; and courts 21, 24; and minor leagues 22–24; politics and 6; and relocation 19
Antonnuci, John 170
Argyros, George 157
Arizona Diamondbacks 4, 36–37, 59, 74–78, 169–170
Armour, Mark, *Paths to Glory* 104–105

Armstrong, Jack 105
Atlanta Braves 28, 49, 64, 69, 72
attendance, decline in 52

Baerga, Carlos 105
Baltimore City Online 113
Baltimore Orioles: American League 111; and Angelos 112–116; and free agency 89; local media money 11; new stadiums 80–81, 103, 108; payroll discrepancies 69; purchase price 8; and "S-curve methodology" 104–105; and sabermetrics 104–105; stadium revenues 4; World Series 1983 111; *see also* Memorial Stadium; Orioles Park at Camden Yards
Bando, Sal 64
Bank One Ballpark 98
Barger, Carl 162, 164, 169
Baseball America 181
Baseball Prospectus (Perry) 69, 160, 171, 182–183
Batista, Miguel 136
Bavasi, Peter 110
Beane, Billy 66–**_67_**
Beckett, Josh 179
Beinfest, Larry 78, 181–182, 183; *see also* Florida Marlins
Bell, Derek 101
Belle, Albert 106
Benton, Oren 170
Berardino, Mike 181

"Black Sox" 1919 27
Blanco, Hugo 121
Blue Jays *see* Toronto Blue Jays
Blue Ribbon Commission Report 9–10
Boles, John 169, 173
Bonify, Cam 101
Bonilla, Bobby 114, 173, 174
bonus payments: amateur draft 64–65, 106–107, 131–132, 137–138; Cleveland Indians 107; escalation of 63, 66, 131; and Loria 182; Seattle Mariners 64
Boone, Aaron 100
Boras, Scott 131
Boston Red Sox 3, 8, 11, 67, 175, 180
Boyer, Clete 26
Braves *see* Atlanta Braves
Bronx Bombers 33
Brooklyn Dodgers: operating revenue 26; pre-free agency era 14–15; relocation of 53, 153; television and radio rights 52
Brown, Kevin 172, 175
Buckner, Bill 64
Burk, Robert 25
Burnitz, Jeromy 114
buscones 5, 121–122, 123–124, 139, 140

Cabrera, Miguel 179
Cabrera, Orlando 136
Cagan, Joann 90–91, 95–96
California Angels model 171
Cangelosi, John 173
Cardinals *see* St. Louis Cardinals
Carpenter, Chris 172
Carr, Chuck 172
Carrasquel, Chico 146–147
Carroll, Parke 26
Castillo, Luis 179
CBS TV 12, 107, 130
Celler, Emanuel 153
Central Market Gateway Project 93–96
Cerv, Bob 26
Cey, Ron 64
Chicago Cubs 28, 58, 157, 175
Chicago White Sox 64, 164
Cincinnati 99–100
Cleveland, city of 93–96, 97–98
Cleveland Indians: bonus payments 107; financial crisis 1980 109–110; and free agency 106–107; and minor league franchise 22; new stadium 82–84, 112; ownership (1986–1999) 109–112; and player development 105–106, 108; and "S-curve" methodology 104–105; and sabermetrics 104–105; stadium revenues 4; World Series (1997) 177; *see also* Hart, John
Colangelo, Jerry 36–37, 74, 75–76, 77; *see also* Arizona Diamondbacks
Cole, Alex 105
collective bargaining agreement (2002): 70, 185; and Florida Marlins 180; luxury tax 188; with Players Association 9, 30; stadium expense clause 189–190
Colorado Rockies 70–71, 150, 156, 166–168, 170; *see also* Denver; Wirth, Tim
Comerica Park 81, 98, *103*; *see also* Detroit
commissioners: bonus escalation 131; expansion 148, 157–158; and free agency 32; and globalization 129–131; and Japanese players 128; and Loria 180; Major League Baseball Players Association (MLBPA), relationship with 45; revenue distribution 53; and revenue imbalance 78; and worldwide amateur draft 126; *see also* individual commissioners names
competitive index 14–16, 48–50
competitiveness: amateur player draft (1965) 63; balance 1–2, 32, 108, 139; decline of 47–48, 184; factors 13–14, 50–51; free agency and 14–15, 16, 20, 30–31, 51, 62–63; golden age (1940s and 1950s) 8–9, 19, 20, 51; golden age (1980s) 19, 47–48, 50, 107, 184–185; imbalance 32–33; and Latin American players 134; National League 13; National Scouting Bureau 63; and national television money 16–19; and payroll 184; post–World War II era 47; and revenue 54; trends 179
congress: and antitrust exemption 29, 149–150, 154, 155, 158–159; congressional committee (2001) 28; congressional hearings (1953) 24, 51, 53; congressional legislation (1986) 88; congressional subcommittee on monopoly power (1951) 153; Selig testimony 2001 28, 57; Senate Task Force on the Expansion of Major League Baseball (1987) 148–149, 158, 160

Continental League 153
contracts: English-only 122, 123; Latin players 5; *see also* television
Cook, Dennis 105, 173
Coors Field 170
Costas, Bob 31–32
cradle to grave reserve system 20, 21
Cronin, Joe 154
Cubs *see* Chicago Cubs

Daley, William 155
Daugherty, Pat 169
debt/value ratio 36
DeConcini, Dennis 158
deMause, Neil 90–91, 95–96, 189
Denver *see* Colorado Rockies
Denver Baseball Commission 165
Denver Baseball Committee (DBC) 156–158
Denver Baseball Symposium 156
Denver Metropolitan Stadium District 161–162, 167
Denver Stadium Authority 165
Detroit, city of 41, 99–100; *see also* Comerica Park
Detroit Tigers 5; *see also* Dombrowski, Dave
Dewey, Donald 25
Diamondbacks *see* Arizona Diamondbacks
Ditmar, Art 26
Dodgers *see* Brooklyn Dodgers; Los Angeles Dodgers
Dombrowski, Dave (Detroit Tigers general manager) 100, 101; dismantling of Florida Marlins 74, 177; expansion draft picks of Florida Marlins 171–173; and Montreal Expos 169–170; organizational style 183; player development 179
Dominican Republic *see* Latin America
Duren, Ryne 26
Durson, Ed 157

Easley, Damian 101
Eastern League Waterbury 22
Ehrhart, Steve 170
Eisenreich, Jim 173
Erickson, Scott 114
ESPN: revenue, affect on 107, 184; strike (1994) 55; television contracts 3, 11, 17–18, 34, 57, 73, 185

expansion: Colorado Rockies 156; commissioners and 148, 157–158; draft selections (1992) 166, 168; factors 150; Florida Marlins 150, 156, 162–164, 165, 171–173; Kansas City Athletics 154; National League 160; politics of 5–6
expansion committee (1985) 157–158

farm system *see* minor leagues
Federal League 22
Fehr, Donald 133
Fermin, Felix 106
Fernandez, Alex 64, 173, 174
Fernandez, Sid 112
Fernandez, Tony 146
Fetter, Henry, *Taking on the Yankees* 108–109, 169
Fetzer, John 54
Fidler, David 141, 143, 146
Financial World 85
Finley, Charles 21, 154
Florida Marlins: collective bargaining agreement 180; dismantling of 4, 37, 74, 177; expansion of 150, 156, 162–164, 165, 171–173; financial crisis (2001) 179–180; and free agency 173–174; organizational strategies 74–78; ownership swap 180–181, 183; payroll 175–177; player trades 70–71; post-1997 season 177–178; sale of (1998) 178–179; success factors 151–152; trades 182, 183; World Series (1997) 151, 171, 173–177; World Series (2003) 178; *see also* Beinfest, Larry; Henry, John; Huizenga, Wayne; Loria, Jeffrey; Sports Channel
Floyd, Cliff 182
Forbes 29, 58–59
Fort, Rodney 51, 54, 55
Fox TV: contracts with MLB 3, 185; Florida Marlins, contract with 184; revenue growth and 11, 18–19, 34; revenue sharing 57, 73
franchise success ratios 17, 18
free agency: Arizona Diamondbacks 4; and Baltimore Orioles 89; and Cleveland Indians 106–107; commissioners and 32; competitiveness and 14–15, 16, 20, 30–31, 51, 62–63; and Dombrowski 172; and Florida Marlins 173–174; and Players Association 44,

108; reserve system 21; and revenue 44, 62–63; six-year rule 21, 31
Freeman, Orrin 169
Frick, Ford 153

Garcia, Freddy 135
Garvey, Steve 64
Gateway Corporation 96
Gebhard, Bob 169, 170
Giamatti, Bart 149, 157, 158, 159, 160–161
Gillick, Pat 113–114, 115
globalization 129–131, 160–161; *see also* worldwide amateur draft
Gonzalez, Alex 179
Great American Ballpark 99, 100
Grieve, Ben 124
Griffey, Ken, Jr. 64
Grim, Bob 25–26
Guerrero, Vladimir 136
Guevara, Arturo 141, 143, 146
Guillen, Carlos 135
Guillen, Jose 100

Hamilton, Bruce 85
Hammonds, Jeffrey 114
Hampton, Mike 71, 181
Hargrove, Mike 113
Hart, John 105–106, 111–112, 113, 116; *see also* Cleveland Indians
Haupert, Michael 80
Henry, John 77–78, 162, 178–179, 180, 183; *see also* Florida Marlins
Hernandez, Carlos, E. 135
Heyman, Jon 115–116
Hidalgo, Richard 135
Higginson, Bobby 101
Hill, Glenallen 105
Hillings, Patrick 153
Hoffman, Trevor 172
Hoiles, Chris 114
Houston Colt 45's 153
Howard, Thomas 106
Hudson, Tim 68
Hughes, Gary 169
Huizenga, Wayne *163*; and Barger 169; *see also* Florida Marlins; Pro Player Stadium
Huizenga Holdings 167–168; strike (1994) and 163; World Series (1997) 176–178

Illitch, Mike *103*
IRS rules 28

Jackson, Henry 155
Jackson, Reggie 64
Jacobs, David H. 109, 111
Jacobs, Eli 86, 89, 112
Jacobs, Paul 170
Jacobs, Richard 94, 109, 111, 112
Jacobs Field 96
James, Bill 41, 42–43, 67, 135
Japanese Professional Baseball League 126–128, 140
Joe Robbie Stadium 162
Johnson, Arnold 26
Johnson, Charles 70, 181
Johnson, Davey 113–114
Jones, Chipper 64

Kahn, Peter 85
Kansas City Athletics 154
Kansas City Royals 154
Kauffman, Ewing 154
Klein, Alan, *Sugarball* 121
Klein, Joe 111
Knowles, Glenn 80
Kohl, Allen 164
Kohl, Herbert 164
Kohl, Sydney 164

labor laws, violation of 120, 122, 124–125, 126, 141–142
Lachemann, Rene 173
Landis, Kenesaw Mountain 24
Larsen, Don 26
Lasorda, Tom 126
Latin America: academies 5, 123, 126, 141; *see also* buscones; globalization
Latin Players Association 146; Presidential Decree 1984 121; recruitment 143–145; Venezuelan Professional Baseball Association 142, 146; violation of labor laws and MLB 120, 122, 124–125, 126, 141–142; and Win Shares point system 135–136; worldwide amateur draft 5, 132–133, 134, 139–140
League Championship Series (LCS) 15
Lee, Derek 179
Leiter, Al 172, 175
Levitt, Daniel 104–105
litigation: Acosta with New York Yan-

kees 141–142; MLB and Major League Baseball Players Association (MLBA) 131; Morsani with MLB 164–165; violation of labor laws and MLB 120, 122, 124–125, 141–142
Littlefield, Dave 101
Lockman, Whitey 169
Lofton, Kenny 106
Lopes, Dave 64
Lopez, Hector 26
Loria, Jeffrey: bonus payments 182; Florida Marlins 4, 73, 78, 180–181; Montreal Expos, sale of 77; World Series (2003) 178
Los Angeles Angels 64, 153
Los Angeles Dodgers 8, 27–28, 64, 69
Lowell, Mike 179

Mack, Connie 165
MacPhail, Andy 169
Magnusson, Warren 155
Major League Baseball (MLB): age requirement 120, 143; and buscones 123–124; financial crisis 7, 8–9, 10, 57–58, 60; Fox TV, contracts with 3, 185; geography and 52–53; globalization strategy 129–131; IRS rules 28; Japanese Professional Baseball League 126–128; litigation with Major League Baseball Players Association (MLBPA) 131; litigation with Morsani 164–165; low payroll franchises and owners 61; metropolitan regions 38–40; Mexican Professional League 126, 129, 136, 140; payroll and profit 60; post–World War II 25, 26; relocation of teams 53; violation of labor laws 120, 122, 124–125, 126, 141–142; World-Wide Draft Subcommittee 133
Major League Baseball Players Association (MLBPA): and amateur draft 138; commissioners office 45; formation of 1; and Latin Players Association 146; luxury tax 45; revenue sharing 35, 43, 44; salary cap 34, 43–46; split pool concept 35; straight pool plan 35; World-Wide Draft Subcommittee 133; see also amateur players draft; Players Association
Major League Rule (MLR) 4(e) 125
Manfred, Rob 133
Mariners see Seattle Mariners

Maris, Roger 26
Marlins see Florida Marlins
Martinez, Carlos 106
Martinez, Jesus 172
Maryland Stadium Authority 82, 85, 87, 90
Maryland State lottery 84–85, 87, 90
McDowell, Jack 64
McHale, John 63
McMorris, Jerry 170
Meares, Pat 101
Memorial Stadium 86, 87, 90–91; see also Baltimore Orioles
metropolitan regions 38–40
Metzenbaum, Howard 158
Mexican Professional League 126, 129, 136, 140
Miami see Florida Marlins
Miller, Floyd 155
Miller, Kurt 172
Miller, Marvin 21, 36
Miller Park 81, 99, 117, 119; see also Milwaukee, city of
Milwaukee, city of 81, 99–100, 116–119
Milwaukee Braves 175
Milwaukee Brewers: competitive index and 16; relocation of 154; Seattle Pilots 16; and Selig 40, 118–119, 154
Milwaukee Bucks 164
Minnesota Twins 33, 40, 119, 178
minor leagues: AA Toledo 22; academies 5, 123, 141; antitrust exemption and 22–24; Cleveland Indians 22; decline in 65–66; Eastern League Waterbury 22; farm system 24–25, 62, 65, 175; Federal League 22; Latin America 5, 120, 123, 141; reserve system 20, 62; Rickey, Branch 22, 24, 65, 66, 69; St. Louis Cardinals 22, 65; six-year rule 21, 31; Southern League New Orleans 22; training facilities 5
Minute Maid Park 98–99
Modis, Theodore 104
Monday, Rick 64
Monfort, Charles 170
Montreal Expos 2, 33, 37–38, 77, 169–170, 180
Monus, Mickey 170
Mora, Melvin 135
Morsani, Frank 164–165
Moscone, George 156

Mulder, Mark 68
Municipal Stadium 97–98
Murdoch empire 27–28
Murphy, Tom 102
Mussina, Mike 114

Nagy, Charles 105
National League 13, 14, 16, 49, 160, 166
National Scouting Bureau 63, 122, 137
NBC TV 17, 184
Nen, Robb 172
New York Giants 53, 153
New York Mets 59, 153
New York Yankees: Acosta litigation 141–142; competitive index 49; dominance of (1950s) 52; local media money 11; operating revenue 26; player development 72; pre–free agency era 14–15; revenue 3, 51–52, 56; spending 2, 25, 69, 74; Venezuelan labor law case 141–142; World Series (2003) 178; YES network 2, 72
Neyer, Rob 67
Nichols, Rod 105
Nielson surveys 130

Oakland Athletics: college draft 64, 68; payroll 178; player development 68–69, 71; sabermetrics 4, 67
O'Brien, Dan 100, 110–111
Olin, Steve 105
O'Neill, Patrick 109, 110
O'Neill, Steve 109, 110
Orioles *see* Baltimore Orioles
Orioles Park at Camden Yards 82–84, 90, 99; *see also* Baltimore Orioles; Maryland Stadium Authority
Otto, Dave 105

Pacific Bell Park 98
Palmeiro, Rafael 112, 114
Palmer, Dean 101
Palmer, Pete 67
Pappas, Doug 59
Park, Chan Ho 130
Paths to Glory (Armour) 104–105
Paul, Gabe 109, 110, 111
Pavano, Carl 182
Payne, Ulice, Jr. 118
payroll 176; and competitiveness 184; discrepancies 69, 175–176, 178–179; disparities 33–35; imbalance 33; tax 72

Pena, Federico 156, 161
Penny, Brad 179
Perez, Rafael 143
Perry, Dayrn, *Baseball Prospectus* 182–183
Peters, Hank 111–112
Philadelphia Athletics 26
Philadelphia Phillies 3, 28
Pierre, Juan 70, 181
Pittsburgh, city of 41, 99–100; *see also* PNC Park
Pittsburgh Pirates 5, 8, 169
Players Association: Blue Ribbon Commission Report 9–10; collective bargaining agreement 9, 30; and competitive balance 108; and free agency 108; litigation with MLB 131; six-year rule 21; *see also* Major League Baseball Players Association (MLBPA)
Players Associations: six-year rule 31
PNC Park 81, 99, *102*; *see also* Pittsburgh
Pohlad, Carol 40
pre-free agency 14–15, 17, 20, 168
Pro Player Stadium 75, 77, 171, 176, 177; *see also* Florida Marlins; Huizenga, Wayne

Quinn, Bob 110

Rawnsley, David 139
Red Sox *see* Boston Red Sox
Redman, Mark 71, 182
Reichardt, Rick 64
reserve system *see* minor leagues
revenue: competitive balance and 54; disparities 25–26, 48, 54–55; distribution 3, 44, 53–54, 73–78; and free agency 44, 62–63; gate 27, 52, 55–56, 80; imbalance 55–56, 60, 78; local media, and 10–11, 12, 56–58, 80; marketing strategy, MLB 130–131; media 27, 52; merchandising 27; post–World War II 26; stadium 4, 81–84, 89; strike (1994) 17, 55–56, 130, 136, 167; and tax losses 176–177; trends 55; *see also* television
revenue sharing 186, 187; American and National Leagues 166; collective bargaining agreement (2005) 57; and competitive balance 30; Major League Baseball Players Association (MLBPA)

35, 43, 44; salary cap 43; 2003 185–190; *see also* television
Rickey, Branch 22, **23**, 24, 65, 66, 69
Ripken, Cal, Jr. 86, 114
Rodriguez, Ivan 71
Rodriguez, Pudge 182
Rodriguez, Wilfredo 135
Rosentraub, Mark 94

"S-curve" methodology 104–105, 114
sabermetrics 4, 66–69, 104–105, 135, 182
Sabo, Chris 112
Safeco Park 81, 98
St. Louis Cardinals 11, 19–20, 22, 40, 65
salaries: escalation of 8; inflation 106–107
salary cap 30, 34, 35, 43–46
salary floor 34, 43
Samson, David 181
San Francisco, city of 81
SBC Park 81
Schaeffer, William Donald 84, 87–88
Schott, Marge 114
Schwarz, Alan 67
scouts *see* buscones
Scudder, Scott 105
Seattle, city of 81, 155
Seattle Mariners 64, 155–156
Seattle Pilots 16, 154–155, 155
Seaver, Tom 31
Seghi, Phil 110
Selig, Bud: congressional testimony 2001 28, 57; financial crisis, MLB 7–8; and *Forbes* Magazine 58–59; and Milwaukee Brewers 40, 118–119, 154; and Minnesota Twins 119; replaces Vincent 45; *see also* commissioners
Selig-Prieb, Wendy 118
Senate Task Force on the Expansion of Major League Baseball (1987) 148–149, 158, 160
Sexson, Richie 100
Shantz, Bobby 26
Sheffield, Gary 172
Sherony, Keith 80
six-year rule 21, 31
Slaughter, Enos 26
Smiley, Don 173, 176, 177
Smith, Lee 112
Smith, Randy 101
Somers, Charles 22

Soriano, Dewey 155
Soriano, Max 155
Soriano, Milton 155
Sorrento, Paul 106
Southern League New Orleans 22
Spira, Greg 160
split pool concept 35
Spooneybarger, Tim 71
Sporting News 1, 115–116
Sports Channel 76–77, 162, 167–168, 177
Sprague, Ed 101
stadiums: publicly financed 11–12, 29, 40–42, 84; revenues from 4, 81–84, 89; *see also* individual club names
Stark, Jayson 36
Steinbrenner, George 41, **42**, 189–190
Stouffer, Vernon 111
straight pool plan 35
strike (1994): Blue Ribbon Commission Report 9–10; and Huizenga 163; revenue 17, 55–56, 130, 136, 167; television contracts 80, 108; World Series, cancellation of 27
success ratios 49
Sugarball (Klein) 121
Suzuki, Ichiro 27, 130
Symington, Stuart 154

Taking on the Yankees (Fetter) 108–109, 169
Tampa Bay Devil Rays 2, 152
Tampa Bay/St. Petersburg, city of 164
taxes, luxury 30, 45, 57, 188
Taylor, Brien 66
Tejada, Miguel 116, **124**
television: ABC TV 17, 54, 184; CBS TV 12, 107, 130; contracts 2–3, 37–38, 79, 189, 190; ESPN, contract with 3, 11, 17–18, 34, 57, 73, 185; ESPN, revenue affect on 107, 184; ESPN and strike (1994) 55; Fox TV, contracts with MLB 3, 185; Fox TV and Florida Marlins 184; Fox TV, revenue increases and 11, 18–19, 34; Fox TV, revenue sharing 57, 73; NBC TV 17, 184; and radio rights 52; and revenue decline 6, 136; revenue disparity 80; revenue, distribution of 18–19, 53–54; and revenue growth in MLB 2–3, 26–27, 185; revenue, predictor of competitiveness 16, 34; revenue sharing 10–11,

107–108, 159, 168; Sports Channel 76–77, 162, 167–168, 177; strike (1994) 80, 108; WGN TV 28, 58; YES network 2, 72
Tenace, Gene 64
Terry, Ralph 26
Thomas, Frank 64
Thorn, John 67
Thrift, Syd 113, 115
Toronto Blue Jays 59, 67, 151, 155
training facilities *see* minor leagues
Turley, Bob 26
Turner/AOL/Time Warner 28
Twins *see* Minnesota Twins
Tygiel 27

Ueberroth, Peter 129, 131, 149, 156, 157, 158
Urbina, Ugueth 136

"value over replacement player" (VORP) 182–183
Vargas, Angel 121, 142, 146
Vasquez, Angel 169
Venezuela *see* Latin America
Ventura, Robin 64
Vincent, Fay 45, 93, 94, 149, 158–159, 166

Walt Disney Corporation 59
Warner, John 158
Watkins, Donald 28
Weiss 26

Wells, David 114
WGN TV 28, 58
White, Devon 172
White, Michael 93, 94
White Sox *see* Chicago
Whiten, Mark 105
Widger, Chris 114
"wild card" playoff 31
Willers, Katherine 82–83
Williams, Edward Bennett 88–89
Wilson, Lionel 164
Wilson, Preston 70, 181
Win Shares point system 135–136
Wirth, Tim 158–159, 161, 165; *see also* Colorado Rockies
World Series: (1983) 111; (1994) 27; (1997) 151, 171, 173–178; (2003) 178
worldwide amateur draft: Alderson and 132–133; and Latin America 5, 132–133, 134, 139–140; and rules violations by MLB 126; *see also* amateur players draft; globalization
World-Wide Draft Subcommittee 132–133
Wren, Frank 115, 169

Yankees *see* New York Yankees
YES network 2, 72

Zimbalist, Andrew, Jr. 12, 58, 75, 91, 119
Zito, Barry 68

www.ingramcontent.com/pod-product-compliance
Ingram Content Group UK Ltd.
Pitfield, Milton Keynes, MK11 3LW, UK
UKHW042004140426
5217IPUK00015B/967